Towards a normative theory of international relations

When is war justified? When is intervention in the domestic affairs of other states justified? Is international terrorist activity ever justified? Is the policy of nuclear deterrence morally defensible? These questions are clearly of the utmost importance, yet scholars in the discipline of international relations have for the most part avoided moral theory. Part One of this book examines the reasons put forward (or implicitly accepted) for ignoring moral theory, and finds that none of them stands up to close scrutiny. In Part Two a start is made towards the construction of a normative theory which will be useful in seeking answers to the crucial questions listed above. The theory put forward is called constitutive theory, and it is argued that this is more satisfactory than utilitarianism, order-based theories or rights-based theories. In the final chapter constitutive theory is applied to the moral problems surrounding international terrorism.

Towards a normative theory of international relations

A critical analysis of the philosophical and methodological assumptions in the discipline with proposals towards a substantive normative theory

MERVYN FROST

Senior Lecturer, Department of Political Studies
Rhodes University, Grahamstown

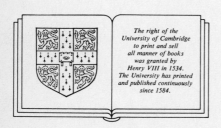

The right of the
University of Cambridge
to print and sell
all manner of books
was granted by
Henry VIII in 1534.
The University has printed
and published continuously
since 1584.

CAMBRIDGE UNIVERSITY PRESS

Cambridge
London   New York   New Rochelle
Melbourne   Sydney

Published by the Press Syndicate of the University of Cambridge
The Pitt Building, Trumpington Street, Cambridge CB2 1RP
32 East 57th Street, New York, NY 10022, USA
10 Stamford Road, Oakleigh, Melbourne 3166, Australia

First published 1986

Printed in Great Britain at the University Press, Cambridge

British Library cataloguing in publication data

Frost, Mervyn
Towards a normative theory of international relations: a
critical analysis of the philosophical and methodological
assumptions of the discipline with proposals towards a
substantive normative theory
1. International relations
I. Title
303.4'82   JX1395

Library of Congress cataloguing publication data

Frost, Mervyn
Towards a normative theory of international relations.
Based on the author's thesis (PhD) – University of stellenbosch, 1983
Bibliography: p.
Includes index.
1. International relations – Methodology. 2. International
relations – Research. I. Title.
JX1291.F76 1986   327'.072   85–15165

ISBN 0 521 30512 8

Contents

vi   *Contents*

viii   *Contents*

Acknowledgements

This book originated in a D.Phil. thesis submitted at the University of Stellenbosch in December 1983. In the course of my research I received help from many quarters. My major academic debt is to André du Toit in the Department of Political Philosophy at the University of Stellenbosch who, as my supervisor, meticulously read and commented on many drafts of this work. My debt to him, though, goes deeper than this. It was he who, together with his colleague Johann Degenaar, originally introduced me to the joys (and showed me the practical importance) of taking philosophy seriously. I could not have wished for better teachers.

I am grateful to Ronald Dworkin of University College Oxford in whose jurisprudence seminars I learned a particularly bold, yet elegant, model of reasoning. In London in 1982 I had a useful discussion with him about my idea of applying that model to the wider context of international relations. I hope he does not consider this book a misapplication of his method.

I spent the 1981/2 academic year as a research student in the Department of International Relations at the London School of Economics. The International Political Theory Group provided what I consider to be the ideal environment for academic research. It achieved a rare combination of academic stringency and social conviviality. In particular I benefited from discussions with James Mayall, Barrie Paskins, John Charvet, Cornelia Navari and Michael Donelan. They helped iron out many mistakes. The ones that remain are my own.

I am grateful for the financial assistance I received from the following institutions: the Human Sciences Research Council in South Africa, the British Council and Rhodes University.

I wish to thank Lola Frost for her support and encouragement throughout this and my earlier efforts at normative theory.

I dedicate this book to my father, who died before it was finished.

Rhodes University   MERVYN FROST
Grahamstown
January 1985

Introduction

One very striking feature of the modern discipline of international relations is that in spite of the fact that most scholars within the discipline claim to be motivated by an urgent moral concern for the well-being of the world polity, there has been very little explicit normative theorizing about what ought to be done in world politics.[1] Most scholars have sought to provide explanatory theories rather than normative theories and, indeed, this is taken to be the hall-mark of international relations as a "scientific" discipline.[2] They have sought to explain why wars occur, how international organizations operate, how growing economic interdependence affects the traditional international order, and so on.[3] Yet they have for the most part avoided theorizing about how the world ought to be arranged; they have avoided such questions as: "When is war justified? When is intervention in the domestic affairs of other states justified? Is international terrorist activity ever justified? Is the policy of nuclear deterrence morally defensible? Is the system of sovereign states morally preferable to some sort of world state?" Key questions then are: "Why is it that within a discipline founded on such moral concern there is such a dearth of normative theory?" and "Are the reasons for this lack of normative theory good ones?" Part One of this book will seek to answer this question. The aim will be to evaluate critically the main reasons for the dearth of normative theory within the discipline of international relations.

In the course of Part One I shall argue that the main reasons for the dearth of normative theory in international relations are to be found in the underlying philosophical and methodological assumptions implicit in the main approaches used by scholars in the discipline. It is these assumptions which are responsible for the prevailing doubts about the worth of normative theory relating to international relations generally. Teasing out these assumptions is an essentially philosophical task. It is not one which appeals to the training or temperament of scholars in the field, who, for the most part, see themselves as concerned with the real world of politics which they take to be far removed from the abstractions of philosophy. Nevertheless, the examination of these underlying assumptions is of fundamental importance. Unless they are brought to light and unless their bearing on the possibility of normative theory is examined, no start can be made towards providing a serious answer to the critical question which scholars acknowledge as crucial to their discipline: "What ought to be done in international relations?"

In the course of Part One it will become apparent that there is not one single underlying philosophical or methodological assumption which can account for the lack of normative theory in international relations. Instead we find that there is a congeries of separate, but related, assumptions. It will be the aim of this section to trace the underlying connections between these assumptions and to indicate how they account for the prevailing dearth of normative theory within the discipline.

Part Two of the book is of a more positive nature. Here the aim is to make a start towards the building of a satisfactory theory which will enable us to provide answers to the hard questions of normative theory which confront the discipline of international relations. In Chapter Three I list some of the more pressing normative questions in contemporary world politics and suggest that these concerns can be encapsulated in the question: "What in general is a good reason for action by or with regard to states?" This question serves as a useful point of departure in the subsequent quest for a normative theory. But prior to constructing such a theory I consider the contention that the question cannot be answered at all. An attempt is made to counter those who argue that conflicting answers to this question are inevitable, since in seeking an answer one necessarily becomes involved in a conflict of ideologies within which no rational solution is possible. I also consider the natural law/community of mankind approach to the pressing normative questions in international relations and indicate why it is not satisfactory.

I then proceed in the latter part of Chapter Three to outline a constructive approach to normative theory which will, I argue, enable us to find answers to the difficult normative questions facing us in world politics today. In seeking to do this my point of departure is that, although there is no agreement amongst the actors involved in international relations about how to handle the difficult cases, nevertheless there is substantial agreement on a whole range of normative matters. For example there is widespread agreement that the preservation of the system of states is a good, that intervention in domestic affairs of a sovereign state is normally wrong, that peace between states is better than war, and so on. My argument is that this area of agreement provides a foundation from which we may start reasoning towards a solution of the difficult cases. I introduce a method of argument for doing this which was developed by Ronald Dworkin within the narrower context of jurisprudence. This method of argument involves, first, listing what is settled within the domain of discourse in question, second, constructing a background theory which will best justify the list of settled beliefs within that domain, and, third, using this background theory to generate answers to the contentious cases.

In Chapter Four I start by listing what may be taken as the settled norms in international relations today. After that I consider three possible background justifications for the list of settled goods: the justification which stresses the primacy of order, the utilitarian justification and the contractarian rights based justification. All of these are found to be wanting in specified ways.

In Chapter Five I articulate a background justification which I call the constitutive theory of individuality and give reasons for preferring it to the others. This justification involves us in a strikingly different mode of theorizing from that used in the other three justifications considered. There is, of course, considerable overlap between the different modes of theorizing, but for the sake of analysis the distinctions between them are drawn as sharply as possible.

Finally, in Chapter Six I seek to show how the mode of theorizing developed in Chapter Five can be used to answer one set of pressing questions in world politics, such as those relating to unconventional modes of violence (like sabotage and international terrorism). I suggest that this mode of reasoning can be successfully used in seeking answers to other hard cases mentioned in Chapter Four, but demonstrating this is beyond the scope of this book.

NOTES

1 It is standard practice for works in international relations to begin with some general statement of moral concern such as the following:

Karl Deutsch, *The Analysis of International Relations* (Englewood Cliffs, Prentice-Hall, 1978), p. 1: "An introduction to the study of international relations in our time is an introduction to the art and science of the survival of mankind. If civilization is killed within the next thirty years, it will not be killed by a famine or plague, but by foreign policy and international relations. We can cope with hunger and pestilence, but we cannot yet deal with the power of our own weapons and with our behaviour as national-states."

A. F. K. Organski, *World Politics* (New York, Alfred Knopf, 1968), p. 1: "The importance of its study today is obvious. None of us cares to come to his final rest as a bit of fall-out."

Most books on international relations start with such professions of concern for the well-being of the world polity.

2 This is not to say that there has been no normative theory produced

within the discipline. There has been some. Recent examples are: Charles Beitz, *Political Theory and International Relations* (Princeton University Press, 1979); C. B. Joynt and J. E. Hare, *Ethics and International Affairs* (London, Macmillan, 1982); Barrie Paskins and Michael Dockrill, *The Ethics of War* (London, Duckworth, 1979); Michael Walzer, *Just and Unjust Wars* (New York, Basic Books, 1977).

3 Kenneth Waltz, *Man, the State and War* (New York, Columbia University Press, 1954); R. Keohane and R. O. Nye, *Power and Interdependence* (Boston, Little, Brown, 1977).

Part One

The positivist bias: a philosophical assumption which accounts for the dearth of normative theory in the discipline of international relations

1 Introduction

Actors in the realm of international relations are regularly faced with normative questions. They are often called upon to decide what, given the specific situation, would be the right thing to do. The problem is not, or not only, the one of deciding upon the best means to an approved of end; that is, the problem is not purely technical. The moral problem is to choose the ends to be pursued and to decide upon what means might legitimately be used in pursuit of those ends.

The kind of problem which faces actors in the realm of international relations is well illustrated in the present day Middle East. Israeli politicians have to decide on the right thing to do with regard to the Palestine Liberation Organization (PLO). The Lebanese and Arab leaders, the governments of the United States and the USSR, each have to decide what rights, recognition and support (if any) ought to be accorded to the PLO. The normative nature of the problem is not dissolved by suggesting that the actors always do (and will) act according to their respective self-interests. What is to count as self-interest is partially determined by normative considerations. For example, where Israel defends a particular course of action on the ground that she is defending her self-interest, part of what is being asserted is that this particular interest ought to be recognized as a *legitimate* one, as one which *ought* to be defended.

Some further examples of normative questions which have faced actors in international relations recently are: the British government had to decide what ought to be done in response to the Argentinian invasion of the Falkland Islands; the USA had to decide what to do about increased communist activity in several states of Central America; the South African government had to decide what to do against neighbouring states which harbour those seeking to subvert the present political order in South Africa by force of arms. Such examples can be multiplied. They all involve questions regarding the right thing to do in some normative sense.

Not all actors in world politics are office bearers in government. Most of us are actors in world politics in one capacity or another. Individuals, whether as ordinary citizens or as members of some non-governmental organization (such as a church, multinational corporation, international agency or welfare organization) also have to make important normative decisions relating to international relations. I mention but three. Citizens called upon by their governments to fight in a war (be it a conventional war or a counter insurgency war) are often faced with difficult choices regarding their obligations. Ought they to agree to fight, ought they to refuse to fight or ought they to protest against the order in some way? Shareholders are called upon by certain pressure groups to influence a given company to withdraw its investment from a particular state for moral or political reasons. Voters in democracies have to make some decisions about normative foreign policy questions in order to cast their vote intelligently at election time. Again these examples could be multiplied.

So far we have been concerned with the ways in which normative questions are important for actors in world politics. But normative issues are important for students of world politics too. Every agent acts upon some understanding of the situation in which he finds himself and since such an understanding requires some study of the situation (however rudimentary it might be) every actor in international relations must, perforce, be both a practitioner in, and a student of, international relations. Furthermore, since we are all in one way or another actors in international politics (merely to be a loyal citizen of a state in a time of war or in a time of peace is to be an actor in international politics), all students of international politics are also actors in international politics and are thus likely to be confronted with some of the pressing normative issues which arise in the domain of world politics.

Given the centrality of these normative questions, what is striking is that within the discipline of international relations very little work is done towards answering them; normative theory is generally eschewed. In international relations as a scientific discipline it is generally taken for granted that the aim should be primarily descriptive and/or explanatory. Scholars are supposed to provide analyses which are above all firmly grounded in the *facts*; they should not become involved in *normative* arguments. This has become so much the accepted practice in the discipline that it is simply taken for granted without any attempt at justification. The fact that a discipline so centrally concerned with normative questions should itself consistently eschew all normative argument is a paradox that calls for critical investigation. I shall contend in this and the following chapter that there are two main types of reason for this dearth of serious argument about values. First, there is the particular epistemological and methodological bias held by most scholars in the field of international relations in common with scholars in many of the other social sciences. This may be called the *positivist bias* and it rests on a radical distinction between facts and values which accords epistemological priority to factual knowledge.[1] Second, there are some prevalent views regarding the characteristic features of moral arguments (such as their alleged non-cognitive status, an amoralist implication which is a supposed consequence of this status, and the general irrelevance of moral arguments in the face of naked power relations) which are held to make moral discourse in general, as well as normative arguments within the discipline of international relations, not worthy of serious intellectual consideration. This type of reason may, for convenience' sake, be caught under the heading *moral scepticism*. I shall be considering this latter type of argument in Chapter Two. In this chapter I shall consider only the first type of reason – the widespread positivist bias within the discipline. This will involve a critical investigation of the methodological and philosophical assumptions underlying the positivists' approach. It is these underlying assumptions which supposedly provide reasons for eschewing normative theory in international relations.

The argument proceeds by looking at some general developments in the philosophy of the social sciences where the dominant positivist orientation of an earlier stage has been critically challenged from more than one direction. These philosophical developments have been very influential in other social sciences (e.g. sociology, anthropology, political science and social psychology) and, in fact, in many cases the hold of the positivist paradigm has been broken. However, these developments seem to have had no impact on the study of international relations. In fact, though, the issues raised in these other disciplines and by the philosophy of the social sciences in general are highly relevant to the study of international relations as well. One purpose of this book will be to rectify this unfortunate backwardness of international relations. Moreover, the critical reflection upon the philosophical assumptions of international relations which is overdue has important implications for our understanding of the very nature of the discipline itself. The main conclusion to which I shall argue in Part One is that it is not possible to study international relations without becoming involved in substantive normative issues. It is the positivist assumption implicitly subscribed to by many practitioners of international relations which brought them to eschew any involvement in substantive normative theory; once this assumption is challenged it will become clear that international relations must of necessity involve normative argument.

2 The positivist bias against normative theory in international relations

The discipline of international relations, as distinct from the more traditional disciplines of history and law, is a comparatively new one. Like most academic disciplines within the social sciences, international relations is plagued by an ongoing dispute about the proper methods to be employed by its practitioners. Probably the major cleavage in this new field is that between the so-called classical and scientific approaches to the subject. In the post Second World War era the scientific approach has come dramatically to the fore. A few of the well known scholars committed to the scientific approach are Morton Kaplan, Richard Rosecrance, Klaus Knorr, Sydney Verba, Karl Deutsch, James Rosenau, J. W. Burton, Stanley Hoffman, Charles Kindleberger, Charles McCelland and J. D. Singer.[2] The classical approach is the approach pursued by most British scholars. The term "classical" is somewhat misleading, suggesting as it does an ancient lineage and a Greek connection. In the debate within the discipline of international relations "classical" is used to identify a predominantly British group of scholars who combine the methods of the liberal historian, the Oxford philosopher, the international lawyer and the political theorist. Some well known names include E. H. Carr, Martin Wight, Hedley Bull and D. C. Watt.[3] What is at issue between these two different approaches to the subject is primarily the question of the proper method for the study of international relations. The classical theorists see the subject as akin to history, whereas the scientific approach seeks, as the word "scientific" suggests, to make the study of international relations more rigorous. Following the example of many theorists in the other social sciences, they aim ultimately to follow the paradigm of the natural sciences. In practice this means that they stress the use of clearly formulated hypotheses and the testing of these against observable data using quantitative methods as far as possible. The distinction between classical and scientific approaches to the study of social phenomena is thus not confined to international relations, but has occurred in other areas of social study as well, for example within the disciplines of history, political studies, anthropology, sociology and so on.

There are important debates within and between both of these approaches to international relations in the area of social studies at large. Furthermore, there are debates between these two approaches to international relations and a third, as yet not very well developed, approach to the discipline, viz. the Marxist one.[4] There is a considerable literature concerning the precise nature of good historical scholarship which has a bearing on the historical approach to the study of international relations and hence to the "classical" tradition in the discipline.[5] However there has been very little explicit debate about the theoretical assumptions underpinning the classical approach to international relations. For our present purposes, though, the important thing to notice is that, for the most part, those who see themselves as pursuing the traditional approach belong, broadly speaking, to the empiricist school of thought.[6] The dominance of the empiricist tradition has important implications for the topic to be discussed, viz. the epistemological bias against normative theories in international relations. These will become apparent later.

In the scientific approach to international relations there is a broad commitment to explanatory and descriptive goals, but little consensus about the precise nature of the method to be pursued. There are disputes about what ought to be analysed, and about the methods to be used in doing the analysis.[7] International relations should provide explanatory theories firmly based on facts, but ought the aim to be the establishment of general theories or ought the researcher to aim initially at middle range theories? Ought the focus to be on data collection or on the formation of hypotheses?[8] The details of these controversies are not our concern here. More important, for our purposes, are certain underlying assumptions of the "scientific" approach in general, which it in fact shares with the "classical" approach.

There is, despite their apparent differences in orientation, a broad measure of common ground linking the liberal historical approach and the bulk of the scientific approaches. I have decided to identify this rather broad common ground with the brief label *positivist bias*.[9] Both the classical and the scientific approaches stress some or all of the following related things: their methods, it is claimed, are in the final instance objective, they seek to verify their conclusions by reference to "the facts," which are in some sense "hard" and there for all to see (i.e. ascertaining the facts does not require an interpretative effort on the part of the investigator and the facts are ascertainable by the investigator without his having previously adopted any particular theory), and the links between conclusion and evidence (or hypothesis and verifying data) are intersubjectively verifiable.[10] Both stress that the results of their studies do not derive from subjective, relative or conventional judgements. Such judgements are in sharp contrast to value judgements which are held to be subjective, relative or conventional. In short, common to both approaches is a radical distinction between the status accorded to factual judgements, to which the discipline of international relations should aspire, and that accorded to value judgements.[11] Facts are given epistemological priority. This forms the core of the positivist assumption underlying both the traditional and the scientific approaches to the study of international relations.[12]

The core of the positivist assumption is to be found in the distinction between fact and value and the different cognitive status accorded to each. On the positivist view what distinguishes facts from values is the characteristic which the former have of being intersubjectively verifiable, i.e. accessible to the senses of anyone who would observe them. Moreover, factual statements are informative; they give us knowledge about the world. Some positivists argue that there is a congruence between factual statements and reality.[13] For them, the matching or picturing guarantees (in some way) the objective basis of factual knowledge.[14]

Positivists may view normative theories in any of a number of different ways. They may adhere to emotivist, expressivist, prescriptivist or some other theory of normative discourse.[15] For example on one positivist view, viz. the emotivist one, a value judgement may be seen as purely arbitrary, i.e. it may be seen as a judgement for which a person simply opts.[16] It is neither right nor wrong, but is simply what the person has chosen. Alternatively, such judgements might be looked upon as conventional, i.e. as being in accordance with criteria which have been agreed upon within a given community. Here there may be talk of the judgements being right or wrong in terms of the conventions. Yet there is nothing beyond the conventions which can be referred to as final proof of the matter to somebody who rejects the conventions. In the final instance there is no possible verification for value judgements.

I contend that this positivist assumption is the most basic reason for the persistent neglect of normative questions which is common to both the traditional and scientific schools in international relations.[17] To demonstrate this conclusively is, of course, difficult. Biases tend to be assumed rather than explicitly stated or argued for. But a glance through the literature will suffice to show that such a bias is indeed implicit in the approach of most of the scholars referred to.[18] Often authors do acknowledge that values will inevitably influence their findings in some way. Typically they admit that value orientations might colour the way in which the data are perceived, they might influence the choice of the initial problem to be studied, they might influence the selection of data, and so on. But in each case the intrusion of personal values, at all or some of these points, is seen as something negative, something to be guarded against. Furthermore, the values which intrude are typically seen as personal values, as values subjectively chosen by the actor. On this view, then, values are choices and are not true or false in the way that factual judgements are.[19] It is this pervasive view which follows from the positivist assumption.

3 Positivism challenged

A critique of the positivist assumption and of the fact/value distinction would open the way for serious debate about values and thus for the possibility of constructive normative theory. In all the social sciences, except international relations, just such a challenge is already under way.[20] Indeed, a major part of the discussion about methodology in such disciplines as political science, sociology, anthropology, economics and psychology has increasingly been concerned with challenges to the supposed objectivity of positivist social science. What is remarkable is that this debate has had no significant impact within the field of international relations. Let us look at the outline of the debate which has taken place in the philosophy of the social sciences and consider whether the main thrust of the argument does have a bearing on the discipline of international relations.

3.1 The 'Verstehen' critique

The primary assumption of positivist social science is, as we have seen, the belief that there is an objective domain of facts. These facts are supposed to be objectively given; i.e. they are given to the senses independently of interpretation or theory. Such facts, according to the positivist model of science, provide a touchstone against which the hypotheses and theories of the investigator can be tested. It is of particular significance for our problem that a major challenge to the positivist approach to social science has been posed by what may be called the *Verstehen* school of social science. This approach is also referred to as "interpretative social science" and some-times as "humanist social science." The origin of the approach is to be found in the work of two independent German social theorists, Max Weber and Wilhelm Dilthey. In 1958 Peter Winch, an English philosopher, combined the insights of these earlier theorists with some of the implications of the philo-sophical work done by Ludwig Wittgenstein in his later period. Winch published his conclusions in his seminal work, *The Idea of a Social Science.*[21] This modern version of the *Ver-stehen* approach involves a rejection of the positivist assump-tions about the nature of social reality. Essentially the posi-tivists supposed that social reality was, in principle, knowable in a direct way which need not involve the investigator in any interpretation or prior commitment to any particular social theory. Furthermore, the observation of this reality was, in principle, no different from the observation of the natural reality with which the so called "hard" sciences were con-cerned. Winch denies that this is an adequate account of the nature and status of societal facts. He argues that social science is primarily concerned with the analysis of the *actions* and *interactions* of people and that actions are not givens which are immediately observable in the way that the data of the physical sciences are.

Let us look more closely at this distinction between the data of the physical sciences and the data of the social sciences. The difference is not that human behaviour cannot figure as the object of physical science, or that the latter is exclusively con-cerned with other data than that of human behaviour. The physical aspects of human behaviour can quite appropriately provide data for physical science as well. But the point is that such data have a different relation to scientific concept for-mation from human actions which comprise the data of social science investigations. In investigating some aspect of the physical behaviour of humans, a physical scientist can introduce the appropriate scientific *concepts* relative to the purposes of his investigation. Thus an orthopaedic specialist who seeks to study the various mechanisms involved in running requires an appropriate concept of "running" for his purposes, e.g. he would have to specify what is to be counted as a single unit of running. There may be good reason for him to look at a whole sequence of two strides or more as the unit to be analysed. If he is interested in taking a single stride as the unit to be investigated, he would have to specify exactly what is to count as a "stride," and so on. The important point here, though, is that the investigator has a degree of freedom in concept formation; relative to his scientific research purposes he can specify what items are to count as the data being studied. He cannot be said to be right or wrong in making this decision. A unit of "running" adequate for the purposes of one investigation may be inappropriate for that of another. The movement of the human body in running is not naturally divided into several discrete units. The investigator can divide it up into separate components in any number of ways dependent on his purposes and requirements in various scientific contexts.

Winch, and social scientists in the *Verstehen* tradition, deny that *actions*, which are the basic data of the social sciences, can be individuated in this way. For an event to be individuated as a specific action according to the interpretative approach, it needs to be *understood*. On this view the act of, for example, marching, cannot be understood as an action (and distinguished from other similar actions like walking, strolling, etc.) if the physical properties only are identified from the point of view of some external observer like an orthopaedic specialist.[22] What makes an action an act of marching is not adequately accounted for by saying that the legs move a certain distance and the arms rise to a specified height. Imagine that a scientist is provided with a set of data which specified that a subject had been carefully observed whose legs had been moving rhythmically through x degrees, that each arc had swung through distance y, that the arms had swung up to height z, and so on. The scientist is asked to determine whether the subject was marching or not. The *Verstehen* theorists argue that on the basis of this kind of data it is not possible to determine whether the subject observed was marching or not. For the data could equally well be consistent with an act of walking (albeit in an unusual way), an act of marching, or an act of pretending to march, and so on. The *Verstehen* theorists insist that in order to determine whether someone was marching or not, it would be necessary to understand the action from the participant perspective as well, i.e. in terms of the agent's own individuation of what he is doing.

Let us demonstrate this point by looking at a hypothetical example from the realm of international relations. Before any observer (be he a social scientist or a historian) can recognize a piece of human behaviour as an example of, let us say, a summit meeting between heads of state, he must be able to understand that behaviour from the point of view of the people involved, i.e. from the internal point of view.[23] In order to identify this particular action the investigator needs to have some knowledge of the practice of summit meetings from the point of view of a participant. Let us consider a hypothetical summit meeting between heads of state in more detail. An external observer with no knowledge of the practice of high level diplomacy with its elaborate rules of protocol, but restricted to the observation of the physical aspects of the event, would be able to record the arrival of a large aircraft, which was met by crowds assembled beside a strip of red carpet. He would record that when a man emerged from the aircraft, lights popped and bands played and that then the man walked up and down rows of men all uniformly dressed in unusual clothes. The observer might individuate pieces of the observed data in ways that seemed useful or significant to him. For example, he might specify as significant pieces of data the appearance of a person at the door of the aeroplane immediately followed by intense flashings of light sources amongst a certain section of the people on the tarmac. If he observed several such occasions he might find a high correlation between the appearance of figure X and the bursts of light from group Y. But to individuate and correlate events in this external fashion is not to make sense of them. To make sense of the proceedings he would need to understand the practice of international summitry from the internal point of view. He would need some understanding of what a state is, he would need to know what a head of state is, he would need to know how states conduct their relations with one another, he would need to know what a guard of honour is, what press photographers are, what red carpets symbolize and so on. Understanding a guard of honour requires some understanding of the role the military play in inter-state relations. To comprehend the presence of the photographers and journalists he would need to know what the press is and something of the relationships which hold between the press, public opinion and the state.[24] In this way, the individuation of all *actions* (and actions are the basic data of all social sciences) presupposes participant understanding.[25] The concept formation of the social scientist is rooted in the conceptual structure of such participant understanding.

What are the implications of the *Verstehen* approach to social science? There are several interrelated ones worth mentioning. First, *Verstehen* requires that the investigator adopt a participant perspective as the basis of his investigation. This requires that his interpretations be tested against the self-understandings of the investigatees.[26] It precludes the social scientist from remaining an external observer in the way that positivists supposed social scientists ought to be.

Second, this approach stresses the importance of the constitutive *language* of the investigatees. For it is patent that any understanding of a social practice must rest upon a detailed understanding of the characteristic language of the practice in question. What is called for is the identification and classification of actions in terms of the participant language. Thus, for example, no worthwhile comparison is possible between modern day summitry between heads of nation states and the ways of meeting between feudal lords without an appropriate understanding of the languages characteristic of the two different practices. The reference here is not to any particular natural language like English or French. For the language of a given practice (modern inter-state diplomacy or feudalist diplomacy) may be articulated in various natural languages. The point is rather that the social scientist must learn to know what would count as, for example, an "insult" (or any other important term) in the practice of international diplomacy. Whether the term used to designate this action is the English one "insult" or the Afrikaans one "belediging" (or the French, German, Italian, etc.) is neither here nor there. The stress on language is important in the following way: it highlights that what is to count as an "insult" in the practice of international diplomacy cannot be determined by identifying patterns of physical behaviour or by finding out what went on in the mind of any particular actor (this would be a psychologistic approach), but by the rules implicit in the practice as a whole as best exemplified in its characteristic language.

Third, there is an important holist implication of the *Verstehen* approach. As our example of the summit meeting shows, it is not possible to have a proper understanding of the single act of a meeting between the heads of state without a knowledge of the whole practice of diplomacy and of inter-state relations and of the ways in which the parts of this practice cohere. This is in sharp contrast to the positivist approach in terms of which particular theory-verifying (or theory-falsifying) facts are supposed to be available to the senses as discrete entities; individual data which can be identified independently of theory and interpretation.

Fourth, the interpretative approach stresses the permanent possibility of misunderstanding actions. An investigator's understanding of a given act is always *corrigible* or *defeasible*.[27] For example, what he at first took to be a summit meeting might turn out to be a rehearsal for a film of a summit, or a meeting between men claiming to be heads of state who are not in fact that. The investigator is faced not merely with the task of recording the immediate events of the summit meeting; he is also faced, if only implicitly, with the problem of determining when a person really is head of state. In many cases (for example, Rhodesia immediately after UDI) this might be a very contentious issue and one which cannot be resolved merely by scrupulous observation of the "facts" of the meeting. Here we find the interpretative school challenging the supposed "hardness" of social facts, which on the positivist view were held to be ascertainable as correct in a direct manner. Of course, positivists acknowledge the possibility of misperception, of being under an illusion and so on. However, for the positivist such cases must be the result of a malfunction in the perceptual apparatus of the observer. Correcting such a malfunction may be likened to refocusing a telescope; it is a matter of adjusting the instrumentation properly. For the *Verstehen* school clearing up a misunderstanding involves the observer in something quite different. It involves the investigator entering into a discussion with the participants in order to sort out the possible misunderstanding. This discussion will be about the correct interpretation of the action concerned; it will be about the meaning of the act and will refer to the norms, rules, principles and maxims of the practice in which the action took place.

Fifth, *Verstehen* requires that the investigator take notice of the value system of the investigatees. He cannot avoid this, for all actions have an ineluctable normative element. Let us demonstrate this by referring back to the example of the summit meeting. To make sense of the summit, the summit watcher needs to know what states are, what heads of states are, what pressmen are, and so on. To understand the importance attached by the participants to the summit, he would need to understand the underlying set of values which inform their judgement that such summits are important. This in turn would require at least a rudimentary knowledge of the participants' political philosophy, that is, of how states are supposed to protect certain values. Such a political philosophy would no doubt refer, *inter alia*, to the value of national security, which in turn could be shown to be linked to the value of the security of the individual. It is knowledge of this background value system which makes it possible for the investigator to predict the range of future actions open to people within a practice.

Although the interpretative approach challenged the foundations of positivism in the social sciences by showing that the assumptions on which positivism had been founded were suspect in certain specified ways, this approach does not yet lead to the full reinstatement of normative social theory. This will become clear if we consider the interpretative approach to participant values more closely. The interpretative approach does not require the social scientist to accept or evaluate the values of the participants. It requires merely that he understands them. In a sense his understanding may still be said to be objective and compatible with the basic dichotomy between facts and values. There is a sense then in which the interpretative approach is descriptivist. The argument here may be put slightly differently as follows: the *Verstehen* theorists make a valid point when they show that the data of social science are not observable in the way that the data of the natural sciences are; when they show that understanding is required. But this does not undermine the positivist distinction between scientific inquiry and moral judgement. The data of social science, viz. understandings, like the data of the natural sciences, are either right or wrong according to non-subjective criteria. In short, on this view *Verstehen* leaves the fact/value distinction intact. Ironically, the interpretative approach, itself an attack on positivism, is open to criticisms which show it to be positivist in a different but related way. It is positivist in that a proper understanding, according to this school, is achieved where the investigator's insight properly matches the rules of the practice being investigated. A correct understanding depends on a positive match between the understanding of the investigator and the self-understandings of the investigatees.

This positive match does not require any serious theorizing about matters of value on the part of the theorist. Indeed, the *Verstehen* theorist may charge the positivist with not being value-free enough. The positivist is charged with interpreting the social data through the filter of his own value system rather than through the interpretative criteria provided by the value system of the investigatees.

This criticism of the supposed value-freeness of the interpretative approach can be clarified by means of the following example. Consider a social scientist investigating the behaviour of the South African government during the Angolan War. (In 1975–6 the South African government secretly decided to send in a large contingent of the South African armed forces into Angola, in order to aid the anti-communist UNITA movement in its civil war struggle with the USSR-backed MPLA (Popular Movement for the Liberation of Angola). The decision of the South African government, once it became known, raised a storm of protest both internally and internationally.[28]) Any scholar seeking to explain the action would first need to *understand* the action of the South African government: why (i.e. for what reasons) did the South African government intervene in the Angolan civil war in this way? Clearly part of what has to be understood is the set of values held by members of the Cabinet and the military leaders. One possible interpretation would depend on an understanding of the anti-communist values adhered to by some ministers and generals. A clear understanding of such values is necessary in order to account for the Angolan decision, but this understanding in no way depends on the social scientist himself subscribing to (or critically evaluating) the values in question. He may personally be highly critical of anti-communist values, but his own stance is irrelevant to the investigation. It is, on this view, possible to understand values in a value-neutral way.

From the foregoing it is clear that the interpretative approach to social science maintains a strong distinction between doing social science and arguing about normative theory.[29] The fact/

value distinction is essentially maintained. It follows that the debate in the philosophy of the social sciences which we have considered thus far has not yet indicated the necessity for (or the unavoidability of) serious normative theory in international relations and the other social sciences. It is only in the next phase of the discussion that the necessity for social scientists, *qua* social scientists, to become involved in debate about normative issues will be demonstrated.

3.2 *Critical social science: the merging of social science, political practice and normative theory*

The *Verstehen* approach to social science has been severely criticized on numerous counts. Many of these criticisms have come not from positivists seeking to rebut the criticisms levelled at positivism by the interpretative theorists, but from theorists who essentially agree with the main thrust of the anti-positivist attack launched by the *Verstehen* school. This approach seeks to push the anti-positivist attack even further than did the earlier school and we may for convenience' sake call it the *critical approach*.[30] This approach is critical in several different ways: first, it does not accept the self-understandings of the investigatees as being beyond criticism. According to the interpretative approach, once the social scientist has understood an action from the point of view of the actor, that is all there is to be done. The theorist would not be warranted in "finessing" the self-understandings of the investigatee; the agent's self-understandings are incorrigible.[31] In a critical approach the scientist would examine the self-understandings of the subject in the context of the practice as a whole and in the context of its history. Such an examination might reveal that the subject's self-understandings help uphold a system within which he (the subject) is being disadvantaged in terms of his needs and purposes and thus that his understanding is defective in important ways.[32]

Second, the approach is critical in that it does not presume coherence in the practice within which the subject understands his act. The *Verstehen* approach sought to understand actions within the context of a practice which was presumed by the participants to be a coherent whole. A critical approach takes seriously the possibility of there being deep-seated internal contradictions within a practice. This has profound political implications. Pointing out such contradictions indicates the kind of actions necessary for a changed practice. Interpretative theory is implicitly conservative in so far as it seeks only to understand the existing practice, not change it.

Third, the critical approach rejects the conception implicit in the interpretative approach about the relationship between theory and practice. Because interpretative theory sought to understand a practice from the internal point of view and because it disallowed the "finessing" of the self-understandings of the investigatee, theory had always to be seen as following practice and could not be seen as having any particular role to play in the development of future practices.

Our particular interest is in the way a critical social inquiry rejects the *descriptivism* inherent in the interpretative approach. Interpretative theory is descriptivist in that it portrays the social scientist's task of being the description of the self-understandings of the subject being investigated. The method precludes the social scientist from passing judgements on the self-understandings of the investigatees. Understanding is a method which allows the investigator to arrive at the proper description of an act. But description does not require the social scientist to become involved in any evaluative enterprise. His task is to understand the practice in question and not to judge it. Although part of what the social scientist seeks to understand will include certain value positions held by the subjects under investigation, the *Verstehen* method does not require the social scientist, *qua* social scientist, to enter into normative argument about the values of the investigatees. A critical approach denies that it is possible for social scientists to proceed in such a neutral way. Let us explore this contention more fully.

The core of the critical approach's attack on the descriptivism of interpretative theory lies in the rejection of the interpretativist rule that the subject's self-understandings may not be finessed. The critical social inquirer asserts that a subject's self-understandings may be wrong in important ways. What the critical approach takes over from the *Verstehen* method is the conviction that no proper understanding of a subject's actions is possible without engaging in a dialogue with the subject. But the critical approach does not accept as sacrosanct the initial self-understandings of the subject, for it may well be the case that, in the course of the dialogue between the investigator and the subject, the latter comes to see that his original self-understanding was wrong in some fundamental way.

In order to make clear what the implications of the foregoing are for our topic (we are concerned to show why social scientists *qua* social scientists must necessarily be involved in questions of substantive normative theory), let us engage in the following thought experiment. Imagine a social scientist in international relations studying the Soviet invasion of Afghanistan. She seeks to answer the question: "Why did the Soviets do it?" Accepting the primary canon of the interpretative approach to social science, she realizes the primacy of achieving a proper understanding of this act from the point of view of the leadership of the USSR. A necessary prerequisite for explaining the Soviet invasion of Afghanistan is that she achieve some measure of participant understanding. Let us suppose that she has learned Russian, has access to the Politburo and seeks to understand this particular act in terms of the reasons and aims provided by the Soviet leaders themselves. It is more than likely that amongst the actors involved (we assume that they tell her what they take to be the truth and do not deliberately lie) she will come across more than one version of what the USSR intended to do in invading Afghanistan. One might stress that it was an action aimed at settling domestic political problems (e.g. the secessionist aspirations of the nationalities) by focusing attention on a foreign venture.

Another might interpret the act as giving aid to an unstable Marxist government. Another might focus on Afghanistan's strategic importance as a link in the cordon of satellite states which acts as a bulwark against capitalist imperialism. It might appear as if these interpretations are compatible one with another. However, they are incompatible at least in the sense that each interpretation suggests a different set of standards for evaluating the act, suggests a different prediction about the future, and a different set of immediate policy implications. Consider the first version (the invasion of Afghanistan as a device to quell domestic unrest). On this view the success of the action must be judged by looking at internal politics. Furthermore, the longer the war continues the better it will serve its purpose and this consideration will guide policy-making with regard to the conduct of the war. Contrast these implications with the implications of the third version (the invasion as a strategic move against US imperialism). This implies that the criteria for judging the act are to be found in the reactions of US military policy-makers. Furthermore, it implies that the stabilization of Afghanistan will be a major priority and that great military and economic resources will be committed to achieve this end. In various circumstances the rival participant understandings of the act may in fact turn out to be incompatible and it will become a matter of participant conflict to establish the "correct" interpretation in actual practice.

Our social scientist, in seeking to penetrate the practice of Soviet foreign policy-making, finds that there is no one clear understanding of the act, but rather several competing understandings. Her own preferred understanding is simply one of the competing understandings. It follows, and this is the crux of the matter, that our social scientist, in seeking a proper understanding of the invasion, has to join the argument with the actors involved about just what was actually done and why. This argument is not a neutral one about the proper label to hang upon an object.[33] Describing it in one way rather than another is itself a normatively charged act. As we have seen, describing it in one way rather than another involves evaluating it in one way rather than another.[34] The debate between those members of the Politburo holding competing views about the purposes of the act (and between them and our social scientist) is not an objective/scientific one, but rather of a political/normative nature. The social scientist is, and cannot avoid being, involved in this normative discourse.

The point being made here was made trenchantly by Charles Taylor in an article entitled "Neutrality in Political Science."[35] There he argued that in political science the description of an action as an x had within it an implicit value slope. Thus disputes about the proper description of the "facts" are partly arguments about matters of value. Neutrality is not possible. If it is claimed, it is an illusion. It follows that social scientists, and scholars in international relations as well, cannot avoid becoming engaged in normative questions and must face up to the challenge of normative theory.

3.3 Participant understanding, critical inquiry and moral argument: a possible dialogue

It emerges, then, that contrary to what we might have thought following the *Verstehen* approach, practices should not be assumed to be coherent sets of rules which enable us, once we have adopted the internal point of view, to understand any action within the practice in a straightforward way. For within the practices there is often conflict about the proper identification of an act. The social scientist must necessarily become involved in this conflict and in the moral argument it entails. This engagement with moral questions is not something which follows social scientific understanding, but has to be undertaken in order to obtain an understanding of the action in question. Within the confines of this work it is not possible to go into all the many questions which a full investigation of this problem would require. Instead, let us demonstrate the form of this involvement by means of an imagined dialogue.

A social scientist seeks to understand South Africa's involvement in the Angolan War. For the sake of argument let us suppose that the decision was taken by one man, Mr Foster. The critical social scientist (hereafter referred to as Critic), recognizing the importance of the internal point of view, engages in the following dialogue with Mr Foster:

Critic: Mr Foster, can you help me to understand why South Africa invaded Angola? In your view, which of the following would best describe South Africa's incursion into Angola:

1. An act of imperial aggression for material gain.
2. A defence of South Africa's national security against a communist expansionist policy which is aimed at international domination.
3. An act of aid to a movement favourably disposed towards South Africa.
4. An opportunistic attempt to win diplomatic favour with the USA?

Mr Foster: Description 2 is the best. The Soviet drive towards world domination is well known. What we sought to do in that war was to pre-empt a potential threat to South Africa's long term national security.

Critic: I accept your account, for after all you made the decision and you must know best what your reasons actually were. However, I find it difficult to understand how you could have seen the internal civil war in Angola as a threat to South Africa's national security. Surely national security is a phrase which cannot be used to cover just any action a government undertakes?

Mr Foster: Obviously not. What I am saying is that at the time the actions of the Soviet-backed MPLA constituted a real threat to South Africa's long term security.

Critic: Then you agree that there are clear cases where one *can* and clear cases where one *cannot* talk of "real" threats to national security warranting intervention?

Mr Foster: Of course, only a fool would deny that.

Critic: For example, the phrase "national security" could not properly be used to cover a South African attempt to destroy the United Nations building in New York. Similarly, there are clear cut cases where the phrase "national security" is applicable. For example, were Mozambique to mount a conventional attack on South Africa with the express purpose of incorporating her territory into the Mozambiquan state, this would be a clear threat to South African national security. More difficult are the borderline cases: a legal opposition party which seeks to transform the whole form of government (e.g. the communist parties in western Europe are sometimes thought to be such) and the exiled political movements who do not seek to overthrow the state, but merely strive for a voice in central government. Which of these constitute threats to national security?

What criteria are operative here? Would Zimbabwe be justified in interfering militarily on the side of Inkatha [a Zulu nationalist movement in South Africa] on the grounds that by so doing she [Zimbabwe] was defending her national interest? Would you not count that as interference in the domestic politics of South Africa? If so, why was the South African incursion into Angola not similarly condemnable?

Mr Foster: You are full of questions and your questions are all about what is right and what is wrong. Such questions are not pertinent to our discussion. What is to the point is that I and my government perceived in the communist involvement in Angola a threat to our long term security interests.

Critic: The rights and wrongs of the matter are very much to the point. Let us return to the imaginary example of the Mugabe government militarily aiding some or other Black opposition group within South Africa on the grounds that by so doing a long term threat to Zimbabwe's security was being pre-empted. Would Mugabe's perception of a security threat be correct simply because he had it?

Mr Foster: Clearly not.

Critic: In seeking to explain such a Zimbabwean incursion would it be important to determine whether his perception was correct or not?

Mr Foster: Definitely. For if it could be shown that he was mistaken in perceiving a threat to Zimbabwean security, this would explain why the international community of states did not support his venture, and vice versa.

Critic: By the same token, then, if it can be shown that your perception of a security threat in the developing Angolan situation was wrong, this would explain the international outrage which followed.

Mr Foster: Yes. Conversely it would expose the double standards of the international community if we are shown to have been right.

Critic: Indeed, if you can show that your perception was right this would show the international reaction in another light altogether. It would show it to have been perverse. For they would then be seen to have condemned an action which was upholding a rule (in this case, the right to protect national security) to which they themselves subscribe.

Mr Foster: That is just what I am saying.

Critic: If, then, as we have agreed, it is important to establish whether a perceived security threat really is one, then it is most important to determine the precise criteria by which such threats are properly identified. Do you agree?

Mr Foster: Yes.

Critic: What criteria are relevant, do you think?

Mr Foster: National security is threatened where the sovereignty of a state is threatened, for example, where one state invades another with the express purpose of conquering it.

Critic: What would you say about the following difficult case, viz. the

1982 Israeli invasion of Lebanon? The Israelis claimed that the invasion was an attempt to counter a threat to Israeli national security posed by the presence of Palestine Liberation Organization fighters in Southern Lebanon. The PLO claimed it was an unjustified act of aggression against their movement. Given these divergent perceptions, which one was correct?

Mr Foster: I cannot answer that "off the cuff" without going into the details of the case.

Critic: What sort of details would be relevant here? Is what is called for an empirical investigation of the details of what actually happened "on the ground," so to speak?

Mr Foster: Well, if I could establish that the PLO had in fact been raiding across the border into Israel, this would support the Israeli claim that their national security was being threatened.

Critic: Suppose that the PLO claimed that they were not seeking to undermine Israel's national security with their acts of force, but rather aiming to get Israel to agree with the establishment of a Palestinian state on the West Bank territory occupied by Israel in the 1967 war. Pursuing this line of argument, the PLO point out that the cause of their attacks against Israeli targets is Israel's failure to recognize the legitimate right of self-determination of the Palestinian people. Thus any threat to Israel stems from an initial failure by Israel to respect the rights of the Palestinians. If this argument were valid, would it influence your understanding of the Israeli invasion?

Mr Foster: Yes, of course, for were it true, it would show Israel to be doing something quite different from what she initially claimed to be doing. Instead of defending her national security we would now have to see her as overriding, with force of arms, another group's right to self-determination.

Critic: We have now reached the position where the Isreali claim, "We are defending our national security," is ranged against the Palestinian counter claim, "You are denying us our legitimate rights." Furthermore, we have established that the matter cannot be settled by simply looking at what in fact happened. How would you decide between these two claims?

Mr Foster: In terms of our earlier discussion, we have agreed that the matter cannot be settled by finding out what the parties in fact perceived their acts to be, for their perceptions might be wrong. I have to do something else. I have to evaluate their perceptions in order to determine which is correct.

Critic: Yes. How would you do this? What sorts of considerations would be relevant?

Mr Foster: The Palestinian claim is that they have a right to self-determination. I would have to determine whether, indeed, they do have such a right. I would have to find out under what conditions a group of people (like the Palestinians in this case) do have a right to a state of their own. The Israeli government, of course, would deny that the

Palestinians do have such a right. The Israeli denial of the right must rest upon some view about when such claims are legitimate and when not, for, after all, the Israelis themselves claimed just such a right when modern Israel was established. In short, I would have to determine whether the Israeli claim that the Palestinians have no such right is correct.

Critic: Do you agree then that you cannot come to a proper understanding of what the Israelis did in this case without coming to some conclusions yourself about the type of issue you have just been mentioning?

Mr Foster: Yes.

Critic: Do you agree that this kind of issue (whether the PLO do have a legitimate claim to self-determination) will involve you in an investigation of an essentially normative nature, a discussion about what is right and wrong?

Mr Foster: Yes, though I still say, with regard to the Angolan case, that we were right to do what we did.

Obviously this dialogue could be continued in many different ways. For our purposes it merely serves to indicate that it is not possible to properly identify an act as a threat to national security without getting involved in essentially normative questions. In this case the disputants are called upon to come to grips with the notion of justice.

4 Conclusion

In the foregoing discussion we have seen how the critical approach expands and develops the insights of the *Verstehen* method. The critical approach takes over the central insight of the interpretative approach (which is that it is not possible to describe social actions without understanding them), but argues that in many of the issues that most concern students of international relations it would be artificial and damaging to deny that participant understanding is inseparable from normative discourse, that is, discourse in which the "observer" is a *legitimate* contributor to deliberation about key normative issues. There are several implications of this approach which we must take note of.[36]

First, the critical approach requires the theorist to become seriously involved in the practice under investigation. At first glance this may seem no different from the requirement of the *Verstehen* approach that the theorist adopt the internal point of view. However, the involvement required for a critical under-standing amounts to more than the adoption of the internal per-spective. It requires the investigator to actively participate with the investigatees in a discussion about the proper reasons and purposes of their actions. Such a discussion will often involve argument about fundamental values. The interpretative assumption about the incorrigibility of people's self-understandings is dropped.

Second, there is what might loosely be called the "demo-cratic" dimension of critical understanding. In the long run the people being theorized about are the validators of the theory. For where critical investigators get involved in disputes about the proper understanding of an act the arguments turn on values which might be said to be immanent within the practice. The test which will show whether a given interpretation is based on values immanent within the practice is whether those within the practice can be brought by argument to see that, all things considered, it is so. Thus, for example, the critical approach to women's liberation is to some extent tested by the extent to which it is seen, after due consideration, to be true by women themselves. The point being made here is easily open to misinterpretation. It is not being suggested that theories may properly be tested by first publicizing them and then subjecting them to a vote. Rather the point is that for critical understand-ing the subject's considered reaction to the theory is of vital concern in determining its validity. The critical approach does not focus on the unreflective or immediate reaction of the subject, but is more interested in the subject's considered response which will follow from a critical dialogue with the investigator. A proper understanding of an action thus requires critical self-awareness on the part of the subject and on the part of the investigator. It follows that this method requires unhin-dered communication between theorist and subject.

Third, the method of critical understanding has the effect of bringing theory and political practice closer together. We have seen that critical understanding requires a sustained dialogue between the theorist and his subjects. We have also seen that during this dialogue a critical investigator will often have to become involved in arguments about fundamental values. A theory about political change within a given practice is itself a politically charged act within that practice. A consequence of this is that both the inquiry and resulting theory must be seen as interventions within the practice being investigated. The distinction between political scientist and political activist is a much more blurred one for critical understanding than it is for positivist social science or for the *Verstehen* approach. Gadamer suggests that the method of critical understanding is not a particular method in social science, but is essential "to the original character of the being of human life itself."[37]

A central conclusion of this chapter is that a crucial preliminary to any study of international relations is a proper understanding of the acts being investigated. We have seen that coming to understand an act is often a difficult task which positively requires that the investigator become involved in normative discourse with those in the practice being investigated. If the argument of this chapter is correct, the present practice of most scholars in the field of international relations leaves much to be desired. It is seldom the case that scholars analysing wars, interventions, actions in defence of the national interest, hot pursuits, multinational corporation involvement in the affairs of states (and so on) explicitly discuss the substantive normative theories in terms of which they are able to identify the actions in question as being of this or that kind (e.g. as being an intervention in the domestic affairs of another state). They continually give the impression that they are merely *describing* actions.[38] Yet in so far as they are identifying actions as being of one kind rather than another, they must implicitly be drawing on some normative practice. It is time that this implicit normative component be made explicit and be subjected to critical scrutiny.

NOTES

1 I am using the phrase, "positivist bias" here in a wide sense to include such diverse theories as objectivist theories of knowledge (according to which an item will not count as a piece of knowledge unless it corresponds to an item in the world), empiricist theories of science, verificationist theories of science, falsificationist theories of science, *and* value-free approaches to social science. These theories are obviously not always compatible with one another and adherence to one does not indicate an adherence to them all. Nevertheless, they all have this in common: that they are all premised upon a strong distinction between facts and values.

2 The distinction between the classical and scientific approaches was first made by Hedley Bull, "International Theory, the Case for a Classical Approach" in *Contending Approaches to International Politics*, ed. K. Knorr and J. N. Rosenau (Princeton University Press, 1970). The following is a list of some of the main works by the scientific theorists mentioned in the text: J. W. Burton, *International Relations: A General Theory* (Cambridge University Press, 1965); K. W. Deutsch, *The Nerves of Government* (second edition, New York, Free Press, 1966); Stanley Hoffman, *Contemporary Theory in International Relations* (Englewood Cliffs, Prentice-Hall, 1960); Morton Kaplan, *System and Process in International Politics* (New York, John Wiley, 1957); Charles P. Kindleberger, "Scientific International Politics," *World Politics*, Vol. 11, No. 1 (1958), p. 83; K. Knorr and Sydney Verba, *The International System* (Princeton University Press, 1961); C. A. McCelland, *Theory and International System* (New York, Macmillan, 1966); R. Rosecrance, *International Relations: Peace or War* (New York, McGraw-Hill, 1973); J. N. Rosenau, *The Adaptation of National Societies: A Theory of Political System Behaviour and Transformation* (New York; McCaleb-Seiler, 1970); J. D. Singer, *Human Behaviour and International Politics* (Skokie, Rand McNally, 1965).

3 It is probably fair to say that most British students of international relations are more classical than scientific in their approach to international relations. Hedley Bull, *The Anarchical Society* (London, Macmillan, 1977); E. H. Carr, *The Twenty Years Crisis* (London, Macmillan, 1942); D. C. Watt, *A History of the World in the Twentieth Century* (London, Hodder and Stoughton, 1967); Martin Wight, *Systems of States* (Leicester University Press, 1977); Martin Wight, *Power Politics*, ed. Hedley Bull and Carsten Holbraad (Harmondsworth, Penguin Books, 1979).

4 For some Marxist writings pertaining to international relations see the article and bibliography by Tony Thorndike, "The Revolutionary Approach" in *Approaches and Theory in International Relations*, ed. P. G. Taylor (London, Longman, 1978), p. 54. Also see V. Kubálková and A. A. Cruickshank, *Marxism–Leninism and the Theory of International Relations* (London, Routledge and Kegan Paul, 1980).

5 Access to some of these debates may be had through: A. Dogan, *Philosophy of History* (New York, Macmillan, 1965); P. Gardiner, *Theories of History* (Glencoe, The Free Press, 1959); and W. H. Walsh, *An Introduction to the Philosophy of History* (London, Hutchinson, 1967).

6 In this connection see: Hedley Bull, "International Theory"; and Morton Kaplan, "The New Great Debate" in *Contending Approaches to International Relations*, ed. K. Knorr and J. N. Rosenau, p. 39.

7 In this connection see J. D. Singer, "The Level of Analysis Problem in International Relations" in *The International System: Theoretical Issues*, ed. K. Knorr and S. Verba (Princeton University Press, 1961), 77–92; K. N. Waltz, *Man, the State and War* (New York, Columbia University Press, 1959); and K. N. Waltz, *Theory of International Politics* (London, Adison-Wesley, 1979).

8 "In the present stage of its evolution, international theory is engaged in an extremely costly, laborious, and slow process of accumulating data which do not, so far, clearly fit into any plausible general framework." Joseph Frankel, *Contemporary International Theory* (London, Oxford University Press, 1973), p. 19.

9 See note 1 above.

10 For example, A. F. K. Organski, *World Politics* (New York, Alfred Knopf, 1968), p. 5, writes, "A scientific study must be concerned with empirical facts, that is, it must be testable by evidence available to the senses." Also, "but during the course of his investigation, the scientist lays aside his values and treats his data objectively as if it did not matter to him what he found." Relevant here, too, is Karl W. Deutsch, *The Analysis of International Relations* (second edition, Englewood Cliffs, Prentice-Hall, 1978), p. vii, who writes, "As the practice of international relations has become more difficult and decisive, its study has moved to keep pace. The dramatic advances in the field over the last three decades include changes in basic concepts and theories, changes stimulated by a meeting of the newer behavioural sciences of psychology, sociology and anthropology with the longer established disciplines of political science, history and economics. These changes in theory have been accompanied by the development of new methods of research, the development of statistical procedures for analysis and the growing availability of *testable empirical data*" (emphasis added). On the next page he writes "knowledge is different from values. Values motivate the search for knowledge and make some of its results more salient to us than others. Knowledge tells us which of our values may conflict and where and when our means begin to injure and destroy our ends instead of serving them. My own values are made plain throughout this book. *You may share or reject them*" (emphasis added).

See also K. J. Holsti, *International Politics* (Englewood Cliffs, Prentice-Hall, 1967), pp. 13–24, where he distinguishes between the traditional approach to international relations and modern scientific ones, in terms of different "organizing devices" for ordering and making sense of the "facts." He ends Chapter 1 by admitting that no observer can avoid reflecting "certain biases." This affects, he says, even the most "objective scholar." His ideal (which he recognizes as unattainable) is objectivity and a value-free approach to the subject matter.

11 For a discussion of the distinction see Fred M. Frohock, *Normative Political Theory* (Englewood Cliffs, Prentice-Hall, 1974), Chapter 1; W. D. Hudson (ed.), *The Is–Ought Question* (London, St Martin's Press, 1969); Karl Popper, *The Open Society and its Enemies* (London, Routledge and Kegan Paul, 1945), Vol. 1, p. 62; Peter Winch, *Ethics and Action* (London, Routledge and Kegan Paul, 1972), p. 50.

12 The two approaches, the traditional and the scientific, differ in their respective claims about what can be done with the facts; about the way the facts can be incorporated into an explanation. The traditionalist claims that it is not possible to subsume the facts under general theories, whereas the scientific approach views the production of covering laws as the final goal of the enterprise. See Hedley Bull, "International Theory," and J. David Singer, "The Behavioural Science Approach to International Relations: Payoff and Prospects" in *International Politics and Foreign Policy*, ed. J. N. Rosenau (New York, The Free Press, 1969), p. 67.

13 They made a distinction between factual propositions which picture reality and analytic propositions which do not. The distinction was most forcibly argued by the logical positivists of the Vienna Circle. See John Passmore, "Logical Positivism" in *Encyclopaedia of Philosophy*, ed. Paul Edwards (New York, Macmillan, 1967), Vol. 5, p. 52.

14 The distinction between fact and values is not only of importance to the social sciences but is, according to many empiricist philosophers, at the core of all science. The supposed factual base of science has been subject to critical scrutiny by philosophers of the social sciences and of the natural sciences. For an example of the latter see Paul Feyerabend, *Against Method* (London, New Left Books, 1975), especially Chapters 5–9.

15 See W. D. Hudson, *Modern Moral Philosophy* (New York, Doubleday, 1970) *passim*.

16 Vernon Pratt, *The Philosophy of the Social Sciences* (London, Methuen, 1978), p. 93.

17 This is not the only reason for the characteristic avoidance of debates about norms. Other reasons are discussed in Chapter Two below.

18 See especially the sources cited at notes 2 and 3.

19 See the quotations at note 10 above, where Organski writes of the scientist laying aside "*his* values" (emphasis added), and Holsti writes about the "*biases*" (emphasis added) of scholars in international relations.

20 For a good bibliography of some of the literature see Brian Fay, *Social Theory and Political Practice* (London, Allen and Unwin, 1975).

21 Peter Winch, *The Idea of a Social Science* (London, Routledge and

Kegan Paul, 1958). The *Verstehen* approach was originally worked out by Wilhelm Dilthey. See his *Selected Writings*, ed. H. P. Rickman (Cambridge University Press, 1979), Part IV, esp. p. 218 and following pages, and Max Weber, *The Theory of Social and Economic Organization*, trans. A. Henderson and T. Parsons (London, W. Hodge, 1947), Chapter 1. The topic is critically discussed by Jurgen Habermas in *Knowledge and Human Interests* (London, Heinemann, 1971). See also the set of discussion papers edited by Marello Truzzi, *Verstehen: Subjective Understanding in Human Sciences* (Reading, Mass., Addison-Wesley, 1974).

22 This example and the following ones are my own, not those used by Winch.

23 The notion of the "internal point of view" was introduced by H. L. A. Hart, *The Concept of Law* (London, Oxford University Press, 1961).

24 It is not the case that any such act can be *identified* from a non-initiate point of view, but only properly *understood* from the point of view of an initiate. To identify the act requires that the investigator be at least partially initiated into the practice. Of course, further initiation into the practice will bring a deeper understanding of the act.

25 A partial appreciation of the importance of the internal point of view has been achieved by some behaviouralist scholars in international relations who have articulated a need to take note of the different *perceptions* of different actors in world politics, e.g. Robert Jervis, *Perception and Misperception in International Politics* (Princeton University Press, 1976). But interpretative social science would see this approach as too individualistic and psychologistic and would argue that in order to determine how, for example, policy-makers in the USSR perceive the USA, what is called for is an understanding of the practice within which the actors are participating.

26 Brian Fay, *Social Theory and Political Practice*, Chapter 4; John Hughes, *The Philosophy of Social Research* (London, Longman, 1980), Chapter 5; Peter Winch, *The Idea of a Social Science*, p. 89.

27 John Hughes, *The Philosophy of Social Research*, p. 83.

28 See R. W. Johnson, *How Long Will South Africa Survive?* (London, Macmillan, 1977) Chapter 8.

29 A. R. Louch, *Explanation and Human Action* (Oxford, Blackwell, 1966), p. 207.

30 Following the example of Brian Fay, *Social Theory and Political Practice*, Chapter 5, I use the labels "critical theory," the "critical approach," and "critical social science," to refer to a rather broad class of thinkers; a class broader than those contained within what has come to be called the Frankfurt School. I am aware too of the great differences between the thought of the different scholars within the tradition of critical theory. Aspects of the differences are well set out in David Held, *Introduction to Critical Theory* (London, Hutchinson, 1980). In this section I do not intend to portray the main features of the

critical approach, but merely look at one aspect of the approach which is pertinent to our endeavour.

31 Charles Taylor, "A New Realism" (lecture given in the Department of Political Studies, Rhodes University, Grahamstown, South Africa, 25 September 1980).

32 For a portrayal of the main features of the critical model see Brian Fay, *Social Theory and Political Practice*, p. 92.

33 John Hughes, *The Philosophy of Social Research*, p. 83; David Held, *Introduction to Critical Theory*, p. 310, where he discusses Habermas' rejection of descriptivism.

34 John Hughes, *The Philosophy of Social Research*, p. 84; A. R. Louch, *Explanation and Human Action*, Chapter 4.

35 Charles Taylor, "Neutrality in Political Science" in *The Philosophy of Social Explanation*, ed. Alan Ryan (London, Oxford University Press, 1969), p. 139.

36 The general points made about the implications of the *Verstehen* approach (pp. 21–3 above) are relevant here too.

37 Quoted in David Held, *Introduction to Critical Theory*, p. 311.

38 On descriptivism see J. N. Rosenau, Gary Gartin, Edwin P. McClain, Dona Stinziano, Richard Stoddard and Dean Swanson, "Of Syllabi, Texts, Students, and Scholarship in International Relations," *World Politics*, Vol. 29, No. 2 (January 1977), p. 263.

Chapter Two

Sceptical and realist arguments against normative theory in international relations: a critical appraisal

1 Introduction

In the previous chapter I discussed in some detail the general positivist bias of much international relations theory as one of the main reasons for the lack of normative political theory in the discipline. I showed how positivism, and the fact/value dichotomy on which it rests, has come under serious attack in the philosophy of the social sciences and I showed how the main thrust of that attack indicates that it is not possible to do social science without to some extent becoming involved in arguments about the substantive issues in normative political theory. But this positivist bias of the discipline is only a partial explanation for the poverty of theory in this field. It is the aim of the present chapter to look at certain other common assumptions held by theorists in international relations which prevent their taking normative theory seriously. In particular I shall examine certain pervasive assumptions regarding the nature, status and use of substantive value judgements and moral theory in international relations.

There can be little doubt that most scholars in the field of international relations do consider substantive moral arguments and normative theory to be not a worthwhile endeavour and to be suspect in certain ways. If asked to give reasons for their scepticism with regard to normative argument and theorizing, the answer would most likely be something akin to the following. Such theories are *soft* in that they fail to take account of the realities of international relations. A main contention of the present chapter will be that when normative theory is thus accused of being "soft" it is often far from clear in what precisely this softness is supposed to consist. I wish to argue that when the charges are isolated and examined many of them will be found to fail.

The arguments considered in this chapter may all be comprehended under the general rubric of sceptical arguments. Yet they are sceptical in different ways. Some are sceptical about the epistemological status of normative arguments, while others derive their scepticism from other than epistemological considerations. Yet others are sceptical about the applicability and relevance of normative theory irrespective of its epistemological status. It will be the aim of this chapter to consider the underlying problematic and the proper implications of this charge of moral scepticism.

In order to indicate some of the diverse ways in which scepticism about normative theory has been expressed in international relations let us start with a long list of its alleged shortcomings:

1. Value judgements simply express the theorists' own attitudes, whims, emotions, tastes, etc.
2. The propositions of normative theory are not capable of being true or false because there are no normative facts.
3. Normative theories cannot be verified or falsified in the same way that scientific theories, properly so called, can be.
4. Theories about the way the world ought to be are produced by the world as it is. They are epiphenomena of the way the world is. They cannot guide the world, but rather serve as *post hoc* rationalizations.
5. Normative theories are utopian and cannot be realized in practice.
6. In the real world of sovereign states, each state seeks to maximize its power unfettered by considerations of principle. In such a world normative theory is otiose, for the pursuit of power by states is not governed by norms.

7. In the actual world there are diverse sovereign states and a multiplicity of moral orders. This in itself rules out the possibility of a universally agreed normative theory of international relations which would in fact require a universal world order maintained by a single all powerful sovereign. Things being as they are, this is highly unlikely to materialize. If a sovereign were *mirabile dictu* to appear, he would be able to implement whatever normative code he pleased. Thus theorizing about the merits of different normative codes is pointless. At best it may be seen as enjoyable in itself; as akin to the appreciation of art.

8. In their relations with one another sovereign states use normative arguments as tools of policy. States will always find some normative rationalization to suit whatever purposes they have. Thus the only worthwhile investigation to be done concerns the effectiveness of different normative theories as rationalizations. The question of the truth or falsity of the norms invoked is irrelevant.

9. The system of states is one way of organizing relations between groups of people. A morality is a kind of ordering which exists between men as individuals. The ordering principles of a state system are quite incompatible with those involved in a moral order properly so called. Consider the following typical differences:

   a. A typical moral order will sometimes require people to act against their self-interest in specified situations. A morality which *always* coincided with one's own interests would not be recognized as a morality at all. In sharp contrast to such moral constraints the practice of international relations assumes that governments will generally pursue the self-interest of the state. Governments will generally not sacrifice national interest for the sake of some high principle.

   b. Several moral orders take the well-being of individuals as the ultimate value, whereas the rules of the international practice demand that reasons of state take priority over reasons referring to the well-being of individuals. Indeed, in terms of the accepted practice of international relations states are often called upon to sacrifice the well-being of individuals for the good of the state within the system of states.

c. A further example of the difference between the reason of states and moral reasoning is that a requirement of the latter is that individuals ought to be treated equally. In international relations statesmen are required to benefit their own citizens, often at the expense of others, viz. foreigners. The interests of foreigners are often not considered equally or not brought into the equation at all.

d. All moralities count honesty as a virtue, but in international relations governments are often called upon to use deceit. This is considered justified if it serves the self-interest of the state.

e. Moral reasoning typically requires that people be treated as ends and not as means to desired ends. States often act contrary to this principle where this is required by the overriding interest of the state.

f. Moral reasoning requires that agents act on principle and not for the sake of expediency. Within the system of states this principle does not make sense.

This list makes no claim to being exhaustive, but it is quite sufficient to reveal the diverse ways in which it may be alleged that normative theory in international relations is not worthy of serious consideration and of the various forms which scepticism about the status and use of moral discourse can take within this discipline. The arguments in the list can usefully be classified into the following three broad categories. First, there are the arguments which make philosophical claims about the status of normative assertions (items 1–3 on the list). Second, there are arguments about the relationship between normative theories and political practice (items 4–8 on the list). Third, there are arguments about the supposed distinctions between the rules guiding behaviour within the sphere of private morality and the rules guiding behaviour in the sphere of international politics (item 9 on the list). These different kinds of argument against normative theory in international relations are often run into each other and are rarely separated out. Let us now evaluate each of the three broad classes of argument in turn.

2 Non-cognitivism as the philosophical basis for scepticism about normative theory

Objections 1–3, i.e. those regarding the philosophical status of value judgements, are not confined to the discipline of international relations, but may be seen as applicable to normative discourse generally. Thus someone who is convinced by the sceptical arguments that value judgements cannot be true or false and thus have no cognitive substance will be convinced of the worthlessness of moral arguments generally and not merely as they pertain to international relations.[1] A proper discussion of the issues raised by such value non-cognitivism would involve a major work in meta-ethical theory which is beyond the scope of the present study. Here we shall concentrate on one or two central issues.

2.1 Amoralism as a consequence of moral scepticism

The core of all non-cognitivist positions is that about matters of value (in sharp contrast to the position about matters of fact) there can be no truth of the matter. The moral sceptic then proceeds to draw certain implications from this conclusion. I shall evaluate scepticism indirectly by examining this second step first. Let us start by considering one possible implication of non-cognitivism, viz. the amoralist implication. The amoralist implication follows directly from the denial of cognitive status to value judgements: if about matters of value there is no truth or falsity to be had, then an actor is warranted in ignoring traditional moral injunctions and following the dictates of self-interest or prudence or, indeed, any other imperative at all. The core of amoralism, then, is that any reasons are good reasons for action. A person convinced by the amoralist position would deny that an actor ought to be bound by rules of the form "In situation X you ought to do Y." Although the amoral attitude is not often found among individuals, it is often supposed that it is well displayed in international relations. It is often said that in the real world states have no reason to follow rules of the form "In situation X states ought to do Y," except where it is in their national interest to do so. This latter constraint is hardly considered a constraint at all, for states may determine what is to count as the national interest as they will.

Bernard Williams shows that on closer scrutiny a consistent amoralist individual could hardly be considered a sane man.[2] For a consistent amoralist may pursue his own whims, but his philosophy precludes him from ever criticizing the behaviour of others on moral grounds. He may not claim to have been wronged on grounds of unfairness, injustice, deceit, cruelty, etc. All he can say in terms of the logic of his own philosophy is that he likes some of the things which happen to him and dislikes some of the others. Notice that if the amoralist tries to avoid these consequences of his position by saying, "I am not bound by moral rules, but I expect others to be," then his case is lost because he must then be arguing a moral position with special permissions built in it for him. The amoralist might find it in his interests to encourage others to believe themselves bound by moral rules whereas he, himself, is not. However, he cannot make serious moral judgements about others if they, too, would deny that these moral constraints apply to them.

Does the argument applied to the individual case have the same force when applied to states?[3] Would it also be a contradiction in terms for a state to be consistently amoralist? Construct a picture of a practising amoralist state. It could, by definition, never level charges of unfair, unjust, deceitful, inhuman (and so on) actions against other states. If it did so it would have to acknowledge that such charges were mere posturing, empty moralizing. Conversely, it would have to deny the validity of any similar charges against itself, not as being wrong, but as pointless. It is patent that states in general are not overtly amoralist. In their dealings with one another they talk the language of right conduct; they abide by the conventional discourse of international relations. For example, there are disputes about "hot pursuit" raids. Typically they are justified as necessary for the maintenance of national security or condemned as unwarranted violations of the sovereignty of a neighbouring state; they are depicted in terms of justifiable self-defence or unjustifiable aggression. There is often disagreement between states about what constitutes right conduct in a particular situation or about what the proper standards of right conduct are. But of the fact that all states acknowledge that there are some standards of right conduct there can be no doubt.

Might it not be the case that states are all covertly amoral?[4] This suggestion, although initially plausible, will not stand up to critical inquiry. The charge by state A that it has been wronged by state B will only be meaningful if it is the case that there exists a practice in which the alleged wrong is generally recognized as a wrong and if both A and B are members of that practice. Consider the rule "States ought not to invade the boundaries of other states except under the following specified conditions ..." Appeals to this standard, even hypocritical ones, can only be made because, in general, it actually is accepted as a binding norm within the practice of states. Hypocritical appeals to the norm are dependent on a non-hypocritically adhered to practice. In short, the occasional act of covert amoralism is dependent on the existence of a functioning and open moral practice.

Finally, someone arguing for the amoralist position with regard to the states might argue that states find the whole practice of right conduct an expedient fiction. Whenever they appeal to moral norms of right and wrong, they are actually merely acting *as if* they were moral. This argument fails because it misunderstands the connection we have been trying to establish between being a state and recognizing rules of right conduct for states. The hypocritical-state argument suggests that there are entities called states which can be conceived of as choosing to pretend to play the game of right conduct for states. My argument is that it is not possible to conceive of something as a state independently of it making and recognizing claims based on some code of right conduct. Recognizing such rules and being recognized in terms of them is what is involved in being a state. Those arguing the case which I have been attacking need to give some plausible account of what the state is, which account does not contain within it any reference to rules of right conduct (such as the right of sovereign control over a given territory, the right to declare war and the right to make treaties, etc.). I do not think that this is possible. In Chapter Five I discuss in some detail the way in which the notion of statehood is situated within the context of a set of rules within which the parties reciprocally recognize one another in specified ways.

We may summarize this section thus: the person or state who acted as a consistent amoralist would not be recognizable as a man or a state properly so called. This does not imply that all individuals and all states are at all times moral. It also does not imply that any specific moral stance is the right one. What is being argued is that individuals and states must have *some* moral position, for having such a position is partially constitutive of what being a person or being a state is.

2.2 The compatibility of non-cognitivist scepticism and serious moral argument

There is a philosophical position which is non-cognitivist with regard to the epistemological status of moral discourse, but which does not draw an amoralist conclusion from the non-cognitivist premise. An example of this form of moral scepticism is provided by John Mackie in his book *Ethics: Inventing Right and Wrong.*[5] He is concerned to defend the proposition that there are no objective values. His argument is primarily ontological. He says, "values are not objective, are not part of the fabric of the world."[6] As reasons for this conclusion he appeals to what he calls the argument from diversity (which asserts that since there is such a multiplicity of moralities in the world, it is implausible to suppose that there is a single true morality) and to the argument from queerness (which says that if there were objective values they would have to be entities, qualities or relations in the world which could only be seen by some special "queer" faculty quite out of the ordinary).[7] However, Mackie's scepticism does not preclude the possibility of serious argument about values between people who share certain basic premises. But where disputes about these fundamental premises arise there is no objective base which may be referred to in order to settle the matter. This sceptical position is put forward against Plato, Kant and Sidgwick, amongst others.

Scepticism of this type is perfectly compatible with conventional moral behaviour (where such behaviour includes the having of serious moral arguments). Indeed, John Mackie in his book reaches certain substantive moral conclusions. It is thus possible to have moral beliefs and to adhere to a moral code based on them while at the same time being sceptical about the ultimate ontological status of moral statements.

A crucial question is what (if any) normative implications follow from a non-cognitivist position like Mackie's? An important implication is hinted at in the subtitle of Mackie's book which refers to inventing right and wrong. If values are not objective, then they must be man made. It is this implication which is unacceptable to many and leads to the general belief that serious theorizing about values is not worthwhile. Is this belief justified?

I have already indicated that it is quite possible to be a sceptic and consider oneself bound by a moral code. Still, noncognitive scepticism of this kind easily gives rise to the supposition that if there is no ultimate objective standard in terms of which moral propositions may be judged true or false, then ultimately moral judgements must be *subjective*. Scepticism about values then allegedly commits one to moral subjectivism. Finally and crucially, this is then taken to warrant an "anything goes" approach to life and to the conduct of affairs in international relations as well; it is seen as a warrant for amoralism. What we have here is an unwarranted slide from a noncognitivist epistemology to an amoralist position.

It is easy to see what dire consequences this belief could have within the discipline of international relations. First, on this view there could be no serious discussions of right and wrong with regard to international conduct. Second, there could be no argument with the view (widely held in international relations) that might makes right.

The link between non-cognitivism and subjectivist amoralism is not warranted. There are ways in which an assertion may not be ultimately traceable to an objective basis, yet may still not be *merely* subjective. We have already seen one way in which this may be so. A value judgement may be validated or invalidated in terms of a set of premises held in common by a group of people. These premises may not be, in any ontological sense, true, but simply be premises to which the people involved are committed. Here I want to argue as I did earlier that what is involved in being a person or being a state cannot be explicated without some reference to a common commitment to some such set of shared normative principles – be it a liberal Western set or a primitive tribal one.[8] We would not recognize as a person someone who did not claim that certain kinds of conduct towards him were right whereas others were wrong, and who did not recognize similar claims against him in terms of a conventionally shared morality. The same point applies to states. As a matter of fact we find all people and all states making just such judgements about their own and others' conduct. It is in the making of such judgements that moral disputes arise. Subjectivism (amoralism) consistently maintained would have to hold that ordinary moral practice is nonsensical, based on a lie, or some such thing. I have already indicated how any suggestion that individuals and states may be seen as hypocritically moral may be countered.[9]

A sceptic may well be prepared to accept this argument

against the subjectivist position, but argue that although his scepticism does not imply subjectivism, it does imply *relativism*. The relativist position is that the moral discussions all take place within and are relative to a specific moral practice. Within such a practice there is a wide base of mutually agreed upon premises. The arguments within such a practice are about the application of those premises to a given situation. Thus some statement of a moral position may be shown to be true or false *relative* to the basic premises held in common by the disputants within the practice. But where inter-practice disputes arise there can be no truth of the matter.[10] Applied to international relations this line of reasoning leads to the following kind of conclusion. We can conceive of moral disputes among liberal politicians and statesmen. Such disputes may be intersubjectively settled by reference to the conventions which in fact all liberals are committed to. Similarly there may be disputes among messianic statesmen open to intersubjective tests. But there are no objective standards for settling any disputes between members of the two groups. For the relativist there thus comes a stage in moral argument at which conflicting bedrock positions are reached and that is when the dispute transcends the shared conventions.

Sometimes a normative consequence is drawn from this relativist position, viz. that since there are no objective standards for settling inter-practice disputes we ought to be tolerant of the norms and behaviour of those in practices other than our own.[11] What we have here is a relativist attempt to avoid the amoralist implications of relativism. The problem with this conclusion is that it is a non-relative *moral* prescription made by a relativist. Why should we make the jump from the lack of a standard of truth to the moral requirement of tolerance? The relativist's own premises undercut the conclusion urging tolerance. For when the relativist says that we ought to be tolerant, this "ought" must, on his own premises, be a relative "ought." It cannot apply across practices because the situation as defined excludes inter-practice agreement.

Before considering what conclusions may properly be drawn

from the sceptical/relativist thesis, there is one other mistaken conclusion which must be noted. This is the conclusion that because there are so many different moral practices and because there is so little consensus between them, people are justified in withdrawing into a general apathy. Here there is an unwarranted jump from non-cognitivism to a form of amoralism.[12] It does not follow from the sceptical position asserting that there are no ontological moral truths and from the fact that there exist diverse moral practices that there are good reasons for being apathetic. If we take relativism seriously there is just as much reason (viz. no reason) to be the opposite of apathetic (which presumably involves being fanatical in some way). Neither an injunction to be tolerant nor a permission to be apathetic is a necessary consequence of relativism. What may be correctly drawn from the sceptical/relativist thesis is the conclusion that where there is an inter-practice dispute there is no guarantee that a right answer will, in the fullness of time, be found. There is, by definition, no agreement on the criteria for the right answer. If agreement is to be achieved it will have to be created (made) between the disputants. However, this does not imply, for the reasons already given, that we are obliged to accept subjectivism.[13] Saying that moralities have to be built does not imply that the building of a morality is not a worthwhile activity, nor that we ought to refrain from morality building and concern ourselves with more important tasks (like the search for truth through scientific method). It is arguable that we have to do *some* morality building if things are not to go badly with us. In so far as moralities are invented or built they are designed to overcome certain problems which people face in society. For example, any group of people will need some shared morality if they are to co-operate together to achieve those goods which cannot be achieved without co-operation, e.g. maintaining security, upholding property relations, regulating sexual relations and so on. Moralities are answers to predicaments which any society faces. A conflict of moralities is itself such a predicament for which a moral answer must be created.

Let us stand back and look at the argument thus far. We have been evaluating the argument that scepticism about morals undercuts all serious theorizing about values. Without considering the positive arguments for scepticism about values I sought to show that amoralism (which is sometimes taken to be a consequence of non-cognitivism) cannot be coherently maintained in practice. Subsequently I argued that non-cognitivism concerning the ontological status of value judgements does not warrant or imply amoralism, tolerance or apathy. Such scepticism is quite compatible with serious theorizing about questions of value in all disciplines including international relations. Thus far I have not done any substantive theorizing with regard to the evaluation of different normative theories of international relations. I have merely been concerned to show that scepticism about the existence of objective moral values does not entail that normative theory is pointless or worthless. More positively, two things have emerged from the discussion: first, there are many human predicaments which cannot be solved without the building of a normative order. Human flourishing depends on the creation of such orders. Second, the creation of such orders requires the participation of the people involved in the dispute. In sum, then, non-cognitivism establishes certain ways in which normative arguments are different from arguments about facts. It does not establish that normative argument is not worthwhile.

3 Realist arguments against normative theory in international relations

3.1 *Realist arguments based on the primacy of the structure of world society*

There is a widespread tendency in the discipline of international relations to eschew explicit discussion of normative issues on the ground that such thought is derivative from the structure of social reality and is thus of secondary importance. Normative theory always presupposes that actors in the practice of international relations do have alternatives and real choices, and can change their conduct. Only if we accept these presuppositions do ought-statements in the context of international relations make sense. Similarly, normative theory in international relations presupposes that the international order itself can be deliberately changed in specified ways. In short, then, normative theory presupposes that there is an important sense in which people's normative ideas can shape the order in which they live. It is this presupposition which is often regarded as suspect in the discipline of international relations. For many scholars in the field (be they balance of power theorists, interdependence theorists or neo-Marxists) see themselves in some broad sense as "hard headed realists." They are extremely wary of the notion that it is possible in the realm of international relations for people's notions about what is normatively acceptable to shape the order in which they live. Normative theorizing is dismissed as utopian thinking ("soft," "tender minded"). However, if it is the case that in international relations people's normative ideas do not play any major part in shaping the international order in which they live, there must be implicit in this general position some other view of the link between political reality and normative ideas. The general assumption implicit in such "realist" views is that the normative ideas people have are determined by the general structure of the social and political reality in which they find themselves. There is an underlying notion that the political structures are "autonomous" in some sense. They are "autonomous" in so far as they are supposed to be independent of the normative ideas held by those in the international practice and not able to be changed by these ideas. The nature of the structures is portrayed differently in different theories. In neo-Marxist theories the structure is presented as the material base of society. In political realism the fundamental structure is called the real structure of power. In interdependence theory it is the international economic system which is presented as the determining basis of world politics.

In what way is the structure of the social reality supposed to be independent of normative ideas and in what way does this supposed autonomy have a bearing on the worth of normative theory? The precise nature of this structure is a core problem for all the theories mentioned. Although there is clearly some assumption about the primacy of these structures and although it is assumed that the nature of the structures has a bearing on the worth of normative argument, it is far from clear what the positive content of these assumptions about the autonomous/determining/underlying social "reality" are. Yet it is possible to give an approximation of its general features.

First, society as a whole is conceived of as some sort of social system. A system may be defined as a set of parts which are interdependent in certain specified ways. There are wide variations in the way that different theorists conceive of the social system. Some conceive of it as a whole within which there is a general equilibrium between the parts. According to one such model the modern world is an emergent system of technological and economic interdependence between peoples. Within the context of state bound economies it is no longer possible to sustain economic growth. Growth can only be sustained where new patterns of co-operation between states develop. This ever more complicated pattern of interdependence will have the effect of making the sovereign states, as we know them, increasingly less sovereign, less independent. There will thus emerge from this process a new form of world polity to replace the system of sovereign states.[14] Other theories each operate with their own different concept of system. Historical materialist theories argue that there is indeed a global system of interrelated parts, but the parts, far from existing in a state of harmonious equilibrium, are pictured as being in a process of change caused by fundamental contradictions within the system. The reference here is, of course, to Marxist and neo-Marxist accounts of the international order; to theories of imperialism, neo-colonialism, theories of underdevelopment and the like.[15]

Second, it is supposed that the way in which the system

operates is independent of any single person or group of people's wishes.[16]

Third, it is supposed that the actors in the system are, in some sense, determined by it. Both their behaviour and their thoughts (what they tend to do *and* the prescriptive rules/ norms specifying what they ought to do) are in some way thus determined by the underlying structure. The implications for normative theory now become clear. The system determines the ideas (including the normative ones) which people have. Normative theorizing can thus not be of any importance; the system operates independently of such theories and itself determines whatever operative normative notions arise. As I said at the outset, normative theory always presupposes that it is possible in some way for actors, guided by their normative ideas, to change in significant ways the order in which they live. If it is the other way about, i.e. if their normative ideas are determined by the underlying structure, clearly normative theory is of no consequence. At best it is enjoyable for its own sake, as in art.

There are many examples of this way of thinking. Let us look at two: one an equilibirum model and one a system-in-conflict or structural model. The equilibrium model is the one pre-sented by Kenneth Waltz in *Theory of International Politics*.[17] In this work he develops a theme he himself had made famous in an earlier work which is now a classic in the field.[18] There he had stressed the need for different levels of analysis in inter-national relations. A narrow focus on either the individual or on the state – although both are important levels of analysis – would not permit a full explanation of international phenom-ena, unless it was supplemented with a systems-level analysis. This three-levels-of-analysis approach is now the conventional wisdom in the field. For Waltz it is the systems level of analysis which is primary. Without it a proper analysis of the other two levels would not be possible. *Theory of International Politics* is devoted to further exploration of this fundamental level – the systems level.[19]

A systems theory, Waltz says, is one which explains the interactions between the parts of the system without reference to the specific character of these parts. It would explain war in general without referring to any particular states or statesmen. Crucial to the enterprise is the notion of *structure*. It is the underlying structure of international affairs which, in Waltz's view, is a primary determinant of the actions of states and individuals within states. What is a structure? It is distinct from a *device*, which is something consciously designed to produce a given result. A structure is not a direct cause, but acts as a set of constraining conditions; as a selector.[20] Systems (composed of structures) are thus supposed to emerge from our interactions, without our intending them. Once they have emerged they constrain our actions. The market is such a system. The international order between states is another one. Notice that what is crucial for Waltz is that structures not only develop spontaneously and are unintended, but serve as determining constraints on our actions and our intentions. Once developed, structures reward and punish actors according to whether these actors uphold the system or not.[21] It is clear that Waltz envisages the structure of the international system as being, in some sense, the fundamental determinant of world politics; as being in some way independent of the ideas men happen to have. The international order as a structure of this kind is thus assumed as some kind of basic political "reality" and it is, moreover, one which clearly diminishes the possible relevance of normative theory.

Historical materialism, too, is a theory in terms of which there is a determining and in some sense autonomous base which determines the ideas of the participants in international affairs. Although there has been and continues to be an extended debate about the proper definition of historical materialism, there is little doubt that most scholars pursuing the historical materialist method would agree that "world society emerges in this view not as a consequence of 'power' relations or decision-making routines or the rest of the paraphernalia of a traditional approach, but as a function of or reaction to the world economy."[22] As an example of historical materialist method applied to international relations let us look briefly at Lenin's theory of imperialism.

Lenin sought not merely to explain the First World War, but to provide a general theory of why wars occur in the modern capitalist world. His aim is thus very similar to that which later inspired Waltz to develop his systems-level analysis. Lenin's view sees the capitalist world order as being shot through with fundamental contradictions which will in the long run lead to the demise of that system. Lenin's classic work on this topic is entitled *Imperialism the Highest Stage of Capitalism.*[23] In it he argues that in the modern world capitalism has taken on a significant new form. It has left the free market phase and has entered the monopoly phase. The main features of this phase are: first, the formation of production cartels or monopolies within the major capitalist countries of the world. These monopolies have seized control of the most important sources of raw materials within these states. Second, in this stage of capitalism the role of the banks changes significantly. Instead of being modest middle men through which funds could be channelled they have become monopolistic controllers of finance capital. Third, as a result of this formation of monopolies in business and banking there arose in capitalist states a surplus of capital for which new avenues of investment had to be found. Opportunities for investing this surplus were found in the colonies. Fourth, as the major capitalist countries were all seeking outlets for their surplus capital and the available territories for expansion were limited, these countries came into competition with one another in their imperialist projects. It is this imperialist competition which explains the outbreak of wars in the modern world. The First World War is shown, according to this theory, to have been a war "for the division of the world, for the partition and repartition of colonies and spheres of influence of finance capital, etc."[24]

Lenin gives some empirical data to show that the businesses

and banks of the capitalist powers had become increasingly monopolistic during the latter half of the nineteenth century and early twentieth century. The accuracy and details of these contentions need not concern us here. For my purposes it is the way in which he portrays the link between the underlying processes of capitalism and the political results thereof which is relevant. "The capitalists divide the world not out of any *malice*, but because the degree of concentration which has been reached *forces* them to adopt this method in order to get profits."[25] A few lines later he writes:

The epoch of the latest stage of capitalism shows us that certain relations between capitalist associations grow up, *based* on the economic division of the world: while parallel to and in connection with it, certain relations grow up between political alliances, between states, on the basis of the territorial division of the world, of the struggle for colonies, of the "struggle for sphere of influence."[26]

For Lenin the political aspects of imperialism are thus a necessary outcome of the basic economic processes at work. He argues vehemently against those like Hobson and Kautsky who deny the "inevitability of imperialism."[27] He writes, "Whatever the political system, the result of these tendencies is everywhere reaction and an extreme intensification of antagonisms in this field. Particularly intensified become the yoke of national oppression and the striving for annexation."[28] The annexations revolutionize the existing social relations in the colonies. At the same time hostility to the annexations is generated, leading to the rise of nationalisms in these areas which will become increasingly hostile to domination by the capitalist powers. Here we see a contradiction emerging which it was predicted would lead to important changes in the future.[29]

The brief outline which I have given of Lenin's historical materialist account of the international order during the "highest stage of capitalism" is sufficient to indicate how Lenin envisages the basic capitalist structure of world society as the *primary determinant* of the actions of citizens and states alike. On this view what happens comes about not through people deciding what morally ought to be done and then doing it, but rather through contradictions within the system becoming more and more sharply defined until some form of revolution results. This is not to say that there is within this theoretical perspective no room left for agency. Lenin was a consummate political activist and wrote a famous piece entitled *What is to be Done?*[30] But the "ought" implied in this title is not indicative of any moral imperatives; rather Lenin's deliberation was of a technical nature, i.e. it was about the best means to agreed upon ends.

Lenin's is, of course, not the only historical materialist account of the international order. There are other more recent examples of this approach to international affairs.[31] These more recent examples are not all of a piece. There are important and sustained disputes between the different theorists. Yet they are all similar in so far as they assert that it is the basic economic structure of society which in the last instance determines what happens in the political, moral, religious and cultural spheres. A superstructure of religious, moral and political ideas is determined by the economic base. A too crude view of this relationship is nowadays characterized as "vulgar Marxism" and rejected as an erroneous interpretation of Marx. Nevertheless, even the non-vulgar theories hold that in the last instance the relations of production are determining of the superstructural elements of society.[32] A feature of these approaches is that normative ideas are characterized as ideological, which is taken to mean justifying of the existing relations of production.[33] On this view ideology is non-autonomous thought; it is thought which reflects the base structure, or rationalizes it, or which is in some or other way an automatic response to it. In such a vision of the world order there is little room for any autonomous normative theory.

We have been looking at theoretical approaches to international relations, which, because they rely on an underlying notion of a determining basic structure, make normative theory otiose. This notion of a basic structure is seriously flawed in that it wrongly supposes that the underlying determining structure (base, system, etc.) is independent of norms; i.e. it wrongly supposes that there is a structure (base, system, etc.) which could be identified without reference to the normative ideas of those participating in it. If it can be shown that the base is itself largely constituted by a set of normative ideas, then the whole determination thesis must fail. It can be easily shown that normative notions necessarily enter into any description of the supposed determining structure of society; normative theory cannot be avoided in any attempt to identify or articulate such a structure.

Consider Waltz's characterization of the international system. Its primary units are, he says, states. But a state is not a political reality that exists independently of the ideas and norms which people adhere to. Amongst other things the existence of a state always implies the existence of a large group of people who are in some way bound together, in large part, by a set of normative commitments and obligations. There could be no such thing as a state without people adhering to such obligations. Against this it might be argued that a state is not wholly (or always) a consensual arrangement in which people see themselves as bound together by mutually accepted rules; a state often rests on coercive elements.[34] This objection misses the point. For us to call a given arrangement a state it must be the case that there exists a practice within which the participants recognize themselves as citizens of a state and that they recognize certain of these citizens as forming a government having the authority to make laws which are binding upon them. In order to recognize themselves in these ways the people involved must acknowledge certain rules. The point may be made by looking at an analogous situation in the context of sport. Rugby is a game and like all such games is played according to agreed upon rules; it is a practice constituted by people recognizing certain rules which they hold to be constitutive of the game rugby. Of any individual rugby player it may well be possible to assert that he plays rugby only because he is forced to by his father. Indeed, we can imagine a situation in which *all* the players in a particular sport play only because they are forced to do so (gladiators). Does this point undermine our immediate argument?

It may be argued that I am paying insufficient attention to the whole question of *power*. A critic at this point may argue that the account ignores (or seriously underplays) the fact that people are often *forced* to obey the rules (laws) of a practice (be it a game or a political arrangement like the state). In order to make this point most forcefully our interlocutor might use the following bloody example: imagine a very powerful group of people *forcing* a less powerful group to participate in the practice of gladiator fighting. This "game" is played by putting a gladiator in a ring with a hungry lion. The rules are: if the gladiator stays alive for five minutes he gets five points and is given a club as a weapon. If he then kills the lion straight away (thus depriving the audience of a good fight) the club is taken away and a fresh lion is brought in. But if instead of killing the lion straight off, he manages to keep the fight going for half an hour before killing it, the gladiator is set free. Here the game consists in the players recognizing and abiding by the rules. Thus in some sense the game may well be constituted by the ideas the participants (including the spectators) have, but this game (this set of ideas) was *forced* upon the gladiators by the stronger group.

This example does not undermine the main thrust of my argument. The argument is not that all practices (including the one we call the state) are voluntarily entered into. Nor is it the aim of the argument to make the notion of power obsolete. My argument is that whatever *structure* (base, system or whatever) is said to force people to act and think in certain ways, this structure itself cannot be identified without reference to some set of constitutive ideas. Applying this point to the gladiator example, my argument is that no adequate account can be given of the power which forced the men into gladiator fighting which does not contain within it reference to the set of ideas in

terms of which the people in question (the Romans?) constituted themselves as a powerful group. Thus Waltz cannot give
an account of the structure of a system of sovereign states
without (if only implicitly) referring to the ideas whereby the
people involved come to see themselves as members of sovereign states within a group of sovereign states. Similarly, neo-
Marxist theory cannot give an account of a determining
economic base of society without referring to the normative
ideas in terms of which the people involved constitute themselves in a given set of property relations, e.g. in terms of such
notions as private property, contract, state property and so on.

The central point, then, is that participating in a practice (be
it a game or a political arrangement) requires that the participants recognize themselves as bound by the rules of the game;
as bound by certain norms. Thus where a state exists there
must be a group of people who see themselves as constituting a
state through their mutual recognition of a specified set of
rules. In this sense, then, a state consists in a group of people
recognizing themselves as bound by a specified formation of
rules. Thus (and here I return to the main point of the present
argument) a state is not a political reality which exists independently of the ideas (including normative ones) which people
adhere to.

I am arguing that states are constituted by people mutually
recognizing one another as reciprocally bound by a certain set
of rules. The argument is that no coherent account of the structure of the state can be given without referring to this practice
of mutual recognition: the set of ideas and rules constituting
the civil and political relationships between them. If the argument is sound then the evaluation of these rules – which
activity I have called normative theory – is clearly of cardinal
importance.

The argument above must not be taken as suggesting that the
way the world is is an intentional product of some person or
group. Nor is it being argued that *any* arrangement men might
wish for in the world could forthwith be brought about. Simi-

larly it is not being denied that the unintended consequences of multiple past actions will influence people's future thought. What is being asserted is that a highly relevant and indeed constitutive feature of social wholes is the set of norms which the participants adhere to. Thus it follows that normative argument and theory must be of central importance in social (and thus international) life.

A critic may retort that all I have established is the centrality of ideas in social wholes, but that this is not the same as establishing the need for normative *argument*, for propaganda can weld a society together just as well. A partial answer to this is that propaganda is parasitic on proper argument.[35] The "arguments" of the propagandist "piggy back," as it were, on practices of sound argument, just as the distorted uses which advertisers make of certain words derive their power from ordinary sound usages. The other part of the answer will be found within the following section in which a different kind of realist argument against normative theory is considered.

3.2 Realist arguments from the primacy of power

At its most general, the conventional doctrine of *political realism* asserts the primacy of power over reason. The political realist is not primarily concerned with the logical or epistemological status of normative propositions; he is not concerned whether such propositions may be said to be true or false. The political realist asserts that even if normative theories are in some ontological/objective sense true, normative theorizing is not worthwhile, because what the theories prescribe can and will always be overridden by those with the power to do so. Consider international relations. The realist argument is that even if it were possible to establish how states ought to behave towards one another, the problem of getting states to behave in that way would still remain. The statement of a reasonable position does not bring about a reasonable order. What is needed, the political realist argues, is the power to implement that order. But, the argument continues, power is not a neutral instrument which can be attained and put to use for good or for evil. Power has its own imperatives which those seeking to gain or maintain power must follow. A power seeker who ignores these and sets out to implement some or other desired normative order does so at his peril, for the imperatives of power are given and he who disobeys these "realities" will either fail to gain power or lose that power which he has.

It is easy to see how this line of argument leads to the conclusion that normative theory in international relations is not a worthwhile activity. For in this view power is required for the implementation of *any* desired order in international affairs, but what is required for the maintenance of power is not dependent on the truth or falsity of a particular normative theory. Indeed the requirements of power often run counter to what is considered an acceptable normative code. The imperatives of power make normative theory otiose.

Modern political realism in international relations may be seen as a reaction to earlier "utopian" thought. The modern realist rejection of normative theory stems largely from the disappointed hopes of the inter-war generation of scholars in the discipline. After the First World War there had been a widespread hope that a new order based on the notion of collective security would introduce an era of lasting peace. Fundamental to this movement was the belief that it would be supported by public opinion which, by the light of reason, would see the wisdom of a collective security arrangement as self-evident. That generation of scholars failed to predict fascism, the breakdown of the League of Nations and the outbreak of the Second World War. Political realists in following generations thus came to blame the earlier thinkers for failing to take note of the irrational aspects of man's nature (nationalism, fascism) and the realities of power.[36] More generally it became the conventional wisdom of such political realism that it is the "realities of power" and not any normative views or theories which are decisive in international affairs.

What are we to make of this seemingly plausible claim that in the final instance might is more fundamental than right? The realist position is an untenable one because might and right (power and value, reality and ideal) are not conceptually and practically distinct in the way they need to be to maintain this position. Evidently this argument is very similar to the one made in the previous section. But let us expand it somewhat by looking closely at the link between political power, on the one hand, and human aims, values, norms, morals, principles and so on, on the other.

The core of the political realist position is that the structure of power determines the appropriate course of conduct for actors in the realm of international relations in a way that is not dependent on the truth or falsity of the values (norms, etc.) which men happen to have. On this view actors in world politics are, at any given time, constrained by the *structures of power* existing in the world. What is crucial for the realist is that the imperatives of power are in some sense objectively given in a way that is not dependent on people's theories about right and wrong. My argument against the realist is that power is always intimately linked up with specific sets of ideas which constrain what that power may be used for. An example will illustrate this. The Ayatollah Khomeini of Iran has power over his followers because he is seen by them as their religious leader within the context of that whole set of ideas which comprises the Muslim religion. Within that context he has power to execute certain decisions. But the range of possible decisions is also limited by the theological context. The Ayatollah is not able to pursue the policies of Mr Sharon (to take an extreme case) for this would be in breach of the principles adhered to by his followers from which his power, in part, derives. Similarly, the power of President Gorbachev is situated in and constrained by the ideas of Marxism–Leninism as manifested in the present day constitutional and party arrangements in the USSR. Were he to attempt to turn to Friedmanite monetarism his power would quickly wane (and he would probably be declared insane). These two examples refer to the ideas which bind a leader to his followers and which constrain his power. Power always exists within a practice which is partially constituted by certain normative ideas. Far from it being the case that the leader has the power to choose what value system (ideology) to implement, he is, himself, constrained by the value system in terms of which he holds power.

Against the argument outlined above a critic may want to argue that this may apply to the leader and his followers, but does not apply to the relationship between a power wielder and his victims. Thus, the critic might argue, the President of the USA is constrained vis-à-vis his followers (i.e. the citizens of the USA) by certain democratic/capitalist ideas, but deny that this applies to the relationship between the USA and the citizens of certain Third World client states. This criticism fails because even in dealing with third parties ideas bind the power holder. As President of the USA, Mr Reagan is obligated to follow policies which are justifiable in a certain kind of way – in the liberal/capitalist/democratic way – rather than in some other way. His is not a power to use according to whim. To put it bluntly, his action is subject to moral criticism and his power may ebb and flow as a result of such criticism. Contrary to the political realist thesis, power analysed in this way accentuates the importance of normative theory.

The critic may not be satisfied with this response. He may claim that all I have shown is that the power wielder is subject to the moral criticism of his allies and followers, but that from the point of view of the victim or subject, normative theory is of no particular relevance. The power of the power wielder is not dependent on the moral approval of the victim. But my argument is not that power relationships exist only where the sufferer sees the power of the wielder as morally unjustified. For example, many Third World states see the economic and political power which is wielded over them by the developed states of the West (especially the USA) as morally unwarranted. My argument is that it is not possible to characterize a power relationship without reference to the ideas (norms, morals, principles, etc.) which the wielder holds *and* to the ideas (norms, morals, principles, etc.) which the subject holds, even though these may be antipathetic to those held by the former. Consider the example mentioned, viz. the claim made by many Third World states that the great Western powers exert unwarranted economic and political power against them. The political power of the Western statesmen depends on their being office holders within the context of their particular respective states. Their political power depends on a whole set of ideas, held in common by the citizens of those states, regulating the relationship between governors and the governed. Similarly, their economic power depends on a set of beliefs, held in common by the same group of people, concerning what is right and wrong with regard to property relationships at home and abroad. Such a power relationship depends, too, on certain sets of political and economic ideas held by those in the subject states. Those in the subject states aspire to be citizens of a state of a certain kind (an independent, democratic one, for instance) and they aspire to participate in a certain set of property relationships (be it capitalist, socialist or communist). If those in the subject states were not bound together in terms of these commonly held notions, then it could well be the case that the power relationship which exists between them and the developed states would cease to be (or turn into something different). Let me make this point by means of an extreme example. Were the people in a given region which is now identified as a subject state to convert to an extremely ascetic and other-worldly oriented religion (i.e. they ceased to believe in the values of statehood, modernization, democracy and ceased to believe in the value of private property) then the great powers, such as the USA, would no longer have the same power over them. The powerlessness of the subject, too, thus cannot be portrayed without reference to the ideas (norms, etc.) that bind those in the subject state together as a community of a certain kind. Thus these states, too, are vulnerable to critical normative theory. Normative criticism may, at least in principle, significantly affect the so called "realities of power."

Once again it will not do to respond to the argument above that although it establishes an important link between power and normative ideas it does not yet establish the importance of serious normative *argument*; that all it establishes is the importance for power wielders of legitimating propaganda. It is important that we consider this response, for it is implicit in many Western theories of power in international relations. These theorists admit that what people think or believe is an important element in determining the power of a state, but they see this as only one element in the overall power structure. This element of power is customarily referred to in such theories as the element of public opinion.[37] On this view governments that want to maintain power must take good care of domestic and international public opinion. This is done through the media, by propaganda. Other elements of power often mentioned are: economic resources, industrial capacity, military strength and so on. If the link between power and ideas is conceived of in this way, i.e. where ideas are merely synonymous with opinions (without any particular link to the other elements of power such as the military and the economic ones) and where opinion is only one of the elements of power, then no clear case is made for the importance of reasoned normative argument at all. Establishing the power of public opinion does not establish the importance of normative debate. The link which I have been seeking to establish between power and ideas is not this one; it seeks rather to undermine it.

The public opinion view of the connection between power and ideas once again assumes the position which I have repeatedly tried to refute, viz. it assumes that power can exist independently of ideas. On the propaganda view of power, the wielder of power "has" power which he may then use to make propaganda to increase his power. On the view for which I have been arguing, the political power of a power wielder consists in part of a norm-constituted relationship between him and his audience. If they did not adhere to these ideas he would not be a leader. Furthermore this is not a point which relates to only one of the "elements" of power. All the so called "elements" of power are partially constituted by people co-operating one with another in terms of some specified set of norms. Thus, in a capitalist country economic strength derives from the members of the country co-operating according to the constitutive norms of capitalism. The same applies to industrial and military power. Power is thus based on co-operation according to norms.[38] Power wielders cannot be indifferent to how those norms are evaluated, and must therefore take normative thinking seriously. If the ideas in terms of which they hold power are eroded, then their power is eroded. Criticism is the acid which corrodes ideas. However, critical scrutiny may also reinforce a given set of ideas and thus reinforce power. So we see that all power holders have an interest in justifying their position and refuting their critics. This is not a peripheral interest as is sometimes suggested by the use of the words "rationalization" and "legitimation." It is crucial, and we thus come to see the normative theorist as a player in the game of power.[39]

It might be thought that I have been blurring crucial distinctions between such notions as power, authority and influence. Although the distinctions between these notions are important for some purposes, they are not crucial to the argument here. The argument is that for any group of people to exercise power over another group, both groups have to be constituted as groups, in terms of some set of ideas (which will include normative ones). No doubt, the members of the power wielding group will see these constitutive rules as legitimate and as conferring authority on the rulers to rule, whereas those subject to the group's power may see the rules as illegitimate (and thus as not conferring authority on that government to do what it does). Settling the controversy about whether the rules are legitimate or not is a matter for moral argument. The details of this argument are not my concern here. I am concerned merely to establish the general point that power relations cannot be characterized without reference to the ideas binding people together.

4 Morality and the imperatives of world politics

I here come to consider a final argument against taking seriously theories about how the world ought to be organized. At its most general the argument goes as follows: in whatever way the world is organized it will always be a political arrangement and political arrangements are always non-moral in important respects. There is, on this view, an irresolvable tension between politics and morality. In the popular mind Machiavelli is the chief proponent of this view. It derives most of its plausibility from the belief that politicians and statesmen are often required to act in ways which breach the rules of private morality. Thus statesmen are often called upon not to act altruistically, not to tell the truth, not to treat individuals as ends rather than means, not to adhere to the principle of equality and so on. In short, politics requires of its practitioners that they act in ways contrary to the fundamental requirements of private morality. On this view, then, politics is necessarily a dirty business.[40]

What are we to make of this position? It is, of course, possible to define "moral" in such an individualistic way that it applies to widely accepted private codes of conduct, but not to codes of conduct governing public office. But stipulating that a word be used in a certain way does not tell us anything about actual moral practice. Such definitional *fiat* is positively harmful if it obscures important similarities between the members of the arbitrarily distinguished classes. It is true that in practice we do consider that the standards for evaluating the conduct of public office holders are significantly different from those used to evaluate our own private conduct. But it is not true that we consider the conduct of public office holders to be governed by a general "anything goes" rule or that the standards of private morality have no application to the public sphere at all. On the contrary, in public debate about the proper standards applicable in the conduct of international relations the traditional vocabulary of private morality is much to the fore. For example, in the North–South dialogue a central concept is that of a just distribution. Reference is also often made to notions such as equality, fairness and desert. Also, there is constant reference to one or other concept of individual rights. Furthermore, we find in international debate that there are references to concepts such as promise keeping and integrity.

Once again it is no answer to say that the public office holders merely pretend to be governed by the standards referred to. As I have mentioned serveral times before, pretending is always a parasitic activity.[41] One can only pretend to be a just statesman because there is a real (not pretended) practice of just statesmanship. Thus there might be one or two politicans who can pretend to be just, but it is incoherent thinking to suppose that all politicans could pretend all the time. There could be no plays were there no real life.

The argument thus far must not be taken as suggesting that a private morality and a political morality of international affairs must be identical. It would be odd if they were. For it would be most implausible to think that a satisfactory moral code for individuals could be the same as a satisfactory moral code for public office holders. We generally consider the former to be responsible only for himself whereas the latter is responsible in a collective and public context. A single example will demonstrate the difference I am trying to illustrate here. An individual may properly decide whether to act courageously in a given situation and to put his well-being at risk by so doing. In contrast we do not think that a political leader has the right to commit a state to a risky action in the same way, for the politician not only puts his own welfare at risk, but also that of the citizens of the state. He acts on their behalf and this places moral constraints on him.

Delineating the precise distinctions between the standards by which private conduct ought to be regulated and those applicable to holders of public office is an important task, but one that I cannot deal with here. For the present I am concerned merely to establish that the standards applicable to the two spheres are different, but related. It is not the case that the standards governing the public sphere are either non-moral or immoral. That there is a common vocabulary in discussions about both private and public morality seems *prima facie* a good reason for supposing that the two spheres share a common concern and are interrelated in some way.

5 Conclusion and recapitulation

In this and the previous chapter I have raised and argued many points. Let us now take stock of the argument as a whole. The main thrust of the argument so far has been to show that normative argument cannot be avoided in the study of world politics. In Chapter One I argued that social scientists seeking to explain international affairs could not but get themselves embroiled in arguments of a normative nature. They become thus embroiled when in the course of their inquiry they characterize what happened as an act of this or that kind. Characterizing what happened as acts of this or that kind is a requirement of *any* explanation of social phenomena. This identification of an act requires of the social scientists that they understand the act in terms of the practice within which it takes place. However, we saw that even in the context of a given practice, what is to count as the proper understanding is often hotly contested. Deciding upon a proper interpretation requires that the investigating social scientist become involved in debate about the most fundamental normative issues within the practice being investigated. In the imaginary dialogue between Mr Foster and a social scientist we saw how the debate about whether a particular act could properly be called "a defence against a threat to the security of the state" could not but lead to a discussion about the nature of justice and rights which are fundamental normative issues.

In the present chapter we have considered a variety of different reasons which have been given for not taking the study of normative theories in international relations seriously and found them all to be flawed. Our major findings in this chapter are that:

1. Amoralism is not a position which can be coherently argued by a man or a state, for to be a man or a state implies the making of moral claims for oneself.
2. The arguments (such as Mackie's) against objectivist theories of morality, even if they succeed, do not lead to (imply) amoralism or a general scepticism about the worth of moral argument. Anti-objectivist arguments are designed to demonstrate that moral assertions lack a *certain kind* of cognitive status, not that they have no cognitive status.
3. Certain realist contentions about normative issues being derivative from power relations and thus being of secondary importance were shown to be wrong in that they are based on a misunderstanding of the relationship between power, norms and normative theory.
4. Although public morality may be different from private morality there is no reason to construe public morality as not a morality properly so called.

These first two chapters have been aimed at dispelling the main reasons which have prevented normative theory being taken seriously in international relations. We have seen that some involvement in normative theory is unavoidable.

NOTES

1 Charles Beitz, *Political Theory and International Relations* (Princeton University Press, 1979), p. 62.
2 Bernard Williams, *Morality: An Introduction to Ethics* (Cambridge University Press, 1972), pp. 17–27.
3 A consistent amoralist person would be considered insane. Can we conceive of an insane state?
4 In the popular mind this is often a position attributed to Machiavelli. Whether or not Machiavelli in fact held this position is not our concern here.

5 John Mackie, *Ethics: Inventing Right and Wrong* (Harmondsworth, Penguin Books, 1981).

6 Ibid. p. 15.

7 Ibid. pp. 36–42.

8 See Section 2.1 above, and Chapter Five below.

9 Ibid.

10 It is to be doubted whether on a strong relativist position there could be inter-practice disputes at all. In order to have a dispute there has to be *some* common ground. Thus disputes imply the existence of a practice (even if it is only an emerging one). Thus wherever there is a dispute, relativism has already broken down; practices are merging.

11 Bernard Williams in *Morality* calls this argument "the anthropologists' heresy, possibly the most absurd view to have been advanced even in moral philosophy" (p. 34). I follow Williams' line of argument in refuting the relativist position. For a detailed rejection of the argument that relativism requires a commitment to tolerance see Geoffrey Harrison, "Relativism and Tolerance" in *Philosophy, Politics and Society*, fifth series, ed. Peter Laslett and James Fishkin (Oxford, Blackwell, 1979).

12 Bernard Williams, *Morality*, p. 40 and following pages.

13 See Section 2.1 above.

14 See, for example, Ernst B. Haas, *Beyond the Nation State* (Stanford University Press, 1964); D. Mitrany, *A Functionalist Approach to World Politics* (London, Martin Robertson, 1975); and J. P. Sewell, *Functionalism and World Politics* (Princeton University Press, 1961).

15 V. I. Lenin, *Imperialism the Highest Stage of Capitalism* in *Selected Works of Lenin* (Moscow, Progress Publishers, 1977); A. G. Frank, *Capitalism and Underdevelopment in Latin America* (Harmondsworth, Penguin, 1971); Samir Amin, *Accumulation on a World Scale* (Hassocks, Harvester Press, 1974).

16 Kenneth Waltz, *Theory of International Politics* (London, Addison-Wesley, 1979), p. 73 and following pages.

17 Ibid.

18 Kenneth Waltz, *Man, the State and War* (New York, Columbia University Press, 1959).

19 In *Theory* Waltz elucidates systemic approaches to international relations. The great merit of his argument is that it articulates the main weaknesses of earlier systemic theories. First, there was a failure to delimit the borders of the international "system" being posited. If these are not clearly defined then it is not possible to explain the interactions between the system and its environment. This makes it impossible to explain either the effect of the system on the environment or of the environment on the system. It also leaves the way open to supposing that everything is included within the system. This makes systems analysis self-defeating, for it is then necessary to assume that the theory of the systems theorist is itself determined by the system and cannot be a good theory or a bad theory, but simply the theory which

the system requires. It becomes definitionally impossible to envisage contending theories of international relations. Second, there was a failure to distinguish between theory and reality. Systems theories are often confusing in that it is not clear whether they are simply describing a system of international relations which exists, as it were, "out there" in the world, or whether this "system" is a theory used to explain the facts of the world. Waltz accuses Stanley Hoffman of not making it clear whether "system" is an analytic postulate or a reality to be investigated. This difficulty is, in fact, one which is common to much international relations scholarship. (See Waltz's discussion of this problem in Chapter 3 of *Theory*. The issue is also well discussed in Charles Reynolds, *Theory and Explanation in International Relations* (London, Martin Robertson, 1973), p. 36 and following pages. The prevalence of this confusion is also commented on by J. Rosenau *et al.* in "Of Syllabi, Texts, Students, and Scholarship in International Relations," *World Politics*, Vol. 29, No. 2 (January 1977), p. 263, in which the authors did a survey of 26 major introductory international relations textbooks and found that the vast majority of authors wrote as if they were *describing* an existing international system.) For, on the one hand, if systems theory is no more than description and redescription of the international system, then there can be no conflict between such systems theories, but only arguments about which description best fits the international system. Either some or all of the parties to the dispute must be mistaken or under some illusion. On this view changes of the international system are not to be explained, but merely noticed. On the other hand, if systems theory is not descriptive, but consists of theories seeking to explain the way things are in the world and to predict changes in the *status quo* by using systemic notions as analytical postulates, then the whole enterprise has to be seen in a different light. In particular a very different process for evaluating such theory itself is indicated. This involves the discrete steps of theory building, hypothesis formation and procedures for confirmation or falsification.

20 Kenneth Waltz, *Theory*, p. 73.
21 Ibid. Chapter 5.
22 Ralph Pettman, *State and Class* (London, Croom Helm, 1979), p. 148.
23 V. I. Lenin, *Imperialism*.
24 Ibid. p. 636.
25 Ibid. p. 689 (emphasis added).
26 Ibid. pp. 289–690 (emphasis added).
27 Ibid. p. 718 and following pages.
28 Ibid. p. 725.
29 Ibid.
30 V. I. Lenin, *Selected Works*, p. 92.
31 See note 15 above.
32 The most famous statement by Marx of his position is contained in the Preface to *A Contribution to the Critique of Political Economy* repro-

duced in *Karl Marx: Selected Writings in Sociology and Social Philosophy*, ed. T. B. Bottomore and M. Rubel (London, D. C. Watts, 1963), p. 51. Marx writes, "In the social production which men carry on they enter into definite relations that are indispensable and independent of their will; these relations of production correspond to a definite stage of development of their material powers of production. The totality of these relations of production constitutes the economic structure of society – the real foundation, on which legal and political superstructures arise and to which definite forms of social consciousness correspond."

33 See Samir Amin, *Accumulation on a World Scale*, pp. 6 and 32.

34 The most widely accepted definition of the state, which is the one proposed by Max Weber, makes the element of coercion *the* major aspect of states which distinguishes them from other modes of organization. On this view the state is that power which successfully claims the monopoly of coercive force within a given territory. See *From Max Weber*, ed. H. H. Gerth and C. Wright Mills (London, Routledge and Kegan Paul, 1970), p. 78.

35 See Section 2.1 above.

36 I am indebted to Cornelia Navari of Birmingham University for this point. The most well known of such utopian thinkers was, of course, Woodrow Wilson. Two of the major figures who reacted against this kind of thinking were Martin Wight and E. H. Carr.

37 For example see P. A. Reynolds, *An Introduction to International Relations* (London, Longman, 1976), Chapter 4; Hans Morgenthau, *Politics among Nations* (New York, Knopf, 1973), Chapter 9; and K. J. Holsti, *International Politics* (Englewood Cliffs, Prentice-Hall, 1967), Chapter 7.

38 Hanna Arendt, *On Violence* (Harmondsworth, Penguin Press, 1970), analyses power in a similar way.

39 Here we see the practice of social science and the practice of politics merging as we did in another context at the end of Chapter One.

40 For more on the distinction between rules governing conduct within the sphere of private morality and rules operative in the political sphere see the selection of articles and sources cited in *Public and Private Morality*, ed. S. Hampshire (Cambridge University Press, 1978).

41 See Section 2.1 above.

Part Two

Normative issues in international relations: the domain of discourse and the method of argument

In the previous two chapters I sought to clear the way for substantive normative theory in international relations. I sought to do so by showing that the reasons often advanced (or assumed) for avoiding substantive normative theorizing within the discipline of international relations are not sound. Indeed, in the course of the discussion it became apparent that scholars in the discipline cannot but become involved in issues of a normative nature. Having completed this preliminary stage of the argument let us now begin with the more positive task of constructing a substantive normative theory.

A first step will be to identify some of the pressing normative issues facing actors and theorists in the sphere of international affairs. This immediately raises the question of how best to settle these issues. Finally we shall have to face the general question: "What is to count as a satisfactory normative theory?" I shall tackle these problems by arguing that the very statement of the list of difficult issues implicitly indicates the existence of an area of agreement between people – a domain of discourse – which gives us a basis from which we might construct an argument towards a substantive normative theory. I shall introduce and use, for this purpose, a method of argument first used in the context of jurisprudence.

But before going on to attempt the construction of such an

argument we must first consider two objections to my contention that there actually is an area of agreement (domain of discourse) in international relations on the basis of which the difficult cases can be settled. After considering these two objections we shall proceed to outline a method of argument which I believe will facilitate a solution to the list of issues mentioned.

1 The normative issues in international relations and the central question for normative theory

What are the pressing normative issues in international politics today? Let us list some of them:

1. Questions relating to the causes and conduct of war. When may states justifiably go to war? Once at war, what are the normative constraints on the belligerents? What are the rights and duties of those states not directly involved in the war *vis-à-vis* the warring states?

2. Questions related to nuclear armaments. When should they be used? How ought they to be deployed? Is a deterrence policy justified? Who should be allowed to have nuclear weapons? What institutions ought to control their proliferation? What controls should there be on the technological research leading to the development of new nuclear weapons?

3. When may and ought individuals to agree (or refuse) to participate in the use of force against other states or other political groupings?

4. How ought states to respond to unconventional forms of violence like international terrorism? Who ought to do what about those who hijack aeroplanes, etc., for political purposes?

5. When is intervention by one state into the domestic affairs of another state justified? What means may justifiably be employed in such interventions?

6. How should those fighting wars of national liberation be treated by the states not directly involved in the conflict?

Ought they to treat the conflict as a war? Or should they treat it as a domestic matter within the state concerned? Are the captives in such a conflict to be regarded as prisoners of war, political prisoners or criminals?

7. How should refugees from one state be treated by other states? Who is responsible for them? Should they be allowed to choose a new home state or are they obligated to eventually return to their state of origin?

8. How should those not fighting for secession of a particular territory treat those who are engaged in such a conflict?

9. When may a state divide itself into several smaller states?

10. Questions relating to the international use and distribution of the resources of the world. Who ought to get what, when, how? Ought a distribution to be achieved by the operation of a capitalist free market in which multinationals are allowed to operate? Or should the distribution be governed by a world wide democratic body of some kind?

11. What kind of international organizations ought to be established?

12. What human rights are there and how ought they to be protected? Ought states to protect them? If a state fails to protect such rights, ought other states to intervene? Should there be international institutions to secure these rights? If so, what are states and individuals justified in doing in order to bring about such arrangements?

These questions are posed in a general form, but in each case it is easy to think of specific cases to which the question could be applied. For example, in Britain the whole set of questions about nuclear arms has been raised recently with regard to the buying (or not) by the government of the Trident II missile system as well as whether or not the USA should be allowed to station new nuclear weapons in Britain. Furthermore, the CND movement recently raised the basic question whether Britain should unilaterally disarm herself. Another example of one of the general questions being given a specific application concerns the proper action to be taken by the surrounding states in response to the liberation movement in El Salvador.

It is possible that someone may want to add further questions to the list of pressing issues in international affairs. But it is highly likely that most people would agree that these normative problems on the list are crucial ones. It is highly unlikely that anybody would want to argue that these problems are not important problems at all. Such agreement on the statement of the main issues is of fundamental significance, for by implication it indicates a common basis from which argument towards a solution of these key problems might proceed. This contention needs further elucidation. What kind of agreement does agreement on the list of problems reveal? How and why is this agreement (if it exists) relevant to finding possible solutions to the key issues mentioned?

Let us consider this latter question first. A problem cannot be formulated as a normative issue except within the context of given practice of normative argument. Normative issues only arise as such within the context of certain shared understandings. This is, of course, a very general point indeed. A similar point can be made by means of an example from sport. The issue of whether or not a given move in a game of rugby is a foul or not can only arise amongst the initiates of the game. It could not arise as an issue at all between people not familiar with the game. In a similar way moral issues do not arise among psychotics because, amongst other things, psychotics have no understanding of the practice of morality as it exists amongst normal people; they lack any concept of moral wrongness. Moreover this point – that normative issues can only arise within the context of a wider area of agreement – has a further significance as well: it indicates to us where we ought to start looking for a solution to such issues, viz. within the area of agreement in which the issue arose. Thus someone seeking to determine whether a given kind of event in rugby is a foul or not must start by acquainting himself as fully as possible with the rules and underlying principles of the game as a whole. Similarly, we, who are seeking answers to pressing normative issues in international relations, must start by seeking an understanding of the area of normative agreement implied by our agreed list of pressing issues. Our task is to outline the relevant *domain of discourse*. A domain of discourse is an area of discussion within which the participants generally recognize (and recognize others as recognizing) many rules as settled. Thus an outline of the domain of discourse pertaining to rugby would involve indicating that range of rules which speakers in the domain regard as settled, such as the rules which determine what is to count as a scrum, a tackle, a pass, a conversion and so on. In our case we are called upon to outline what is considered normal in the domain of discourse relating to the inter-state practice.

This initial step (outlining the domain of discourse within which the issues arise) is, of course, not the same as answering the specific questions or constructing a general theory. Theory building is an attempt to pass beyond what participants within a given domain of discourse normally do, which is to answer the pressing questions which arise in an *ad hoc* way. Theory building is a subsequent stage where an attempt is made to show how all the diverse things accepted by initiates within a given domain of discourse form a coherent and orderly whole and which indicates how difficult cases might be solved. Thus within the sphere of morality, what participants normally do is make individual moral judgements on an *ad hoc* basis. They judge, for example, that killing people, torturing people and so on is bad, and that helping the needy and preventing harm is good. A moral theory would then be a theory which "introduces order and system into our considered judgements over a wide range of positions."[1]

Let us return to the initial step. Within the context of what area of agreement (i.e. within the context of what domain of discourse) do the pressing questions we have identified arise as issues? Imagine a specific application for any (or all) of the twelve questions on our list. Whatever specific application is

thought of for each of the questions on the list (which is far
from being exhaustive), it is certain that it will arise in a context
where reference is made to one, some or all of the following:
states, inter-state relations and citizens of states. Even those
questions which point towards the creation of a new order in
the world (one which might not consist of states) must prescribe what states and citizens ought to do now in order to
move towards a new world order later. Similarly, some questions which on the face of the matter do not appear to apply to
states, for example questions about the proper role of multinational corporations, may, on closer consideration, be shown
to be concerned with states. Thus many normative questions
about multinationals may be better formulated as: "What ought
states to do about multinationals?"

I contend that all normative issues in world politics today
refer, either directly or indirectly, to the state, inter-state relations and the role of individuals as citizens of states. If this is
correct it is then possible to encapsulate all the several normative questions in the one central question: "What in general is a
good reason for action by or with regard to states?" This question clearly covers questions as diverse as: "What ought John to
do when called upon to take up arms against another state?
When ought a state to support another state in a war with a
third state? How ought states to deal with international terrorism?" And so on.

2 The domain of discourse: modern state ordinary language and its alternatives

The domain of discourse within which the listed issues must
be settled has been identified as what might be termed the
modern state domain.[2] Any argument regarding these questions will be within the modern state centric practice.

However, before proceeding I must first consider two objections which might be raised against my argument so far. The
first is that there is no such area of agreement within which the

difficult issues may be situated. On this view the most conspicuous feature of the domain of international affairs is just that there is no such core of consensus which can serve as a base from which to reason to a solution to the more difficult cases, since difficult normative issues typically arise between peoples with radically opposed ideologies. On this view, opposing ideologies are taken to rule out any common area of agreement. This argument is related to arguments already considered when we discussed scepticism, so I shall not go into it in great detail.

The second objection to my approach is not that I am wrong in identifying an area of agreement from which to argue to a solution of the hard cases, but that I have identified the wrong area of agreement. According to this view – the modern natural law view – there is an area of agreement which can give us a base from which to argue. However, it is not situated in the state centric practice. It is situated in a more fundamental community of mankind. Let us consider each of these objections in turn.

2.1 *The conflict-of-ideologies objection*

One way of portraying the modern world is to depict it as a world in which there is little or no moral consensus. Hans Morgenthau, for example, has written of the dissolution of the European international society. In this society, from the Treaty of Westphalia until the beginning of the First World War, an elite consensus about the fundamental rules of right conduct in international affairs had existed.[3] However, on Morgenthau's view the consensus has been eroded since the end of the First World War. In its place there has arisen a diversity of nationalisms which are no longer based upon any set of common norms.

Thus carrying their idols before them, the nationalistic masses of our time meet in the international arena, each group convinced that it executes the mandate of history, that it does for humanity what it seems to do for itself, and that it fulfills a sacred mission ordained by providence, however defined. Little do they know that they meet under an empty sky from which the gods have departed.[4]

On this view, then, far from it being the case that there is an underlying consensus, there has in fact been a retrograde movement to tribalism, irrational nationalisms and fanatical religious zealotry. Writing in a completely different tradition, Michael Walzer makes a similar point. He argues that in the modern world there is no political consensus; that in the modern world man does not experience his political being within a single frame of reference. Instead men have divided political allegiances. His argument is against the applicability of the state centric view according to which man's political being is conceived within a single state centric frame of reference.[5] Writing in yet another tradition, Barrie Paskins and Michael Dockrill argue that "The contemporary world is living with the aftermath of what Nietzsche termed 'the death of god,' that is, the collapse of all consensus on an authoritative political, social, moral and religious order."[6] The outbreak, in recent times, of wars of a fundamentalist religious nature has served to reinforce the position of those arguing that the modern world is best characterized in terms of the absence of any overarching consensus. Although there may still be some minimal "raft of consensus" between, say, Marxist and liberal democratic states, there is, so the argument goes, surely very little consensus at all between liberal democratic states and the fanatically religious states like Iran and Libya. Similarly, the emergence since the Second World War of many new states, the populations of which are not steeped in Western political and cultural traditions, reinforces the view of those scholars in international relations who stress the fundamental absence of consensus in the modern world. This influential perspective on world politics is what Ralph Pettman has referred to as the "pluralist perspective."[7]

According to this view, then, disputes do arise, but they are best seen as being of an *ideological* nature. The disputes are such that the justifications produced by the parties to the disputes pertain to domains of discourse which are in some sense hermetically sealed off from one another. In such ideological conflicts any real argument is not possible because of the lack of any basic consensus between the parties and because of the closed nature of each party's belief system. Thus disputes may arise, for example, between states committed to a liberal democratic view of world politics and states which hold a Marxist–Leninist view of world politics, or between those who hold a Christian view and those who hold a Muslim one. The parties to such disputes will typically justify their positions in terms of frames of reference which are fundamentally opposed to (or incomprehensible to) those held by the opposing states. What I have called the "ideological" aspect of such disputes is sometimes referred to as "nationalistic universalism."[8] Each nation comes to see its own value-set as a universalist frame of reference to be applied to all nations. The alternative value systems invoked by other states are rejected as wrong and pernicious *in toto*. It is this aspect of such conflicts which is so graphically described in the quotation from Morgenthau given above. This approach to normative disputes in international relations was manifested most starkly during the years of the so called "Cold War" when democratic and communist ideologies confronted each other on the stage of world politics.

This view of the international domain of discourse often leads its adherents to conclude that there are insuperable difficulties in the way of finding any rational solution to normative problems. This position may be restated in the following way: because there is no common ground, or because the two sides (Marxist/non-Marxist, Christian/Muslim) have such different points of departure, the matter cannot be settled by argument. If it is to be settled at all, it will have to be settled by power.

My argument against this conflict-of-ideologies approach is that parties to disputes in international affairs do not normally confront one another in this mutually uncomprehending way. They rather tend to confront one another within the context of a well established practice. Their disputes are situated within a

common state centric domain of discourse, and the participants (usually representatives of states, or of non-state groupings confronting a state) share an understanding of the multiple
different actions which can be undertaken within this context.
More specifically, the very nature of their conflicts presupposes that they all understand what it is to make an incursion
over a national border, what it is to threaten war, what is
involved in starting a war, what is involved in staying neutral
during a war, what is involved in forming alliances, what it is
for one state to act as honest broker between two warring states,
what is involved in a ceasefire, in signing an accord, what is
involved in inter-state diplomacy, summitry and so on.
Without such a shared understanding of the basic rules of the
game, no inter-state conflict would be conceivable. Thus,
although it is true that in conflicts between states (or between
non-state actors, like liberation movements, and states) the
opponent is often *portrayed* (by his opponent) as one with
whom argument is not possible, this is, quite paradoxically,
only possible if the conflict is taking place within a context of a
core of agreed upon rules within a given practice. Just as within
a rugby league certain teams may regard one another in a more
than usually antagonistic light, nevertheless to the extent that
they still *play rugby* together they show a mutual commitment
to the rules of the game. Thus although the emergence of
nationalism (with its attendant ideological trappings) has
introduced a new element in the international practice of
states, it is beyond doubt that such a practice still does exist.

I argue, then, that it is not the case that normative disputes in
international relations today can properly be seen as confrontations between members of one ideology with members of
another incomprehensible foreign ideology. The Marxist confronting the representative of the Western liberal tradition is
not in the same position as the Western anthropologist confronting the Trobriand Islanders (or a group of Martians) for the
first time. All the debates about normative issues in international relations take place *within* a common tradition of poli-

tical theory – within what I have called the modern state domain of discourse. Thus it could be shown, for example, that the debate between Marxists and non-Marxists (such as state-centrist or interdependence theorists) is, amongst other things, about how the state system can best be understood. Part of the Marxist argument against capitalist democracies is that they purport to be protecting democratic values while in fact such capitalist democracies entrench certain very undemocratic dependency relationships based on the exploitation of one class by another.[9] The details of the argument need not concern us here, but I must point out that the whole debate is rooted in the common ground of the state centric and modernizing domain of discourse.[10] If there were no such common ground there could be no debate. Some of the central terms of this domain of discourse are: states, citizens, representative democracy, the separation of powers, the rule of law, and that set of terms referring to the creation and distribution of wealth.[11] My argument is not that within this shared language (or, as James Mayall calls it, "a cognitive ethic"[12]) there is absolute consensus on all things. Patently there is not. I simply wish to point to the existence of this world wide domain of discourse as a basic given. There are no significant groupings of people who fall totally outside it. Previously there were such outside groupings. In earlier times it was plausible to characterize the world as consisting of the civilized groups and the barbarians.[13] The assertion that normative disputes are best seen as confrontations between mutually uncomprehending ideologies would have been far more plausible in that situation.

It may perhaps be disputed that democracy is part of this general consensus. Surely only a minority of all states are democracies. But the point is rather that most states do claim to be committed to democratic values. Those that are not in fact democracies justify their form of government as being a special case. The promise is usually made that a democracy will be established as soon as possible. Furthermore there is also widespread agreement on what might be broadly termed the goal of modernization. This includes the goals of technical advance, industrialization and the education of the populace which is necessary to support the former two goals. James Mayall has spelled out some of the components of what he terms the modernization myth: first modernization is used as a central justification for the exercise of power. Second, it involves a commitment to nationalist ideology which is used to destroy traditional forms of power and authority and to advance modernist aims. Third, there is a commitment to the traditional diplomatic forms as an avenue to be used in the pursuit of the modernization goal. Fourth, the language of modernizing development and redistribution is the language of the Western developed world, not that of traditional cultures.[14]

In summary, in this section I have tried to counter the claim that normative argument about pressing issues in international relations is not possible because the basic consensus (which is a precondition for *any* argument) is lacking in international relations. I have outlined, in a very introductory way, the domain of discourse within which argument towards a solution of the listed issues may proceed.

2.2 *The natural law/community-of-mankind approach*

Let us now consider the second objection to my contention that there is a modernizing state centric domain of discourse within which we may seek solutions to the pressing normative questions listed at the outset. This is the objection offered by those who adopt a natural law or community-of-mankind approach to normative issues in international relations. For those in this tradition, the normative evaluation of issues pertaining to the practice of states presupposes that there exists a moral community of mankind. If we are to avoid cultural imperialism (i.e. imposing our values on others to whom they do not apply) and if we are to avoid relativism (which would commit us to maintaining that there are no common standards for evaluating the system of states), then (the argument goes) we must assume the existence of a moral community of mankind.[15] The existence of such a community of mankind is supposed to give us a moral perspective from which the system of states can be judged. Michael Donelan talks of a "primordial community of mankind."[16] The underlying logic of this approach is similar to the one I have adopted in that it stresses (as I have) that no argument is possible in the absence of some underlying community of values between the disputants. However, this approach differs profoundly from mine in the portrayal it gives of the basic community from which argument must proceed. It claims that there is a moral community of mankind which it conceives to be in some way independent of the modernizing inter-state practice, whereas I consider just that modernizing state system as providing the idiom within which normative argument takes place.

The crucial question with regard to this approach is, of course: "In what sense, if any, does such a moral community of mankind exist?" A related question is: "What kind of investigation is called for to establish the existence of that community? Could it be established by an empirical investigation (if not that, what then)?" All would agree that there is in the world today a large number of states. But is there a community of mankind? There are over four billion people, but is it right to call this a community? Would it not be better to say that there are ever so many diverse communities?

The natural law response to this challenge is to argue that there are certain self-evident principles or goods common to all the diverse groupings of people. It is the fact that these are held by all men which entitles us to talk of a community of mankind. One natural law theorist, John Finnis, lists seven such basic self-evident goods. They are: life, knowledge, play, aesthetic experience, sociability, practical reasonableness and religion.[17] He admits that these values are pursued in many diverse ways and take a great variety of forms, but he insists that they are common to all societies whatsoever. His claim is not merely the empirical one that these goods are as a matter of fact considered goods by all men. It is the much stronger claim that it is *self-evident* that the goods are good for all men. "Self-evident" does not mean, says Finnis, "accessible to some weird extra sense which people have."[18] Rather they are self-evident in the sense that they are bound to be implicit in the thinking of anyone, even (and especially) within the thinking of the sceptic who seeks to deny the good in question. According to Finnis, the sceptic who argues that knowledge is not a good is "operationally self defeating" in that his asserting that knowledge is not a good undercuts the content of his assertion.[19] Elsewhere Finnis says the principles are self-evident in that they are necessarily presupposed in the way people act and talk.[20] Thus presumably he would argue that one cannot pursue knowledge without presupposing that it is good to do so. Similarly one cannot play games without presupposing that game playing is a good, and so on through the list of goods.

This way of arguing to the conclusion that there is a moral community of mankind with certain natural (objective) basic values will not do. In the first place Finnis' empirical claim that "anthropologists have shown strikingly similar lists of concerns across cultures" (such as the concern for life, for placing some restriction on sexual practices, for friendship, and for knowledge), while probably true, does not establish that a moral community exists. Consider two cultures (or two individuals) which have strikingly different notions of when life might justifiably be terminated (imagine an argument between a Roman Catholic and a Japanese believer in the hara-kiri ritual). Even if we could show that they both value life in some way, this would not provide proof of any fundamental consensus from which moral argument can proceed. Pointing out that people in different societies face (and have faced throughout history) similar issues does not establish the existence of a primordial moral community of mankind.[21]

In the second place the argument for the self-evidence of such basic values will not do what it is supposed to do. Consider Finnis' argument about knowledge, which says that all men value knowledge in that even the sceptic's assertion that knowledge cannot be had is (if it is anything) a piece of knowledge, so that the sceptic, by making his assertion, shows himself to be valuing knowledge. Donelan reaches a similar conclusion via a different route. He argues that although throughout history there has been an ongoing polemic about the nature of knowledge, nevertheless this polemic itself is "throughout a process of reasoning."[22] He says, "we change our minds from time to time over the centuries about the nature of reason, about how we know and how we criticise: but that we know and that we criticise is confirmed to us in the very procedure itself."[23] Thus both Finnis' and Donelan's arguments get their force from the allegation that the very process of reasoning demonstrates a commitment to knowledge which is constant over time. But it is by no means certain that the scholastics of mediaeval times arguing with one another and the Oxford ordinary language philosophers in the time of John Austin were all committed to the *same* underlying conception of knowledge. It would be interesting to explore this matter. But notice that in order to do so, an investigator would have to understand the scholastic practice of disputation from the internal point of view. Then he would likewise have to understand the practice of the ordinary language philosophers. Only then could he attempt to extrapolate from each practice what the underlying (or presupposed) notion of knowledge was in each case. These notions might turn out to be radically different from each other. Whether or not they would in fact be so different is not important here. I am simply concerned to point out that we cannot infer from the fact that most people in most cultures throughout history have engaged in argument that there is a common commitment to the same value: knowledge. What we can properly infer is that wherever people reason with one another those engaged in this activity must presuppose *some* point or purpose to it. But whether it is the same in each case is a matter for research. In short, the fact that reasoning is ubiquitous does not warrant the conclusion that there is a community of mankind which naturally has this good in common.

Similar arguments may be brought to bear against all the other goods which the natural law theorists identify as objectively given for mankind as a whole, viz. friendship, sociability, religion, practical reasonableness and so on. Consider play. It is no doubt true that something analogous to play (in a very broad sense of the word) might be found in all societies. But on closer scrutiny it might turn out that what was initially identified by the investigator as examples of "play" in different societies were really not very similar at all. The difference may be more radical than that which exists between two different kinds of game (e.g. cricket and bull fighting). It may be the case that within one society the activity initially identified as a game is considered play in that it is an essentially lighthearted pastime. Whereas in another society the game in question is essentially serious; success at it is considered an indication of a man's stature as a "real man," as indicating that he is a genuine member of the society to which he belongs. Finding out such differences involves gaining a participant and holist perspective on the societies being investigated. The investigator will face all the problems of interpretation which I mentioned in Chapter One.

To summarize: the natural law theorists' case rests on their being able to assert that play (or knowledge, sociability, etc.) are the *same* across cultures in some quite profound sense. My argument is that it is not possible to assert this simply on the basis of a superficial glance at the apparent similarities between the different peoples of this world. Finding out whether these actually are similar or not requires extensive research which is fraught with both practical and philosophical difficulties. In sharp contrast my assertion that a state centric domain of discourse exists can be established with comparative ease. It simply is the case that most actors in world affairs would formulate the list of core problems much as I have done and in formulating the list they would necessarily rely on several key common concepts like the state, citizen and community of states.

2.3 The objection that issues arising in the modern state domain of discourse can only be settled from a wider moral point of view

I must briefly consider an objection which is closely related to the one which we have just discussed, viz. the objection that the serious moral issues which arise in international affairs can only be solved from a wider moral perspective. This objection is raised against my contention that the major issues can be solved within the modern state centric domain of discourse. Against this it is argued that in normative theory we require some wider moral perspective which would enable us to evaluate the modern state domain of discourse as a whole. Michael Donelan articulates this objection in his article "The Political Theorists and International Theory," where he argues that *only* if we accept that there is a moral community of mankind is it possible to morally evaluate the state system itself.[24] On his view there are only two possibilities: either the state system (together with its associated domain of discourse) is the primordial given (in which case that state system cannot itself be morally evaluated because there is no wider, more inclusive perspective from which it can be judged) or there is a primordial community of mankind (which gives us the necessary perspective from which the state system can be judged). I have already considered the difficulties involved in the notion of a community of mankind in the previous section. In this section my argument is that Donelan's dichotomy is wrong in so far as it suggests that unless our domain of discourse is based on the assumption that there is a moral community of mankind, it would not be possible to evaluate the major issues which arise in the state centric domain of discourse itself.

Donelan purports to explain why there has been so little normative theory in international relations. This is due to the fact that most political theorists have taken it for granted that man is fundamentally a being who "lives and always will live in a separate state."[25] On this traditional view, international relations is then a moral wasteland between states. "The most that can be said about it is the implications of the theory of the state."[26] For Donelan doing this is a paltry business, not worthy of those interested in serious moral theory. I dispute this. We are not condemned to critical impotence if we accept that the answer to the pressing normative issues in international relations must necessarily be found within the modern state domain of discourse. Neither does it commit us to the maintenance of the *status quo*. Accepting the centrality of this domain of discourse does not imply that there can be no normative political theory of world politics. That there has been little normative theorizing in international relations is true enough, but the reasons for this lack are not because working out the "implications of the theory of the state" is a trivial thing to do. The reasons for the lack of normative theorizing have already been covered in Chapters One and Two. In this section I want to argue that seeking answers within the state centric domain of discourse to the list of pressing questions is a worthwhile activity and that far from being a trivial residue of state theory it is of primary importance. What I take to be involved in this endeavour will be elucidated in some detail in the following two chapters. It involves constructing a coherent background theory justifying the settled norms in the modern state domain of discourse.

It is necessary to be quite clear about what is, and what is not involved in having recourse to the modern state domain of discourse. The language of this domain is the ordinary language of international relations. This language is a functioning whole – not a completely coherent one – which includes within it a mix of the following terms: state, sovereignty, self-determination, citizen, democracy, human rights (individual rights and group rights), and a set of terms connected to the notion of modernization. Asserting the primacy of the modern state domain of discourse for my purposes does *not* commit me to holding that men will always live in states as we know them, or that life in states as we know them is the only proper life for man, or that the way states are organized at present is the best way of organizing them. I simply contend that any discussion about what ought to be done in world politics (be the proposed action a small one or a large one such as, for example, the wholesale reorganization of the global political system) must be conducted in the language of the modern state. No other suitable language is available. Viewed in this way, it will become clear that the various objections against the modern state domain of discourse as the ground of normative theory in international relations fall away as misconceived. There are several such objections which must be confronted.

A first objection which seems inherent in Donelan's approach is that utilizing the modern state domain of discourse in effect sanctifies the state: it assumes that people will always live in states and that it is not possible within such a language to consider alternatives to the system. This objection is not well founded. By having recourse to the ordinary language of international relations I am not thereby committed to argue that the state system as it exists is the best mode of human political organization or that people ought always to live in states as we know them. As I have said, my argument is that whatever proposals for piecemeal or large scale reform of the state system are made, they must of necessity be made in the language of the modern state. Whatever proposals are made, whether in justification or in criticism of the state system, will have to make use of concepts which are at present part and parcel of the theory of states. Thus, for example, any proposal for a new global institutional arrangement superseding the state system will itself have to be justified, and that justification will have to include within it reference to a new and good form of individual citizenship, reference to a new legislative machinery equipped with satisfactory checks and balances, reference to satisfactory law enforcement procedures, reference to a satisfactory arrangement for distributing the goods produced in the world, and so on. All of these notions are notions which have been developed and finely honed within the theory of the modern state. It is not possible to imagine a justification of a new world order succeeding which used, for example, feudal, or traditional/tribal, discourse. More generally there is no world wide language of political morality which is not completely shot through with state related notions such as citizenship, rights under law, representative government and so on.

A related objection might be that accepting the primacy of the modern state domain of discourse implies that serious normative theory about inter-state relations is not possible. The reasoning which leads to this conclusion is roughly as follows: if the language of the modern state is taken as primary, this involves taking the notion of state sovereignty as primary, for sovereignty is one of the key terms in the ordinary language of international relations. A sovereign body almost by definition is not bound by any higher norms, thus any normative theory about how sovereign states ought to treat their citizens or how they ought to conduct their affairs with one another would be otiose.

This line of reasoning is based on some muddled thinking about the notion of sovereignty. The central problem is easily demonstrated without our having to get involved in the interstices of theories of sovereignty.[27] The muddle arises from conflating two assertions about sovereignty, the first true and the second false. It is true that a sovereign state is subject to no higher law making and law enforcing authority. But it is false that the notion of sovereignty implies "not subject to any higher norms *at all*." To say that a state is sovereign does not commit us to saying that it is wrong or pointless to discuss what norms it ought to follow in its dealings with other states.[28] We often do criticize sovereign states for immoral or unjust conduct.

This confusion about the nature and implications of sovereignty may be further clarified if we attend to the distinction between sovereignty and power. To say that a state is sovereign is to say nought about the power relations which may hold between states. A sovereign state may well exist in the sphere of influence of a more powerful state. The realities of such power relations between states are widely recognized, but this is not held to invalidate their status as sovereign states. Where a system of sovereign states exists, there is a practice in which states are held to make their own autonomous decisions; a practice in which states may be held responsible for such decisions of their own irrespective of the unequal power relations involved. But if a sovereign state is held to make autonomous decisions on the right thing to do in a given situation, it does not follow that whatever it decides to do is therefore the right thing to do. The state may well have made a bad decision. My contention then is that it is wrong to assert that where states are considered to be sovereign there is nothing more to be said about the right conduct of states. What has to be determined is: what are the standards of right conduct for sovereign states? More importantly, how, within the modern state centric domain of discourse, do we find out what these standards are?

There are further arguments against the approach which I am advocating (the approach which stresses the primacy of the modern state domain of discourse), but I have to postpone dealing with these until I have developed the method of argument more fully. I shall return to these objections at the end of this chapter.

I have argued that a discussion of normative issues in international relations must take place in terms of the modern state domain of discourse. This view runs directly contrary to the conventional wisdom of the discipline which may be summarized in the following terms:

It is, indeed, the case that there actually is a system of states, and it is true that the existence of such a system of states indicates that there is some minimal agreement on the ground rules of international relations. However, this in no way establishes the feasibility of settling disputes by finding the right answer by means of argument. The most contested issues (which are also potentially the most dangerous) are those for which there are no agreed upon rules in terms of which they could be settled. Historically there once was a community of European powers led by an aristocracy who subscribed to a common set of religious, political and legal ideas. This provided a wide area of agreement and enabled disputes to be settled by reference to agreed upon standards.[29] However, this consensus has now disappeared. There exists nowadays a multiplicity of world views. Since the underlying consensus which is necessary for the rational settlement of international disputes is lacking, there are only two possible ways remaining for resolving such issues: either the parties may strike a bargain or they might resort to force.[30] This account quite closely accords with what happens in international relations.

I accept that the modern state domain of discourse offers us no clear cut rules which dictate solutions to those pressing problems of international relations which were identified in the list. But I wish to argue that there is a way of overcoming the impasse in which the conventional wisdom finds itself when confronted by contentious normative issues. The way out of the impasse has been brilliantly expounded in the context of law by Ronald Dworkin.[31] His theory has, of course, a specifically legal focus, but I believe that it can be generalized to have a much wider application. In particular, a wider interpretation of his theory will be invaluable to our concern with normative argument in international relations.

3 A method for settling contested issues by argument: Dworkin and the example of hard cases in law

3.1 A general outline of Dworkin's method

Dworkin developed his theory of legal argument in order to cope with the problem posed by *hard cases* in law. These are typically cases which come up for decision before a judge and which are not clearly covered by any settled rule of law or precedent. Dworkin developed his position against the orthodoxy of the positivist jurisprudents who argued that where the facts of a particular case did not fall under a settled rule of law, the judge had to *make* new law to cover the case in hand.[32] In such cases, the positivists argued, judges are constrained by the principles and maxims of the law, but nevertheless they use their discretion and *make* the law. In such cases there can, on the positivist view, be no talk of a uniquely right decision. Against this Dworkin argues that even in hard cases there is a method of judicial argument which can lead to the right decision. It is his portrayal of this method, I suggest, which can be of use to us in seeking solutions to the hard cases of international relations.

Arguably the best way to introduce Dworkin's theory of argument is to outline his discussion of the kind of reasoning a referee in chess might follow in trying to decide a hard case that comes up for decision. Chess is, of course, a game with a well developed set of unambiguous rules governing every possible move on the board and established conventions regarding the context of play. Still, contentious issues may arise where no established rules seem to apply. Imagine that a dispute arises between two players because one claims that the other annoyed him unreasonably by smiling at him (evidently the Russian grand master Tal once smiled thus at Fischer). The referee is called upon to interpret the rule which stipulates that a player who unreasonably annoys his opponent shall forfeit the game. We are to suppose that no identical case has previously been decided. Evidently there is no mechanical decision possible, yet the referee is also not called on to make an arbitrary decision favouring one or other player according to his discretion. He is to settle the issue in terms of the "unreasonable annoyance" rule. How ought the referee to go about reaching the correct decision? Or to phrase the question differently: what would count as a good reason justifying a decision in favour of one of the players rather than the other? Dworkin holds that even though in hard cases like this the conventions of chess do not provide ready-made solutions, they still allow a right decision to be reached by argument. It is this aspect of his analysis which is of particular relevance for our purposes.

Dworkin first points out that what the referee is called on to decide in finding for one of the players rather than the other is to confirm or deny an *institutional right*.[33] If a player has been unreasonably annoyed by his opponent then he has a right to be awarded the game. It is institutional in that the player holds it in virtue of his involvement in the institution. In this case the institution is the game of chess. But for his involvement in that institution the player would not have the right in question. The referee is called upon to make his decision in terms of this institution and its constitutive rights. In this hard case the referee faces a situation in which there is no rule which clearly stipulates whether smiling constitutes unreasonable behaviour or not, and yet where the institution still imposes definite constraints on what the referee may or may not decide. He is not entitled to decide on principles taken from outside the institution, for example from general morality. He may not, for example, decide in favour of a player on the grounds that that player needs the prize money more than the other player does. We would, says Dworkin, reject a decision which was made for reasons of general morality because such a decision is not in accordance with the *character* of the game. The correct decision of the referee would be a decision which protects the character of the game. But what is the character of a chess game?

In arriving at a correct decision the referee is thus to be guided by the character of the game. How is he to determine what this is? Dworkin says, "He [the referee] may well start with what everyone knows. Every institution is placed by its participants in some very rough category of institution; it is taken to be a game rather than a religious ceremony or a form of exercise or a political process."[34] Reasoning thus, it will be clear to the referee that chess is generally held to be an intellectual game. In establishing this, we already rule out several potential solutions to the case in hand (for example, it would clearly not accord with the character of an intellectual game were the referee to decide the issue by spinning a coin). But establishing the character of chess as an intellectual game does not yet uniquely dictate a correct decision. The concept of an "intellectual game" is what Dworkin, following Gallie, calls an essentially contested concept, i.e. a concept which admits of several conceptions.[35] The concept in question (chess is an intellectual game) is not univocal, but is capable of supporting different conceptions. In order to decide the matter in hand the referee must choose the correct one. But which one? How is he to choose?

Dworkin argues that the referee must *construct* the game's character (in so far as it has a bearing on this particular case) by putting to himself different sets of questions. Given that chess is an intellectual game, is it, like poker, intellectual in a sense that includes ability at psychological intimidation? Or is it, like mathematics, intellectual in a sense that does not include that ability? In each case, different implications would follow concerning whether the opponent's smile would count as unreasonable annoyance or not. Such questions thus force him, on the one hand, to look more closely at the game, to determine whether its features provide support for one rather than the other of these conceptions of an intellectual game in its bearing on the contentious issue. But, on the other hand, he must also ask a further set of questions. Given that chess is an intellectual game of some sort, what follows about reasonable behaviour in a chess game? Is ability at psychological intimidation or ability to resist such intimidation really an intellectual quality? These questions ask him to look more closely at the concept of intellect itself.[36]

In looking more closely at the concept of intellect itself the referee will find that some conceptions of intelligence do not achieve a fit with the institutional rules of chess. For example, physical grace may be seen by some as embodying a possible conception of intelligence, but it clearly does not fit the practice of chess. However, the referee may find in the end that two different conceptions of intellect seem to fit the settled rules of the game equally well. In this position he is called upon to decide which of the two accounts provides "a deeper or more successful account of what intellect really is." Even so, though such abstract problems are relevant, this does not require the referee to enter the domain of the philosophy of mind for its own sake. He has to determine what institutional rights the players have, and these more abstract arguments are only relevant in so far as they have a bearing on a correct decision regarding the rights at stake. In the last analysis the referee thus has to come to a reasoned decision regarding a specific institutional problem. The context of his decision is the basic fact that once an institution is set up, such that the "participants have institutional rights under distinct rules belonging to that institution then hard cases may arise that must in the nature of the case, be supposed to have an answer."[37] In this case it must be supposed that either the man who objected to his opponent smiling has a right that the smiler forfeit the game to him, or he does not, in which case the smiler has a right that the game continue. It is not the case that the players have a right to whatever decision the referee sees fit to make, i.e. a right to a decision. They are entitled to the right decision about their rights.

What is at stake is a general grasp of the institution as a rule-following practice including the relevant kinds of justification for settling disputes. If the referee is called upon to decide what rights the disputants have, he must "bring to his decision a general theory of why, in the case of his institution, the rules create any rights at all."[38] Obviously in chess this general theory must refer to the consent which the parties playing chess may be presupposed to have given to the rules of the game. Thus, Dworkin concludes:

the hard case puts, we might say, a question of political theory. It asks what it is fair to suppose the players have done in consenting to the forfeiture rule. The concept of a game's character is a conceptual device for framing that question. It is a contested concept that internalizes the general justification of the institution so as to make it available for discriminations within the institution itself. It supposes that a player consents not simply to a set of rules, but to an enterprise that may be said to have a character of its own; so that when the question is put – To what did he consent in consenting to that? – the answer may study the enterprise as a whole and not just the rules.[39]

How is this account of Dworkin's discussion of the referee's struggle with a hard case in chess pertinent to normative theory in international relations? At the end of the previous section I mentioned the conventional view in terms of which it is not possible to settle contentious issues in the modern state domain of discourse. According to this conventional view in hard cases there are no agreed upon rules for deciding the issues; there are no agreed upon criteria for doing this. In the absence of these (so the argument holds) it is not possible to rule that one decision is right and another wrong. With regard to this objection Dworkin's chess example demonstrates several things: first, that where a difficult case arises within an institution, the person called upon to make a decision is not free to make any decision he sees fit, even though in such cases (by definition) there is no clear rule dictating the correct solution. Rather he is constrained by a set of standards (other than rules) which are, we may say, inherent in the institution taken as a whole.

Second, Dworkin's example indicates the kind of procedure that someone called upon to decide such cases may follow in order to bring the inherent standards to light. The crucial features of this procedure are:

1. The requirement that the decision-maker start by inquiring into the *background justification* for the *institution as a whole*.
2. In seeking an answer to 1 he must start with *"what everyone knows"* as the point or purpose of the institution. This inquiry will reveal certain guiding concepts capable of diverse conceptions. Thus, we saw that all chess players would agree that chess is an intellectual game, but there is scope for diverse conceptions of just what this implies.
3. He must seek out that conception of the institution's point or character which best accords with the settled rules of the institution.
4. In the event of his being left (after completing step 3) with two or more conceptions which seem to fit the institution's settled practice equally well, he must decide which gives the deepest and most satisfying account of the concept. This may involve him in more fundamental philosophical ques-

tions about the nature of the basic commitments of the participants in the practice. But these are only of interest to him in so far as they reveal to him the character of the institution to which the participants have consented.

Third, the chess example shows how a background theory which must necessarily be quite general can be used to generate a determinate solution to a difficult case. It is this background theory which allows a correct decision in hard cases.

The last point is at the heart of Dworkin's ongoing dispute with positivist theories of law and with our own refutation of the conventional wisdom outlined at the beginning of this section. Both the legal positivist and conventional wisdom in international relations hold that we can only talk of a "right answer" to a case where there is a determinate rule specifying what the answer is. On this view, where there is no rule there can be no correct answer, but only a choice among several equally reasonable answers. In such cases, reasonable men are not called upon to seek agreement. Against this Dworkin argues that the positivist model of argument, with its heavy stress on mechanical rules, cannot account for the fact that arguments do take place where mechanical rules are not readily available. In the chess example, in hard cases in law and, I want to suggest, in the knotty issues in international relations, people do argue in the belief that what they are arguing for is correct and that the view which they are opposing is wrong. In the chess example Dworkin shows that it is possible to arrive at a correct decision about the rights of the players although there is no clear rule covering the case.[40]

For my purposes the question of whether or not there are right answers to hard cases is of interest in its own right, but it also has considerable further significance. As Dworkin shows, it is possible to settle hard cases (concerning law, chess, international relations or whatever), but not without getting involved in "deep" discussions about the basic justifications for the institutions within which these issues arise. Thus judges in hard legal cases are called upon to get involved in political theory, concerning themselves with such questions as: "What is the underlying justification for the settled rules of the law? Why and when are legislatures justified in creating new rights?" Once the pertinence of such questions is admitted, it is no longer possible to maintain the positivist separation between law and morals. Positivists wanted to maintain this distinction because it made plausible their contention that the law could be investigated objectively, without the investigator becoming involved in normative theorizing himself. In this respect legal positivists are like the positivist social scientists discussed in Chapter One.[41] They are also akin to the realist school of scholars in international relations discussed in Chapter Two. All these approaches seek to give a factual account of the practices under investigation which does not require any involvement in normative theory. Dworkin shows how an adequate account of an institution must explain what happens when hard cases arise, and that in order to do this the investigator must become involved in fundamental normative theorizing.

3.2 Building coherent background justifications

The core of Dworkin's method of argument involves the construction of a background theory for the institution within which the hard case in question arises. Before attempting to apply his method to the hard cases of international relations and in order to make this crucial phase of his method somewhat clearer, let us briefly examine Dworkin's portrayal of the very different background theories which may be constructed to deal with hard cases involving the interpretation of statutes, on the one hand, and hard cases calling for an interpretation of precedent, on the other.

Where a judge is called upon to interpret a vague statute in order to determine whether it is to apply to a hard case or not, he will have to determine what the general justification for the creation of rights by the legislature is (just as in the chess game

the referee had to determine why the players could be considered to have rights *vis-à-vis* one another at all). The background justification for the legislative creation of rights may be
a version of democratic theory, in itself a set of concepts
capable of admitting diverse conceptions. In terms of democratic theory it seems plausible to argue that representative
legislatures are entitled to enact laws implementing their policies and creating new rights. Here a policy is taken to be a
general goal such as the advancement of the aggregate welfare
within the community.

The background justification for taking into account precedents from case law is quite different. Here it is not possible to
construct a theory which would have it that precedents are
pieces of legislation enacted by judges in order to further
certain policy goals. Legislation by a legislature may be said to
be justified in terms of democratic theory because the legislature is well suited to making policy decisions since it is representative, accountable and well constructed to perform an
interest aggregating function. But judges, whose decisions
create precedents, cannot have their law making activity justified by democratic theory in the same way. It is difficult to fit
judicial law making in prior cases into general democratic
theory at all, since judges are not regularly accountable to an
electorate, nor is the institution of the judiciary particularly
well suited to keeping judges in close contact with the felt
needs of the community, and so on. What alternative justification is there for having judges take precedent seriously?
Dworkin's answer is that it will be a concept of *fairness* which
justifies the practice of precedent. If government through the
courts enforces a decision in an earlier case, it is only fair that
in a subsequent case which is similar a similar decision ought
to be enforced. The institution of precedent is thus justified on
the ground that it is fair to be consistent. The general practice of
precedent is justified by the *principle* of fairness. A principle is
a reason which counts against an action even though the action
in question might advance some policy (like the general

welfare). Dworkin points out that principles are often used to protect individuals against action that would advance the general welfare at the individual's cost.[42]

The details of Dworkin's lucid account of legal reasoning in hard cases need not detain us any further. The relevant point for my purposes is the way in which he has shown that different kinds of justifications need to be constructed for different kinds of institution or different aspects of the same general institution. As we have seen, democratic theory justifies the practice of statutory legislation by a representative legislature, but a principle of fairness is required to justify the practice of adhering to precedent in case law. Here then is a model relevant to the problem of resolving the pressing questions in international relations. Evidently I cannot hope to apply Dworkin's specific legal arguments directly to the quite different context of international relations. Rather I shall attempt to adapt his general approach to the specific concerns of international relations. What is the appropriate justification for the institution which we know as the system of states? Following Dworkin's model we need to construct a suitable justification in order to decide the difficult cases identified at the beginning of this chapter.[43]

There is one last feature of Dworkin's method of argument which must be taken heed of before trying to apply it to international relations. This feature, which was first developed by John Rawls, is the technique of *reflective equilibrium*.[44] It will be recalled that according to Dworkin's method of argument a judge seeking a solution to a hard case must start with what everyone knows to be the settled rules of the institution and then proceed to construct that background theory which best accords with these settled rules.[45] The technique of reflective equilibrium is designed to overcome an incompatibility (a lack of fit) between the body of settled rules and the background theory which might arise at this point. To demonstrate the use of the technique let us imagine a judge facing a hard case in law.

The judge must be pictured as seeking a fit (or match) between a whole body of settled law and the justificatory background theory. However, there are several reasons for supposing that it will not be possible to achieve a complete coherence. First, the settled law is extremely complex and was created by diverse judges, legislators and jurists who may well have had divergent educations, abilities and outlooks. It seems plausible to suppose that the law laid down by such a varied group might not easily be subsumed under a coherent theory. Second, the body of settled law was arrived at over a long span of time and, once again, it seems plausible to suppose that earlier rules may not cohere with later ones. Third, the world changes over time and some of the early rules were laid down in a world quite different from that confronting subsequent judges. The rules made for one setting might not easily cohere with those made for another.

Faced with a possibly not fully coherent body of settled law for which he is to provide an adequate background theory, the technique of reflective equilibrium involves a back and forth procedure somewhat as follows: in seeking to construct a coherent background theory to justify the whole body of settled rules, the judge finds that it challenges (calls into question) some bits of the settled corpus of law. He now faces a dilemma: either he must return to the background theory and modify it in some way so that it can encompass these awkward pieces of the settled law, or he must simply accept that the settled body of law is not fully coherent and that these recalcitrant pieces cannot be fitted into the best background theory he can construct. If he chooses to modify the background theory to accommodate these pieces it is likely that other bits of the settled body will in a like manner refuse to fit the new background theory. Thus it is probable that in any piece of legal reasoning the judge will end up with some bits and pieces of the settled law which do not fit the proposed justificatory background theory. In this way bits of settled law will become suspect and may well with time fall into dissuetude. This back and forth procedure is the procedure of reflective equilibrium. By moving back and forth between the settled rules and the background theory the judge seeks an equilibrium. After achieving a reflective equilibrium the final step for the judge is to use the background theory to generate a solution to the hard case in hand.

It is important to notice that recalcitrant pieces of settled law are *not* akin to the bits of evidence which a natural scientist cannot accommodate in his theory. For a scientist such evidence poses a potential threat to the scientific theory; it forms part of the data which either confirm or refute his theory. A good scientist is not entitled to push such evidence aside on the grounds that it does not achieve a nice "fit" with his theory. In the face of such pieces of counter evidence the scientist might decide to wait and see whether more data of the same kind are forthcoming in the future. But he cannot disregard it altogether. The judge's position is quite different. The bits of settled law which he confronts are not data for which he seeks a satisfactory explanation. Rather they are pieces of settled law for which he has to try and seek a single coherent justification. The bits which do not fit even the best justification constructable must be deemed to be suspect although previously considered settled.[46]

I have discussed this procedure of argument in some detail for two reasons: first, it indicates in a general way how we might set about solving the hard cases facing normative theorists in international relations, some of which we mentioned at the beginning of this chapter. Second, it enables us to counter several objections which have been raised against theories of intra-practice argument, some of which I mentioned in Chapter Two. Before ending this chapter let us briefly look at these.

4 Refutation of the critique of intra-practice argument

In the light of the exposition of the Dworkinian model of normative argument it is now possible to deal with some criticisms which have been made of the notion of intra-practice argument.

The method which has been outlined is intra-practice in that the context in which disputes about hard cases are considered to take place is one in which the disputants are pictured as being initiates of a given practice; they are agreed upon the settled rules which constitute the practice in question. Their dispute is about hard cases *within* the practice.

Critics of intra-practice argument, like Ernest Gellner, have argued against approaches such as the one I have been advocating which relies upon the modern state domain of discourse theory that they are "reindorsement theories."[47] Elsewhere he says such theories force us into "uncritical acceptance" of traditional language.[48] Against such critics I would argue that intra-practice argument as outlined above is not inevitably an endorsement of the *status quo*. As we have seen, argument and reasoning within the practice can lead to the practice changing in significant ways over time. In his major attack on this type of approach, *Words and Things*, he says it commits us to "conceptual conservatism,"[49] which in turn, he says, leads to political conservatism.[50] These charges all contain an element of truth in them together with some falsity. The element of truth is that the procedure of argument outlined above is conservative in that it starts from, and is tested against, the settled rules of the particular domain of discourse within which it takes place. What is false is the contention that the method involves an *uncritical* reindorsement of the practice concerned. As we saw in the discussion of the procedure of reflective equilibrium, there is a critical dimension to this process. In seeking an equilibrium parts of the settled corpus come to be challenged and thus over time the practice changes and develops. Everything is not left as it was.[51] However, it is true that on this view criticism cannot but be piecemeal.

Against this it might be argued that Gellner's major concern is not with validating a single decision within a legal system, but with the problem of validating one domain of discourse *vis-à-vis* others. In particular Gellner is concerned to validate the scientific mode of discourse *vis-à-vis* other non-scientific ones, such as Marxist ones. This is true as a statement of what Gellner wants to do, but it in no way undermines the relevance, for my purposes, of the method of argument outlined above. My contention is that argument about the validity of a domain of discourse (e.g. the scientific one), just like argument about the validity of a decision for a hard case in law, will only be possible within an established mode of discourse which has a large component of settled premises from which the argument can proceed. There are two things which reindorsement philosophers (as Gellner calls them) are concerned to deny here. The first is that there is some special philosophical method which can show whether a given domain of discourse is valid or not.[52] The second is that within a domain of discourse it is not possible to doubt *all* the ordinarily accepted as valid usages (unless, of course, the investigator retreats to a higher domain of discourse within which the original domain is seen but as a sub category). However, it is quite possible to come to doubt *some* of the settled usages.

A related but different objection to the method of intra-practice argument which we hope to have countered by portraying the Dworkinian method of legal argument is the objection that theories of intra-practice argument cannot cope with "creativity," "thought," "game change" or "improvement."[53] On Gellner's view reindorsement philosophies (ordinary language philosophies) cannot account for conceptual changes (which undoubtedly do take place in all societies) because they are committed to the premise that ordinary usage is correct as it is. Once again, this objection contains some element of truth. It is true that reindorsement philosophies deny that philosophy can discover critiera which will show *all* ordinary discourse to be wrong. But we have seen how it is possible via the method of reflective equilibrium to show that *some* of our settled usages are wrong. In response to new situations new usages will emerge. These may be tested via the method of reflective equilibrium (the method of intra-practice critique) and thus, gradually, the ordinary language will change and grow.

Finally, the description of the procedure of legal argument has shown how it is that the user of the language in a given domain (in this case the judge) may make a mistake. It was shown that endorsing an intra-practice theory of argument does not involve a commitment to the view that those within a practice can do no wrong; can make no mistakes. What the Dworkinian model of legal argument gives us is an account of what is involved in making a mistake in hard case decisions. A judge may make a mistake in any of the stages of argument which were identified: in the identification and articulation of the settled law, in the construction of a justifying background theory, in bringing this into equilibrium with the settled law, and, finally, in the generation from the background theory of a new rule to cover the case in hand.

In this chapter I have outlined a method of argument which promises to solve some of the pressing normative issues which face us in contemporary international relations. It starts by pointing out that normative disputes only arise within the context of some shared premises, within the context of some settled rules. I showed, following Dworkin, how this body of settled rules may be used, in a step by step procedure, to generate answers to the hard cases which arise within a practice.

Let us now attempt to apply this method of argument to some of those hard cases in international normative theory identified at the beginning of this chapter. As a first step we must identify the settled norms of international relations and then we must proceed to construct the best possible background theory which will justify them.

NOTES

1 John Rawls, *Theory of Justice* (London, Oxford University Press, 1972), Preface.
2 See James Mayall, "International Society and International Theory" in *The Reason of States*, ed. Michael Donelan (London, Allen and Unwin, 1978), especially p. 133 and following pages.
3 Hans Morgenthau, *Politics among Nations* (New York, Knopf, 1973),

p. 259. See also K. J. Holsti, *International Politics* (Englewood Cliffs, Prentice-Hall, 1967), p. 234 and following pages.

4 Ibid.

5 Michael Walzer, *Obligations: Essays on Disobedience, War and Citizenship* (Cambridge, Mass., Harvard University Press, 1970).

6 Barrie Paskins and Michael Dockrill, *The Ethics of War* (London, Duckworth, 1979), p. 207.

7 Ralph Pettman, *State and Class* (London, Croom Helm, 1979), p. 72.

8 K. J. Holsti, *International Politics*, p. 234.

9 See Karl Marx's descriptions of the way in which the "freedom of labour" principle was interpreted in nineteenth century industrial states in *Capital* (London, Dent, 1972), Chapter 8 on the "Working Day."

10 See Ralph Pettman, *State and Class*, Chapter 3.

11 See Michael Oakshott, "The Language of the Modern European State," *Political Studies*, Vol. 23 (December 1975), p. 409.

12 James Mayall, "International Society and International Theory," p. 136. Also Ralph Pettman, *State and Class*, Chapter 3.

13 Maurice Keens-Soper, "The Practice of the States System" in *The Reason of States*.

14 James Mayall, "International Society and International Theory," p. 135.

15 Michael Donelan, "The Political Theorists and International Theory" in *The Reason of States*; John Finnis, *Natural Law and Natural Rights* (Oxford University Press, 1980).

16 Michael Donelan, "Political Theorists," p. 90.

17 John Finnis, *Natural Law and Natural Rights*, Section iv:2. At page 155 he says there is a common good for human beings inasmuch "as life, knowledge, play, aesthetic experience, friendship, religion and freedom in practical reasonableness are good for any and every person."

18 Ibid. p. 71.

19 Ibid. p. 74.

20 Ibid. p. 69.

21 Is it not possible to use a similar argument against the position which I have been arguing? For in support of my argument that there is an international state centric domain of discourse I pointed to the fact that most actors in world politics profess, *inter alia*, a commitment to democracy. Might it not be argued against me that the different actors have widely divergent views of democracy? Against this I would argue that there is a core of concepts common to those who profess a commitment to democracy. There is no such core of common concepts across cultures with regard to the goods isolated by Finnis.

22 Michael Donelan, "Political Theorists," p. 86.

23 Ibid. p. 86.

24 Ibid. *passim*.

25 Ibid. p. 76.

26 Ibid. p. 77.
27 On sovereignty generally see Wladyslaw Jozef Stankiewicz, *In Defence of Sovereignty* (London, Oxford University Press, 1969).
28 Any suggestion that it is probably rests on some confusion about the relationship between power and moral theory akin to that which was discussed in Chapter Two.
29 Barrie Paskins and Michael Dockrill, *The Ethics of War*, p. 207.
30 Where a bargain is struck between two or more parties there is no question of the bargain being right or wrong. It is simply what is agreed to. We may say that the bargain struck favours one party more than the other, but this is quite different from saying that the bargain was wrong.
31 Most of Dworkin's articles on this issue published over a period of years have been taken up in his book, *Taking Rights Seriously* (London, Duckworth, 1981).
32 In particular he developed his position through a critique of the work of H. L. A. Hart, *The Concept of Law* (London, Oxford University Press, 1961).
33 Ronald Dworkin, *Taking Rights Seriously*, p. 101.
34 Ibid. p. 102.
35 Ibid. p. 103. Also see W. B. Gallie, "Essentially Contested Concepts," *Proceedings of the Aristotelian Society*, Vol. 56 (1965), p. 167.
36 Ronald Dworkin, *Taking Rights Seriously*, p. 103.
37 Ibid. p. 104.
38 Ibid.
39 Ibid.
40 This applies even where the institution within which the dispute is being decided has a further rule which specifies that the referee's decision will be final. For a party involved may well accept the decision as binding, yet still argue that it is wrong. In short, any theory of argument which asserts that talk of there being a single correct answer is only proper where there is a clear rule supplying that answer cannot account for most of the arguments people take seriously in chess, the law, international relations, and many other institutions. See also Dworkin, *Taking Rights Seriously*, Chapter 13 and p. 331 for discussion of the "right answer" question.
41 Chapter One, p. 13 and the following pages.
42 Dworkin describes the basic distinction in *Taking Rights Seriously*, p. 22, as follows: "I call a 'policy' that kind of standard that sets out a goal to be reached, generally an improvement in some economic, political or social feature of that community . . . I call a 'principle' a standard that is to be observed, not because it will advance or secure an economic, political or social situation deemed desirable, but because it is a requirement of justice or fairness or some other dimension of morality."
43 At page 82 and following pages.
44 Ronald Dworkin, *Taking Rights Seriously*, p. 159 and following pages; John Rawls, *Theory of Justice*, pp. 48–51.

45 See above, p. 102 and following pages.
46 Ronald Dworkin, *Taking Rights Seriously*, p. 160 and following pages. Note that Dworkin's portrayal of what judges do in hard cases is not supposed to be a description of what judges in fact do in every case. He admits that the task he sets the judge is impossibly huge, thus he calls his imaginary judge "Hercules." Dworkin may be seen as using an ideal type argument.
47 Ernest Gellner, *The Legitimation of Belief* (Cambridge University Press, 1974), Chapter 3. Gellner worked out his criticism against the Wittgensteinian and neo-Wittgensteinian positions and has, as far as I know, never specifically focused on Dworkin's position.
48 Ernest Gellner, *Spectacles and Predicaments* (Cambridge University Press, 1980), Chapter 3, p. 98 and following pages.
49 Ernest Gellner, *Words and Things* (London, Gollancz, 1959), p. 44.
50 Ibid. pp. 247–9.
51 H. L. A. Hart in "Between Utility and Rights" in *The Idea of Freedom*, ed. Alan Ryan (London, Oxford University Press, 1979), comments on how radical (unconservative) Dworkin's rights thesis is and compares it to a much more conservative one, viz. that of Robert Nozick, *Anarchy, State and Utopia* (Oxford, Blackwell, 1974).
52 See the general argument of Richard Rorty in *Philosophy and the Mirror of Nature* (Oxford, Blackwell, 1980).
53 Ernest Gellner, *Words and Things*, pp. 217, 218.

Chapter Four

Towards the construction of a normative theory of international relations

The task of the present chapter, if done properly, would be a task for Atlas. As was shown in the previous chapter, what we are called upon to do in constructing a normative theory of international relations must involve at least the following steps. First, we must list all those norms in international relations that are considered settled in terms of the modern state domain of discourse. Second, we must attempt to construct the best possible background justification for this settled body of norms. Third, following through on step two, we must apply the procedure of reflective equilibrium. Fourth, with the aid of the background theory we must generate answers to some of the hard cases facing international relations theorists. Since none of us have the capacities of an Atlas we must rest content with something less, something altogether more schematic.

1 The settled body of norms in international relations

It is not possible to give a conclusive or very detailed account of what is the settled body of norms within the domain of normative international theory. At this stage a very rough and preliminary list will have to suffice. Since we are listing the parts of what is a settled whole, we must also expect that there will be some overlap between the listed items. The items are not clearly discrete.

I shall regard a norm as settled where it is generally recognized that any argument denying the norm (or which appears to override the norm) requires special justification. Where I claim that a norm is settled I am not claiming that most people (or states) do in fact obey that norm. In other words, the claim that a given norm is settled cannot be disputed by pointing out instances where people (or states) have not in actual fact acted according to the norm. For example, that many states infringe the norm prohibiting one state from interfering in the domestic affairs of another state does not undermine my contention that non-interference is a settled norm of the modern state domain of discourse. It would undermine my assertion if it could be shown that states do not even attempt to provide special justifications for their interferences in the domestic affairs of other states. What people say in support of their actions thus gives us an indication of whether a given item is settled within a specified domain of discourse.

Another indicator of whether a given norm is settled within the modern state domain of discourse or not is provided by the way in which acts which infringe the norm are undertaken. Where acts which infringe a given norm are often (normally) undertaken clandestinely, this is *prima facie* proof that the norm in question is a settled one. For the most part states do not openly undertake and publicly defend actions aimed at destabilizing neighbouring states. This is *prima facie* evidence that there is a settled norm prohibiting such actions. Finally, it must be remembered in the case of each settled norm that it is the concept of that norm which is regarded as settled within the modern state domain of discourse, and not any particular conception of the concept.[1] Let us now consider what is settled, at least in this sense, within the modern state domain of discourse.

1. Within the modern state system it is a settled norm that the *preservation of the society of states itself* is a good. The

claim here is not that everybody would actively promote this as a goal, but that no significant group of actors in world politics would act contrary to this in the conduct of international affairs without invoking special justification. Even though Marxist theory envisages the withering away of the state in a communist society, Marxist states both in their domestic and foreign policies act in accordance with the norm that the preservation of the international society of states is a good. They formulate their own policies and criticize the actions of others in terms of this norm.[2] Those (such as many Third World states) who argue that the present arrangement of the system of states is unfair do not so much call for the abandonment of the system of states (to be replaced by a world government for example), but argue for certain modifications to the system.[3] In particular they demand a new system for the distribution of wealth between states.

2. For the purposes of the modern state domain of discourse it is settled that it is a good for states in the system to be accounted as *sovereign*, where sovereignty refers to an autonomous state ruling over a specified territory. What is involved here is best brought out by contrasting it with the political organization in a very different kind of system such as the feudal one. In the feudal system the relationships between people consisted in sets of mutual and personal obligations of certain conventional kinds. Typically a set of obligations would be established between a nobleman and a group of serfs, in terms of which he would protect them in time of war in return for a portion of the harvest. The nobleman would himself be bound by mutual obligations with other noblemen and so on. Thus in a given area the web of obligation might be quite complicated and also fluid, there being no clear and single centre of government with ultimate authority over all the people in a given territory, but rather this cross-cutting web of personal obligations.[4] In the modern system of states assumptions

regarding authority relations are quite different. Here all the people within the territory of a sovereign state are supposed to fall under its exclusive authority. This authority is assumed to be binding on them for as long as they remain in its territory. A South African cannot be regarded as bound by the law of the Soviet Union while living in Johannesburg. Also a South African cannot be regarded as under the concurrent rule of two or more states. Where a person moves out of the territory of one sovereign state he moves into that of another and thereby *ipso facto* falls under its authority. A further point to notice is that, unlike the personal nature of feudal authority, sovereign states are considered to be in a sense immortal in that the authority of a state over its citizens is not connected to any particular person's life span, but inheres in the enduring political order itself.

3. In their dealings with each other within the international society states clearly proceed on the assumption that war requires a special justification in a way that peaceful relations do not, thus indicating that *peace* is regarded as a settled norm. In setting up the United Nations Organization the founding states made the maintenance of international peace a primary goal. The argument is not that acts of war are never considered justified – they often are – but the point is rather that war is considered to be in need of justification in a way that peace is not. All states going to war take pains to justify their case before the international community, whereas states remaining at peace with other states do not generally go out of their way to justify their position.

4. It is settled that any attempt by one state to achieve a preponderance of power over other states is a bad thing. An alternative formulation of this point might refer to an anti-imperialist norm.

5. Action by states to avoid any drive towards preponderant power by other states is considered good.

6. Preservation of the *balance of power* is a settled norm and acts aimed at furthering this end need no special justification, while those tending to upset it typically do. Thus a state by strengthening its internal economy, morale, army and so on will publicly avow that this is required to maintain the balance of power, but it will not acknowledge the contrary aim. It might seek to stall the drive towards dominance of another state in one or all of several different ways, for example by forming defensive alliances with other states, by seeking to influence world public opinion against the expanding power, or by seeking to undermine the internal stability of the threatening state.

7. Within the modern state domain of discourse it is settled that *modernization* is an approved goal for states. Modernization is regarded as an approved goal in itself (in that a modernized society is preferable to a primitive one) and it is also invoked as a justification for advancing some of the other settled norms which we have mentioned. For example, a state, in order not to fall under the domination of another state, must, amongst other things, strengthen itself internally. In the world as it is presently constituted this requires that the state replace primitive methods of production with modern industrial techniques. This requires a new division of labour, the accumulation of capital, the acquisition of the necessary technology, the building of the necessary infrastructure, the finding and gaining of access to the necessary raw materials, and so on. It is generally recognized that states which fail to modernize successfully make themselves vulnerable to domination by other states.[5]

8. It is settled that *patriotism* is a good thing where the term is understood as referring to a feeling by the citizens of loyalty to, and love for, their state. That this is a good is explained by reference to the need for internal strength required by the threats mentioned in 5. In order to defend itself against a would-be dominant power, a state's

economic and military power depends on the co-operation of its citizens. A state without such a patriotic feeling amongst its citizens would be weak. It is important that this should not be confused with the quite different issue of nationalism. Certainly no point about a mystical entity called the nation is being made here. Nationalism is a recent and very controversial historical development whereas pariotism is essentially contained in the old adage that unity is strength. There is agreement in the world today that such strength of civic feeling between people living within the territory of a state is a good.

9. Another way of opposing an emerging imperial power is for the states in the system of states to establish a *collective security* arrangement for the purpose of maintaining international peace and security and international law. It is settled that attempts to set up such arrangements are good. Thus there is agreement on the worth of international institutions such as the United Nations Organization and its associated organizations, whatever criticisms might be levelled against their actual performance.

10. In order to achieve the goods mentioned in 5 above, what is required is a sophisticated international *institution of diplomacy*. It is settled that such an institution is an instrumental necessity for the preservation of the other goods mentioned in our list. A successful diplomatic apparatus requires arrangements for the protection of the persons of diplomats, the protection of their channels of communication, and so on.

11. It is settled that in the relations between states, lack of agreed upon ways of doing things is a bad thing. Thus the body of *international law* which is designed to overcome this problem is considered a good. Again the problematic status of such law, and the criticisms levelled at various aspects of it, should not prevent us from recognizing that the idea of international law is a settled norm. As the complexity and scope of the interactions between states have

grown, so has the body of settled international law. There are multiple and persistent disputes about diverse aspects of international law, but the modern state domain of discourse assumes agreement on some core body of international law. Underlying this is a deeper agreement on the need for international law.[6]

12. For the purposes of the modern state domain of discourse it is settled that a government's first duty is to protect the interests of its own citizens. The well-being of its own citizens must be considered more important than the well-being of people elsewhere in the world.

13. It is settled that a set of *democratic institutions* within a state is a good. It is recognized that states without such institutions need to justify their not being democracies. Defences of this kind might refer to economic necessity (that temporary autocratic rule is necessary to get the economy on its feet), external threat (that autocratic rule is needed to enable the state to cope with an external threat), and so on. That the democratic norm is settled, of course, does not imply that any states are democracies.

14. It is settled that *human rights* are a good which need to be protected by states and by the international system. Where an infringement of human rights is claimed, the accused party is called upon to deny the charge or produce an excuse for his conduct. Once again we are not claiming that there is international agreement on what the rights are or on how they ought to be protected. But there is agreement that some such rights exist and ought to be upheld.

15. In spite of the pervasive commitment to democratic institutions and human rights mentioned above, it is settled that there are strict limits to what states may do to bring about the above mentioned conditions in a recalcitrant state. I refer here to the rule of *non-intervention* in the domestic affairs of other states. It precludes direct military involvement against other states except where such action is in self-defence or in terms of a defensive alliance. Mili-

tary action in self-defence may be undertaken unilaterally by the attacked state or there may be a multilateral engagement authorized by a collective security arrangement such as the United Nations.

16. In general it is agreed that it is permitted for states, in order to support collective security measures, to use *economic sanctions* against the offending state. But note that such sanctions are normally considered an unwarranted interference in the domestic affairs of another state.

17. It is settled that in the conduct of war, once it has broken out, certain rules ought to be obeyed, i.e. that set of rules usually referred to as the *ius in bello*.

18. It is agreed that some kind of system of *economic co-operation* between states is a good.

The settled items already mentioned may for convenience' sake be called the list of the settled core. To summarize, it is settled that these are good:

1. The preservation of the society of states.
2. State sovereignty.
3. Peace between states and within states.
4. Rejecting domination as a legitimate goal in international relations.
5. Actions aimed at countering a state's drive to domination.
6. The balance of power. Internal economic, political, military strength and war are good when used to uphold the goods mentioned in 1–3.
7. Modernization.
8. National unity within states.
9. Collective security arrangements between states.
10. Diplomatic conventions between states.
11. International law.
12. A state's primary duty is to protect its own citizens.
13. Democratic institutions within the states of the system.
14. Human rights.
15. Non-intervention in the domestic affairs of other states.
16. Economic sanctions in support of collective security.

17. *Ius in bello.*
18. Systems of inter-state economic co-operation.

2 Justificatory background theories for the settled core of agreed norms: a critical appraisal

On reflection, what is striking about the foregoing list is the primacy of the first two items on the list. Most of the other settled goods are in some way derivative from them. Combining the first two items, it appears that the preservation of a system of sovereign states is the primary good. The majority of the other goods mentioned imply a prior acceptance of this good. Thus any satisfactory background theory will have to justify the settled belief that the preservation of a system of sovereign states is such a good. Any acceptable background theory will have to answer this key question: "Why is it a good thing to preserve a system of sovereign states?" An alternative formulation of the question is: "What is the best justification for the preservation of a system of sovereign states?"[7]

What then is the best justification for the system of sovereign states? There are current in the discipline three main answers which we must look at. I am not suggesting that these three are the only possible answers to the question; there may be many more possible answers. But it does seem a good idea to start with answers which are already current in the debate.

2.1 *Justifications invoking order*

Many theorists in international relations have justified the preservation of a system of sovereign states on the grounds that it promotes *order*. This justification has traditionally been given by those theorists preoccupied with theories of balance of power.[8] Such theorists were primarily concerned with explicating and applying the notoriously difficult notion of the balance of power and they were only incidentally concerned with the question of the justification of the system of sovereign states. Their aims were primarily descriptive and explanatory. In so far as they were concerned with justifying the preservation of a system of sovereign states, the problem which they saw themselves called upon to answer was: "Is the system of sovereign states operating according to the balance of power principle justified even though its members are by definition subject to no common law?"

In one way or another the answer to this question was always that the states in the balance formed some kind of ordered society and that the balance of power was justified in so far as it worked towards preserving that society of states. Originally it was argued that this society of states was a Christian one.[9] Let me give a few examples of this type of argument.

Giovanni Botero, writing in the sixteenth century, says that "to effect a balance in politics is simply to prevent others from disturbing the peace and endangering the society of states."[10] In the next century we find Fenelon arguing:

Neighbouring states are not obliged to observe towards each other the rules of justice and public faith; but they are under a necessity, from the security of each, and the common interest of all, to maintain together a kind of society and general republic, for the most powerful will certainly at length prevail and overthrow the rest, unless they unite together to make a counterweight.[11]

He also wrote, "Nor is this injustice; 'tis to preserve itself and its neighbours from servitude; 'tis to contend for the liberty, tranquillity and happiness of all in general."[12] Daniel Defoe, writing about Europe in the late sixteenth century and early seventeenth century, says, "the safety of the whole consists in a due distribution of power ... that no one may be able to oppress and destroy the rest."[13] In the eighteenth century Vattel articulated the justification we are considering most eloquently when he wrote:

Europe forms a political system ... not a confused heap of detached parts, each of which had little concern for the lot of others ... The constant attention of sovereigns to all that goes on, the custom of resident ministers, the continual negotiations that take place, make of modern Europe a sort of Republic whose members each independent, but bound by a common interest unite for the maintenance of order and the preservation of liberty.[14]

More recently Hedley Bull defends the society of states on the grounds that it promotes the goal of order. In *The Anarchical Society* Bull sets out to examine certain institutions such as the balance of power, international law, diplomacy and war. He says: "it is their functions in relation to order that I seek to explain."[15] In spite of the term "function" it is clear that for Bull the system of states may be said to promote order and to that extent it is justified. Bull is careful to state that order is only one value amongst others which the institutions in the society of states may be said to promote. Order is, for example, distinct from the goal of justice. Although Bull makes some confusing remarks about order not being a primary or overriding goal, it is clear from a reading of his book as a whole that in his view the satisfaction of other goals, like justice and welfare, presuppose that the prior goal of order be already satisfied.[16]

The balance of power authors I have referred to thus defend the system of states operating on the balance of power principle on the grounds that it preserves some kind of ordered society ("the society of states," "a kind of society and general Republic," "the safety of the whole," and "a sort of Republic"). My argument will be that this defence of the system of sovereign states is a weak one. It is weak in that it is either circular, or it is a natural law justification masquerading as something else.

Let us look at the first of these criticisms, viz. that this type of justification is circular. Common to the writers we have mentioned we find the following form of argument: "The system of sovereign states operating according to the balance of power principle is justified in that it preserves a kind of society." We are entitled to ask of this justification: "What kind of society does it preserve?" The answer to this often appears to be: "It preserves a system of states operating according to the balance of power principle."[17] This answer is clearly circular in that the argument now becomes: "The system of states operating according to the balance of power principle is justified in that it preserves the system of states operating according to the balance of power principle." Of course none of the writers mentioned makes this argument quite so explicitly. It would be self-defeating to do so. That their argument is a circular one is often obscured by the vagueness of the terms they employ.

2.2 Hedley Bull on order

An influential modern version of this position, open to the same critical charges, is that provided by Hedley Bull. The position of Bull on this point is more difficult in that he discusses three different kinds of order, viz. order, international order and world order. However, after making these distinctions in the Introduction of *The Anarchical Society* he reverts in much of the book to talking of order *simpliciter* so that it is often far from clear which kind of order is being talked about. Let us look at his three notions of order.

Order Bull defines as a pattern preserving three primary goals, which are:
1. The preservation of life.
2. That promises should be kept.
3. That the possession of things will remain stable to some degree.[18]

International order he defines as the pattern of activity that sustains the following primary goals of the society of states:
1. The preservation of the system and society of states itself.
2. The goal of maintaining the independence or external sovereignty of individual states.
3. The goal of peace among the member states of society as the normal condition of their relationship.
4. The common goals of all social life.[19]

World order Bull defines as those patterns of human activity that "sustain the primary goals of social life among mankind as a whole."[20]

A glance at the above mentioned definitions shows that if

Bull wishes to argue that the society of states preserves *international order* (as he defines it) then his justification is of the same circular kind as that used by the traditional authors discussed. Primary goals of international order 1, 2 and 3 all simply refer to the maintenance of the society of states. Thus the justification becomes: "The society of states is justified because it maintains the society of states." At first glance item 4 seems to refer to some other kind of order. But this is not so. For Bull makes it clear that he is referring to the common goals of all social life *as they apply to inter-state relations*. Thus he says states limit violence by maintaining a monopoly of violence in their territories, by respecting one another's messengers, by trying to limit wars to certain "just wars" and by waging wars within certain constraints. The common social goal is served by states generally adhering to treaties. The property goal is embodied in states' mutual respect for one another's sovereignty over a certain area of territory.[21] Thus even with regard to item 4 in the definition of international order we find that order consists in nothing other than the continued existence of the system of sovereign states. On this view international order would only cease to exist where the situation arose in which only one state existed, or where no states existed. The system of states on this view is justified because it preserves itself. No independent reason is given for the creation, maintenance or preservation of the system of sovereign states.

However, there is another way of reading Bull's justification of the system of states. He may be read as arguing that the system of states preserves *order* (as opposed to *international order*) where this notion involves certain higher level norms as spelled out in his list of primary goals. According to his basic definition of order, as distinguished from the more specific notion of international order, order is that pattern of activity which preserves the primary goals of all social life. These are: the preservation of life, that promises should be kept, and that the possession of things remain stable to some degree. If we read Bull in this way, then his justification is clearly not open to the circularity charge. He cannot be interpreted as saying the system of states is justified because it preserves itself. Rather, it is justified because it furthers these more primary goals of order in general. However, this alternative reading of Bull is open to a different objection, which is that order (which involves the preservation of the aforementioned primary goals) is not a criterion which a basic social arrangement can satisfy or fail to satisfy. Order in this sense is, rather, a constitutive feature of all and any basic social arrangement. This constitutive notion of order needs to be explained in more detail.

Consider the following different types of basic political arrangements: a nomadic tribe, a dynasty, a republic, a kingdom, an empire, a federation, a confederation, a communist society, a socialist state. (This list could easily be extended.) Any of the above mentioned social orders, if it is to be an order at all, must satisfy the primary "goals" mentioned in Bull's definition of order. They must all provide ways for coping with violence, contract and property. The precise way in which the different social arrangements deal with these common concerns will obviously vary, but what is not open to doubt is that they must provide *some* solution to the problems mentioned. A traditional tribal order deals with property in a different way to that adopted in a communist society, or a capitalist one, or a feudal one, and so on. It is clear, then, that any of the listed basic social arrangements *in order to be a basic social arrangement or order* must provide ways of coping with violence, contract and property. Where the "primary goals" of order are not achieved, what we have is not an unjustifiable type of order, but no basic social order at all. Where these "goals" are not met, we have social breakdown, chaos, disorder.

The force of my contention that order is a constitutive feature of any and all basic social arrangement now becomes clear. *Whatever* arrangement is advocated for world politics, whether it be world government, a confederation of states, a collective security arrangement, a system of sovereign states or some other arrangement, it will as a form of order have to be some arrangement which provides for the basic goals mentioned by Bull. If it does not provide for these, there will be the absence of order, viz. disorder, chaos, etc. In other words, order does not provide a criterion in terms of which it is possible to evaluate the system of sovereign states as a specific arrangement *vis-à-vis* some alternative arrangement. Rather order provides a criterion for what is to count as a basic arrangement. If any proposal is to count as a proposal for a basic social arrangement then it must satisfy the criterion of order. Once the proposal has satisfied this criterion, an attempt may be made to go on to the next step, which is to make a comparative evaluation of the merits of the alternatives proposed. In this second step questions will arise about the comparative merits of different ways of coping with the problems of violence, contract and property. What emerges from the foregoing discussion, then, is that order is a defining feature of any basic social arrangement, rather than a goal which such an arrangement might realize.

There is another important point to be made here. I have argued that order is preserved in feudal orders, republics, communes, federations and so on, in that in each (if it is to be viable) some way must be provided of coping with the three core problems. It is important to notice, though, that it is not possible to answer the question: "Which arrangement best preserves order?" because order in the feudal kingdom is something quite different from the order of the communist state. Order here is not a measure against which the different arrangements can be tested (it is not akin to speed, which provides a standard against which different kinds of motor cars can be tested), but is a criterion for recognizing certain sorts of arrangements as such. Order as used here enables us to distinguish between basic social arrangements on the one hand, and, for example, social breakdown and chaos on the other.

We have seen in this section that order is not a primary goal of basic social arrangements, but a constitutive characteristic of all of them. Thus it cannot be used, as Bull wants to use it, as a standard by which one way of arranging world politics (for example, the system of sovereign states way) can be comparatively evaluated against another proposed arrangement (for example, a system of world government).

There is a third way in which Bull's justification of the system of sovereign states (i.e. on the grounds that it promotes order) may be interpreted. Bull may be interpreted as arguing that the system of sovereign states protects order where "order" refers to a further set of values which he has not explicitly articulated. Here "order" might be seen as a shorthand expression for some fuller normative theory which is, however, not fully articulated and difficult to reconstruct.

Consider Bull's discussion of *world order*. He argues that *world order* is more fundamental than *international order*. It is more fundamental because

the ultimate units of the great society of all mankind are not states (or nations, tribes, empires, classes or parties), but individual human beings which are permanent and indestructible in a sense which groupings of them of this or that sort, are not. This is the moment of international relations, but the question of world order arises whatever the political and social structure of the globe.

He says too that if "international order has value, this can only be because it is instrumental to the goal of order in human society as a whole."[22] In these rather obscure passages Bull's argument is that world order is more fundamental than international order *because* individuals are "permanent and indestructible." Clearly individuals are not permanent and indestructible in any literal sense of the phrase. Bull must be read as meaning that individuals are to be valued more highly than "groupings of this or that sort." What else could his point be here? Presumably he is arguing against those who would see the well-being of some collectivity, for example a class, as more important than the well-being of the individuals within it. If this interpretation of Bull is correct then there is implicit in Bull's theory a substantive normative theory in terms of which the good of individuals is more important than the good of social wholes (like states, classes, etc.). However, what precisely the nature and implications of this normative theory are is not clear. It could be a theory of human rights (albeit a minimalist one) or it could be a utilitarian theory. The former seems unlikely, since Bull has elsewhere argued explicitly against theories of human rights in international relations.[23] That still leaves us with the latter option. Support for this is to be found in the last chapter of *The Anarchical Society*, where Bull argues against utopian, Marxist and interdependence theories of international relations which all advocate an end to the system of sovereign states and the creation of a new order. His argument against all of these approaches is that there is no guarantee that the new orders will achieve what their advocates claim; that there is no reason to suppose that a suitably modified system of states could not achieve the desired result just as well, and that the costs of bringing about a new order (rather than modifying the old one) would be exorbitant. The reference to the costs of change suggests that he may be thinking along utilitarian lines.

Let us recapitulate the argument so far. We are seeking to evaluate the contention that the system of sovereign states is justified because it promotes *order*. This kind of justification is implicit in many balance of power theories. In order to evaluate this contention we looked at Hedley Bull's *Anarchical Society* where this thesis is explicitly argued. There we found that the justification of the system of sovereign states which refers to order can be interpreted in three ways. On the first interpretation the justification proves to be circular. On the second, it fails because order is a constitutive feature of *all* basic social arrangements and not a criterion in terms of which some basic social arrangements can be judged better (more justifiable) than others. On the third interpretation the order justification is found to be a veiled reference to some deeper normative theory. In Bull's case the deeper theory involves some notion of conferring primary value on individuals. This deeper theory cannot be explicated in terms of order alone. If we seek a justification for the system of sovereign states, we must seek a satisfactory deep theory which goes beyond order.

What we have found is that the order justification fails to justify the first item of settled belief on the list of settled beliefs. Not surprisingly, it will be found to fail with regard to all the other items on our list as well. In particular it fails to provide a background theory justifying our settled beliefs that the following are good: modernization, democratic institutions within states and human rights. What alternative justification is there for our belief that the system of sovereign states is a good?

2.3 The utilitarian justification

Kenneth Waltz in his *Theory of International Politics*[24] argues in defence of the present system of sovereign states and against those who wish to see some or other form of world government. He rests his case on arguments such as the following. A world government would need a massive force to police the world. The cost of such a force would be exorbitant. A world government would be a prize of great value and the struggle to gain control of this prize would in all probability be ferocious. The cost of such conflict would be a price to be paid for whatever benefits accrued from world government. The conflicts which would arise in a system of world government would in all probability be between rival nationalist groups. Such conflicts are likely to be particularly difficult to stop. There is thus a high price to pay for the loss of state freedom.[25] All of these arguments are clearly cost/benefit type arguments typical of utilitarian justifications. What we have here, in embryo, is an attempt to justify the system of sovereign states on utilitarian grounds.[26] For our purposes this leads to the more general question: "Is it possible to construct a utilitarian background theory which will justify all (or most) of the items which were listed as being settled within the modern state domain of discourse?"

I think not. There are sound reasons to doubt the utilitarian enterprise as a whole, as will appear from some of the arguments mentioned below. But more specifically there are a whole host of reasons which, taken together, make a formidable case against a utilitarian justification as a background theory in support of the list of settled norms. In the present context it is not possible to go into all the difficulties inherent in any attempt to construct a utilitarian background theory to justify the list of settled norms in the modern state domain of discourse. I shall briefly indicate a few of the main ones.

A utilitarian justification for the norm that the preservation of the society of sovereign states is a good would be of the form: "This norm is justified because adherence to it will achieve a greater aggregate utility than would adherence to any other alternative basic norm such as a norm prescribing, for example, a system of world government." "Aggregate utility" here refers to the sum of wants of the individuals in the world. Presumably this would include the whole adult population. In order to arrive at this aggregate each person's wants would have to be taken into account without some people's wants being given greater weight than those of others.

There are several major problems facing any such project. A first problem concerns the nature of the wants which have to be taken into account in the calculus of utility. A utilitarian trying to determine whether this norm would maximize utility or not would first have to determine what people's wants were. A problem arises, though, when it is realized that the people whose wants are to be put into the calculus are citizens of sovereign states in the system of sovereign states. What wants these people have will be partially determined by their being citizens of states in a system of states. But wants are not independent variables; they are not unmediated givens. Rather they are socially, historically and institutionally mediated. Thus, for example, a Frenchman's wants will be in part determined by his feeling himself to be a citizen of the French state. This will lead him to favour French interests over, say, Egyptian ones. What follows from this is the implausibility of evaluating two institutions, let us call them A and B, in terms of their want satisfying capability in situations where the wants being measured are in part the creation of the institutions being evaluated. Wants thus provide no independent criterion for evaluating institutions of this kind. Utility calculations make best sense with regard to individual actions, like choosing which car to buy. Here we compare models with regard to price, speed, reliability, economy and so on. Our reasoning may quite closely resemble a utility calculus here. However, the notion of a utility calculus makes very little sense with regard to evaluating social and political *institutions* like the family and the state, because wants are themselves socially and historically mediated by such institutions.

A second major problem besetting utilitarian justifications is that an arrangement is deemed to be justified which maximizes the *aggregate* utility without regard to the distribution among individuals. The only distributive criterion built into the utilitarian procedure is the one which stipulates that in the utility calculus each person's wants must be included and that no weighting of wants is to take place; each is to count for one and only one. This aspect of fairness in the procedure does not, however, alleviate the problem caused by the aggregative nature of the enterprise which insists that if X maximizes utility it is to be preferred to Y, even if Y involves a very inequitable distribution. Thus if the system of sovereign states maximizes utility it would be justified *even if* it causes extreme misery and deprivation to those living in the poor states. This conclusion offends our basic intuitions about fairness and about social justice.[27] More importantly, this conclusion is incompatible with that settled norm on the list which refers to individual rights. Utilitarian reasoning also justifies arrangements which make some marginally better off, whilst making others very much worse off. On this view, if it could be shown that aggregate utility would be maximized by arrangements making advanced countries marginally better off while keeping Third World countries poor, then this strategy would be justified. It is clear that this line of thinking, pursued to its extreme, is unable to accommodate any satisfactory notion concerning the value of the individual. The fact is that according to this way of thinking the individual is important only as a location for measuring utility. Once the measurement has been made he, as individual, is no longer of any great importance. If what he wants does not accord with what the aggregate justifies, he is expendable.[28] Once again this conclusion offends our basic intuitions about justice and it is incompatible with the settled norm referring to human rights.

A third problem with the utilitarian justification is that it fails to cope with the fact that people's wants are of differing intensities. John in the USA might want an arrangement which improves his leisure time opportunities, but not as intensely as Charles from Chad wants an arrangement which will prevent him starving. Or, because Charles from Chad has been reduced by hopelessness to apathy, the intensities of the wants may be reversed. In this latter case we feel John's intensity of want ought to be ignored, while in the former case we feel Charles' intense want ought to be taken note of. Utilitarian thought starts out by stressing the primacy of what people *in fact* want. In many cases we feel (on moral grounds) that discriminations need to be made between different wants which people do have. Utilitarian thought does not allow us to make such discriminations.

A fourth problem is closely related to the third, and concerns our strong conviction that some kinds of wants just ought not to be counted in the calculus at all. For example, few would wish to have people's wants for a racist political order, for a slave owning order, for a sexually perverted order and so on, to be counted in any utilitarian calculus. The conviction that these wants ought not to be counted is reflected in some of the items on our list of settled norms, for example, in the item referring to human rights. The objection against counting these wants cannot be fobbed off on the ground that such "weirdo wants" are always likely to be minority wants and thus outweighed by the sane majority. Most people would agree that even if, in a given group, a majority wished to enslave a minority, it would be wrong to do so. Here, as with the previous problem, the crux of the matter is that when we think about moral issues we want to discriminate between legitimate wants and illegitimate ones. Utilitarian thinking with its narrow focus on *de facto* wants cannot help us make such discriminations. Whatever criteria are introduced to help us make such discriminations, it is clear that they will not be (and cannot be) utilitarian ones.

A fifth problem presented by a utilitarian's justifications for the settled norms in the modern state domain of discourse is this. A utilitarian background theory must argue that the norms on our list are justifiable on utilitarian grounds. His argument must be that by adhering to these norms actors in world politics maximize aggregate utility. His argument must not be taken to be that states ought to stick to these norms *except* where rejecting them (i.e. adopting some other norms) would maximize utility. For adhering to a norm with an exception like this attached to it is not to adhere to a norm at all. Consider the norm on the list which asserts that the protection of human rights is a good. If we understand it as asserting "Actors in international politics ought to adhere to the norms protecting human rights (*a* to z) except where doing so does not maximize aggregate utility" we would be loath to consider them human rights norms at all. A right of prisoners of war not to be executed out of hand which had attached to it the exception "save where doing so would maximize aggregate utility" would hardly be considered a right. For we often assert we have a right in just those situations where denying us the right might have the effect of maximizing utility. Thus we must take the utilitarian to be asserting that actors adhering to the norms listed (without any utility maximizing exceptions attached to them) will have the effect of maximizing aggregate utility. The utilitarian must be arguing that the utilitarian consequence (i.e. the maximization of aggregate utility) which is supposed to follow from adherence to these norms will come about without any of those bound by the norms making his obedience to the norm dependent on a utility calculus in that particular instance. This is another way of saying that the justification must be a rule utilitarian justification; i.e. it is supposed that utility will be maximized by the parties involved following rules and not basing each of their actions on independent utility calculi.[29] The first few norms on our list call upon states to seek the preservation of the society of sovereign states. The rule utilitarian argument is that out of all the sovereignty preserving actions of states, utility will be maximized, without any state actively pursuing global utility maximization. On the rule utilitarian view the good consequences flow from the actors following the rule, not from the actors following the rule only where doing so will maximize utility. The problem here is that we have a utilitarian justification for a set of norms in which no participant may seek to maximize utility. What is rather weird about this position is that we are here presented with a justification for an agreement, which justification cannot ever provide any guide to the parties involved. The actors involved (in our case everybody involved in world politics) could never appeal to this background justification to back up any proposed change in the settled norms. Because if they did appeal to this utilitarian background justification, they would not be blindly following the norms which it is supposed (by rule utilitarians) would bring about the utility maximizing result in some automatic way (i.e. in a way that does not involve the participants deliberately seeking the maximizing result).

Our conclusion must be that if we want a background theory which justifies the first few settled norms on the list and which can be used to generate solutions to hard cases, the utilitarian option must be rejected. It could only be of use to an otherworldly non-participant, perhaps a god.

A background theory like the utilitarian one which fails to justify the first item on our list of settled beliefs in international relations is not likely to succeed in justifying the other items on the list. It is worth noticing that it fails to justify item 13, which asserts that it is settled that democratic institutions within the states of the system of sovereign states are a good. No convincing utilitarian justification for democratic institutions has yet been given. It is true that students of politics often talk of the "interest aggregating" function of representative institutions and this language suggests that democratic institutions are engaged in a utility advancing task. Others argue that democratic institutions, by making leaders stand accountable at periodic elections, ensure that the interests of the governors and the interests of the governed coincide. This too shows democratic institutions to be utility maximizing mechanisms.[30] However, utilitarian justifications for democratic institutions fail because, first, a utilitarian has to provide a plausible account of an independent utility calculus which would show that democratic institutions maximize utility in a way that rule by, for example, autocratic technocrats would not. The many problems which arise in trying to portray what such a calculus would involve have already been hinted at above. Second, a utilitarian justification of democratic institutions justifies these as a means to an end. On this view democratic institutions are justified because they maximize utility. If and when they fail to do so democratic institutions would have to give way to non-democratic arrangements. Most people who support democracy do not see democratic institutions in this way. Democrats are committed to democracy as an end in itself.[31] The utilitarian justification for democracy fails to justify our settled beliefs about democracy.

Finally, it is difficult to see how a utilitarian background justification could be constructed which would both justify the first few norms on our list (which refer to the preservation of the society of sovereign states) and which would justify the item referring to human rights as well as the item which refers to the *ius in bello* (which includes the norm protecting non-combatants in time of war). These latter norms are for the protection of individuals even in those cases where harming a few individuals might well result in an overall increase in aggregate utility. Utilitarian thinking always opens up the possibility of trading off the rights of individuals against a gain in global utility.

2.4 Rights based justifications

In the present state of international relations theory the last main contender as a possible background justification for the list of settled normative beliefs is a theory of individual human rights.[32] A major problem is that there are several quite different possible theories of individual rights which could be used as background justifications for the settled list. I shall come to consider some of these shortly, but for the present let us, in a very general way, consider whether a rights based theory holds any promise at all as a justifying background theory for the list of settled norms.

If we look at the list of settled norms it is immediately apparent that a theory of individual rights is not obviously plausible as a justification for the norms relating to the preservation of the system of sovereign states (item 1 and 2 on our list of settled norms) and those items immediately connected with these, viz. items 3, 4, 6, 7 and 8. By way of a contrast it is easy to see how the beliefs in the goodness of democratic institutions (item 13), international law (item 11), human rights (item 14) and the laws of non-combatant immunity (item 17) could be justified by some or other rights based theory. This is in sharp contrast to the other two background theories which we have considered (viz. the order justification and the utilitarian justification), which were most plausible when used to justify norms concerning the preservation of the system of sovereign states (and related items) and were least plausible as justifications for our settled norms relating to democratic institutions, international law, human rights and non-combatant immunity. What we are now called upon to do is to see whether it is possible to justify norms 1 and 2 by means of a theory of individual human rights; whether it is possible to construct a rights based justification which reconciles in a coherent way the norms referring to the preservation of the system of sovereign states and those norms more obviously related to rights.

At first glance there seem to be many obvious reasons why

the first two settled norms referring to the preservation of the system of states and to sovereignty cannot be justified by a theory of individual human rights. First, sovereign states, it is generally recognized, may and do give overriding primacy to the protection of their national security and to the pursuit of their national interest. In doing this states often act in ways that seem to be in callous disregard for the rights of individuals. Thus, for example, the security principle sometimes seems to justify the killing of the innocent. On this view the civilians killed by Israeli action in Lebanon are victims of state action which may be justified by the national security principle. In short, the suggestion here is that reasons of state are often used to justify what are, on the face of the matter, serious infringements of individual human rights. This suggests that it would be difficult to show that reasons of state (which are reasons closely related to the notion of sovereignty) are ultimately justifiable by arguments referring to individual rights.

Second, to many the very notion of state sovereignty seems to be opposed to any notion of individual human rights. On this view sovereignty refers *inter alia* to the right of a sovereign to decide what basic rights the people under its jurisdiction have. Indeed, there is a basic tension between a theory which accords sovereignty to the state and theories of individual human rights which accord primacy to the individual. It is, on this view, not logically plausible that the norm of state sovereignty could be compatible with a human rights justification.

Third, even a casual student of history would know that, as a matter of fact, states were not in the first instance devised to protect individual rights. There were sovereign states before there were theories of human rights. For this reason historically minded people would be inclined to think any suggestion that the system of sovereign states could be justified on the grounds that it protects human rights is unhistorical.

Fourth, many people would agree that as an institution the state may be well suited to protect human rights within the state and yet they would deny that the *system of sovereign states* is at all suitable for the protection of rights. The state can protect rights because it has the necessary resources and instrumentalities. It has a law making power which it can use to this end. It has a judicial power with which it can adjudicate when disputes about rights arise. It has a police power with which it can enforce judicial decisions about rights. In some states, such as the USA, the basic rights are entrenched in the constitution. However, all of these devices for protecting rights within states are singularly absent within the system of states viewed as a whole. There is no supreme legislature, no supreme judiciary before which all disputes must be settled and there is no co-ordinated police power which can protect and enforce individual rights world wide. On this view the system of sovereign states viewed as a political institution seems particularly ill-suited as a means for protecting individual rights.

Fifth, a characteristic way of justifying particular arrangements in rights based theories seems particularly inapplicable with regard to the system of sovereign states. I refer, of course, to the notion of *contract*. Many theories of human rights justify the authority of the state by postulating a contract (or an agreement based on tacit consent) amongst rights holders. This contract (or tacit agreement) involves the individual rights holders agreeing to transfer some of their rights to the state in return for certain services from the state. Writers as diverse as Hobbes, Locke, Rousseau, Rawls and Nozick all use the device of a contract among the rights holders to legitimize the authority of the state and to set limits to it.[33] These authors vary greatly in the scope of the authority established in this way. There are notorious difficulties involved in the systematic and coherent development of this line of argument which we shall return to later. But for our present purposes the point is that the notion of contract does at least provide a plausible link between individual rights holders and the sovereign state. For it is at least *prima facie* plausible to envisage those within a state as engaged in a joint enterprise which might presuppose some actual or tacit contract. However, the device of such a contract appears to be quite patently not suited to provide a possible link between individual rights holders and the institution of the system of states as a whole. It is not plausible to suppose that the system of sovereign states was, or could be, the result of a real or tacit contract between individuals. Thus the traditional way of justifying institutions by arguing from rights, via a contract, to an institution seems closed to us in our search for a justification of the system of sovereign states as a whole.

Sixth, in the world as a whole, although there is a broad agreement that rights are important, there is little agreement about what specific rights people have. In the face of such widespread disagreement it seems highly implausible to argue that the system of sovereign states is justified because it advances human rights.

It appears, then, that there are many general reasons for supposing that a rights based justification for the two primary norms on the list is not feasible.[34] Thus it would seem that my endeavour to find a background justification which will encompass the items referring to the preservation of the society of states and sovereignty on the one hand, with the items protecting individual human rights on the other hand, must fail. Yet it is clearly of critical importance for my project to find some background justificatory theory that will be able to reconcile and encompass these different kinds of settled norms. For that reason I need to consider more closely the contractarian approach as the standard way in which rights based theorists have attempted to reconcile the settled norms relating to the system of sovereign states and the settled norms pertaining to individual rights.[35] I shall argue that the contractarian approach does fail in this task, but it will provide a helpful background to our own alternative background justification which also seeks to reconcile both sets of norms.

2.5 Contractarian rights based justifications

Rights based theories often seek to reconcile the principle of state sovereignty with the principles referring to individual rights by making use of such notions as contract, consent and tacit consent. They seek to show through the use of these notions that a sovereign power need not be destructive of rights, but indeed may be derived from rights holders freely exercising their rights. In order to make the relationship between state sovereignty and individual rights clear we are customarily told a story about how rights are transferred from individual rights holders to a sovereign. The story starts off by asking us to picture an initial situation in which there are rights holders, but in which there is no sovereign.[36] Locke, for example, portrays this original situation as a state of nature in which individuals had what we would today term a set of liberal rights.[37] In this state of nature, though, such individuals faced certain difficulties. One such difficulty was that they lacked the power to enforce their rights against others (individuals or groups of people) who might have sought to infringe those rights. In order to overcome this difficulty, the story goes on, the rights holders contracted to create a sovereign power who would be able to enforce their rights. In the contract the parties agreed to cede certain of their rights to the sovereign who would then exercise these rights on their behalf. Where each individual on his own had previously been too weak to enforce his rights against those who infringed them, now the sovereign would (through the concentration of powers in himself as a result of the contract) be able to protect the rights of those who agreed to create him sovereign. According to this story there is thus no basic tension between the notion of a sovereign (with the power to rule over his subjects) and the notion of individual rights holders (who are in some sense envisaged as autonomous). There is no tension because the power vested in the sovereign is seen to be derived from a contract freely entered into between the sovereign and his subjects. The power of the sovereign over the subjects is one the subjects themselves have created. The sovereign power is thus a form of self rule. Of course, rights theorists realize that it is hardly plausible to contend that all the citizens of modern states have in fact explicitly contracted with the sovereign power in their respective states that he exercise power over them. For clearly most people have never made any such contract. This poses a problem for contract theorists, for if most people have never actually made any such contract, what right has the sovereign state to rule over the rights holders living within the state?

In order to get out of this difficulty some rights theorists have turned to the notion of *tacit consent*. According to this notion there are situations in which we may suppose that people have agreed to the transfer of rights (from themselves to the sovereign) even though the people in question have never expressly consented to the transfer. The idea is that people, merely by acting in certain ways (for example, by participating in the democratic institutions of a state, or by generally being law abiding) tacitly signify their consent to the authority of the sovereign. But there are serious problems facing theorists who want to argue the case for tacit consent. For it is crucial to their case that they be able to specify which actions will count as expressing tacit consent and which ones will not. It is important for their case to be able to distinguish between those situations in which the citizens of a state may be said to have tacitly consented to the authority of the sovereign and those situations in which they have not. Clearly we cannot argue that *wherever* people obey the laws of a state they may be taken to have tacitly consented to do so. There are many states in the world where there is general obedience to the laws, but where tacit consent theorists would be loath to say that the people had tacitly consented to the authority of the sovereign, since such compliance is coercively induced. They would not want to allow that the theory of tacit consent may be used in this way in authoritarian, oligarchical and totalitarian states. They would not accept that the theory of tacit consent may be used to justify the authority of *any state whatsoever*. For consent theorists want to use their theory to distinguish those states whose authority is legitimate from those states whose authority is not. May we assume that the law abiding citizen in South Africa has tacitly consented to the institutional arrangements of that state

in the same way that the law abiding citizen of Britain has consented to the laws of Britain? Does the mere fact that they both
abide by the laws of their respective countries signify that they
both accord the same amount of consent to the legal system?
Clearly mere obedience signifies no such thing. The Argentinian may obey the law even though he fundamentally
opposes the legal system in his country, whereas the British
citizen may obey the law because he accepts it as basically just.
The notion of tacit consent itself does not help us distinguish
between these two cases. We cannot, as it were, read the tacit
consent (or lack of it) from the outward behaviour of the two
people.

I conclude that it is not possible to achieve the reconciliation
between rights and sovereignty via the device of a contract
(explicit or tacit) for most people have never made a contract
and the theory of tacit consent is fraught with difficulties.[38]

I have been considering the difficulties which rights based
theories which reason via the contract have in accounting for
the sovereignty of states. Essentially similar problems arise
when contract theories are applied to the system of sovereign
states as a whole. These fail to deal satisfactorily with the
tension between sovereignty and individual rights with which
we are concerned. This may be nicely illustrated by glancing at
the liberal theory of international relations expounded by
Michael Walzer in *Just and Unjust Wars*.[39] That Walzer's
theory is in the contract/consent tradition is demonstrated in
several places. Let us look at some of these.

In his discussion of the morality of war he says that it is
wrong to simply classify all wars as hell. For some kinds of war
are not hell; there are those, like feuds and tournaments, to
which the participants have *consented*. He writes, "when ...
consent ... fails ... 'acts of force' ... become the constant object
of moral condemnation."[40] Even surrender is, for Walzer, a
form of consent. Where a soldier surrenders, he promises to
stop fighting in return for certain rights. Walzer's contractarian
thinking comes out too where he discusses the basis of political

sovereignty which, he says, rests on "the right of men and women to build a common life and to risk their individual lives only when they freely choose to do so."[41] In a similar vein he says, "We want to live in an international society where communities of men and women freely shape their separate destinies."[42] Further on he writes, "no one can be threatened with war or warred against, unless through some act of his own he has surrendered or lost his rights."[43] Finally he puts his position in a nutshell where he writes, "States exist to defend the rights of their members."[44]

The string of quotations given above clearly illustrates Walzer's belief that the state's authority is derived from the consent of the governed and that the state's sovereign right to engage in war is thus based, finally, on individual rights. On this view individuals have rights which may be forfeited or transferred only with their consent. The problem with this view, once again, is that it does not reconcile the norms relating to sovereignty with those pertaining to the protection of individual rights. Let us attempt to make the nature of this problem more explicit.

The cornerstone of Walzer's thinking about the moral problems which are posed by war is his notion of the *legalist paradigm* which he uses in developing his theory of aggression. The legalist paradigm is, he says, "the fundamental structure for the moral comprehension of war."[45] He expresses the fundamentals of this paradigm in six propositions:

1. There exists an international society of independent states.
2. This international society has a law that establishes the rights of its members – above all, the rights of territorial integrity and political sovereignty.
3. Any use of force or imminent threat of force by one state against the political sovereignty or territorial integrity of another constitutes aggression and is a criminal act.
4. Aggression justifies two kinds of violent response: a war of self-defence by the victim and a war of law enforcement by the victim and any other member of international society.

5. Nothing but aggression can justify war.
6. Once the aggressor state has been militarily repulsed, it can also be punished.[46]

It is clear that Walzer is thinking of states in the international society as in some ways analogous to individuals within that society we call the state. Indeed, Walzer sometimes refers to the legalist paradigm as the "domestic paradigm." The fundamental feature of this analogy is that we are to conceive of states as having rights in much the same ways as we think of individuals within states as having rights. Within states our rights are for the most part protected by law and are enforced by the police. In the international society of states there is no police force so the rights holders (viz. states) have to enforce their rights in other ways, for example by themselves or with the aid of allies.

Now we do, indeed, find that the international polity in which we live does exhibit the characteristics mentioned in Walzer's legalist paradigm. It is populated with sovereign states who do act as rights holders, who do look upon infringements of those rights as unwarranted acts of aggression, and who do seek to counter aggressive acts of other states in the ways specified in the paradigm. Several of the items on our list of settled norms bear witness to this, especially those pertaining to sovereignty and the preservation of the system of sovereign states. The key point in all of this is that there is a settled norm in international society that infringements of the territorial and political sovereignty of a state are *prima facie* wrong. Any state attempting such an act is taken to be guilty of a wrong unless some special justification can be provided.

Walzer attempts to combine this legalist paradigm with a contractarian theory of human rights. On his view the rights of state which are articulated in the legalist paradigm are, in the final instance, derivable from individual human rights through some or other form of contract. He makes this point explicitly where, referring to the states' rights of territorial integrity and political sovereignty, he says, "the[se] two belong to states, but they derive ultimately from the rights of individuals, and from them they take their force."[47] Later, writing of the same two rights, he says that they "rest ultimately on the right of men and women to build a common life and to risk their individual lives only when they freely choose to do so."[48] On this view, then, there ought to be no incompatibility between states' rights and individual human rights, for in the final instance the one set of rights is derived from the other. However, in *Just and Unjust Wars* looked at as a whole there clearly is a tension between the two. This tension shows itself in several ways.

First, consider one of the exceptions which Walzer allows against the strict legalist paradigm (according to which the only legitimate acts of violence by a state are acts of self-defence and acts punishing an aggressor). He says that humanitarian interventions are justified in those cases where "massive violations of human rights" are taking place, violations which "shock the moral conscience of mankind."[49] He counts the Indian invasion of East Pakistan in 1971 as an intervention which was justified on humanitarian grounds. What is odd about Walzer's argument with regard to humanitarian intervention is that he restricts it to these extreme cases. For, if the right of states to non-intervention is derived ultimately from individual human rights, then surely whenever a state fails to protect the rights of individuals within it that state's right to non-intervention is eroded accordingly. Walzer carefully maintains that only gross infringements of human rights warrant armed intervention in another state. This suggests that there is some inner conflict between the claims which can justifiably be made on behalf of states and those claims which can justifiably be made on behalf of individuals.

Second, in discussing the Finnish war with Russia which took place in 1940, Walzer reveals a commitment to the rights of states which seems to clearly conflict with a commitment to individual human rights. Prior to that war Russia felt threatened by the closeness of the Finnish border to Leningrad. Russia offered a land exchange deal to Finland which was less than just. The Finns were faced with the option of accepting this offer or of going to war. They chose the latter option. They were defeated and forced to accept a settlement worse than the one originally offered them. Walzer argues that their decision to go to war was morally to be preferred to any form of appeasement. What is of interest to us is the argument which he offers for his conclusion. "The 'Munich principle' [an appeasement principle] would concede the loss or erosion of independence *for the sake of the survival of individual men and women.*"[50] Further on he writes, "I don't want to argue that appeasement can never be justified, only to point to the great importance we collectively attach to the values the aggressor attacks. These values are summed up *in the existence of states like Finland* – indeed, of many such states."[51] Here there is a conflict between the importance attached to the right of the state to survive and the importance attached to the right of individuals to survive. There is no doubt that in this context Walzer grants priority to the former. If it were the case, as Walzer contends it is, that the right of the state to survive is ultimately derivable from the rights of individuals, then this type of conflict ought not to occur.

Third, the tension between states' rights and individual rights emerges nicely in Walzer's discussion of the Israeli pre-emptive strike against Egypt in the so called "Six Day War" in June 1967. This kind of war is not justified on the strict legalist paradigm, but Walzer seeks to show that there are moral grounds for allowing this kind of exception to the paradigm. His general formula for this exception is: "states may use military force in the face of threats of war, whenever the failure to do so would seriously risk their territorial integrity or political independence."[52] On Walzer's view this can be extended to cover cases where the state which poses the threat does not intend to attack the threatened state. He explicitly admits that in this case "it is unlikely that the Egyptians intended to begin the war themselves."[53] Egypt might well have been content to close the Straits of Tiran and remain deployed along the Israeli border. But this would have placed a great strain on Israel. In this situation, argues Walzer, Israel would have to attack. Throughout Walzer's account the accent is on Israel's right to exist. The argument is not formulated in terms of the rights of individuals or threats to these rights. In the situation which existed prior to the war no individual rights had been infringed. It may plausibly be argued that the pre-emptive strike had the effect of infringing many of the rights to life, liberty and property of the Egyptian citizens. The only charge which can be laid against the Egyptians who were killed is that their government might have entrenched an army along the Israeli border and this might have been a severe strain on the military resources of Israel. Once again there is an unresolved strain here between states' rights and individual rights.[54]

Fourth, in general Walzer's justification for the legalist paradigm is that it is derived from the individual consent (tacit or explicit) of the individual rights holders. But this basic position of his is not compatible with the way in which he deals with interventions, i.e. with the moral question about when it is just for one state to interfere in violent disputes within other states. Such issues arise with regard to secession, civil war, wars of national liberation and so on. He accepts a position proffered by John Stuart Mill according to which states are to be treated as self-determining communities "whether or not their internal political arrangements are free, whether or not the citizens choose their government and openly debate the policies carried out in their name."[55] On this view a "state is self-determining even if its citizens struggle and fail to establish free institutions, but it has been deprived of self-determination if such institutions are established by an intrusive neighbour."[56] The overall picture which emerges from this account is that states ought to be respected, not because they represent a contract freely arrived at by individual rights holders, but because they are an area within which such a contract might emerge. Thus we see that on this view states have a right which is prior to the contract; the right is not derived from the contract. Reasoning along these lines, Walzer says that within states people have no right to be protected against domestic failure to construct free institutions. They have no right to be protected "even against a bloody repression." Similarly, intervention is not warranted wherever there is revolution for "revolutionary activity is an exercise in self-determination."[57] Here we see Walzer (following J.S. Mill) sketching a picture within which communities/states (he admits there is a problem here, for community boundaries do not always coincide with state boundaries) have a right to self-determination and the right here is not dependent on a prior contract by individuals. He is not happy with this stark position so he introduces several exceptions to the strong non-interventionist rule.[58] I do not intend to examine these now. I merely wish to point out that there is in his theory a strong sense in which states' rights are not derived from individual contract/consent, but are prior to it. Thus his theory does not reconcile states' rights and individual rights in the standard contractarian way.

I have been looking for a background theory for the list of settled norms in international relations. More specifically I have been looking for a background theory which justifies and reconciles the seemingly antipathetic norms relating to the preservation of the system of states and sovereignty on the one hand, with those norms relating to the protection of individual rights on the other. Contract theory sought to do this by providing us with a picture of a free person who then restricted his freedom through contract/consent. On this view the contract/consent brings about a transfer of powers from the individual to the sovereign state. The sovereignty of the state is presented as a limitation which the people have imposed upon themselves. What has emerged from the foregoing discussion is that contractarian rights based theories do not manage to justify and reconcile the norms relating to state sovereignty with those relating to human rights. Is there an alternative way in which this might be done? I think that there is.

NOTES

1 See Ronald Dworkin, *Taking Rights Seriously* (London, Duckworth, 1981), p. 135, for a discussion of the concept/conception distinction.
2 See Vendulka Kubálková, "Moral Precepts in Contemporary Soviet Politics" in *Moral Claims in World Affairs*, ed. Ralph Pettman (London, Croom Helm, 1979), p. 185.
3 See Jan Pettman, "Race, Conflict and Liberation in Africa" in *Moral Claims in World Affairs*, p. 136.
4 See G. Poggi, *The Development of the Modern State* (London, Hutchinson, 1978); Cornelia Navari, "The Origins of the Nation–State" in *The Nation State*, ed. Leonard Tivey (Oxford, Martin Robertson, 1981); Barbara Tuchman, *A Distant Mirror* (London, Macmillan, 1979); and Hedley Bull, *The Anarchical Society* (London, Macmillan, 1977), p. 9.
5 This point was already made forcibly by J. G. Flichte in the last century. See his section on "The Characteristics of the Present Age" in *The Popular Works of Fichte*, ed. W. Smith (2 vols., London, John Chapman, 1849), Vol. 2, p. 221 and following pages.
6 The content of the corpus of international law must, of course, be seen as resting on the norms which have been mentioned in the list.
7 Before considering some possible answers to this question I must attempt to allay certain objections. It may be argued that the primary question in the normative theory of international relations is *whether* the system of sovereign states is a justified way of organizing the government of the world. (Michael Donelan argues in this vein in "The Political Theorists and International Theory" in *The Reason of States*, ed. Michael Donelan (London, Allen and Unwin, 1978).) By contrast my formulation of the primary question might be held to assume that the preservation of a system of sovereign states is justifiable. My formulation would thus seem to avoid the most fundamental problem which is: are the norms referring to the preservation of the system of states and to the value of sovereignty justifiable at all? My answer to this object is implicit in all that I have argued up to now, but it is probably as well to recapitulate two important points. First, a natural lawyer may wish to argue that there exists a practice more basic than that of the system of states, viz. the community of mankind. This, he would argue, provides a basis from which the system of states can be evaluated. Earlier I argued that it is not plausible to assert the existence of such a community. (See the discussion of the arguments advanced by Michael Donelan and John Finnis above, Chapter 3, Section 2.2.) The world is characterized by a diversity of moral communities. There is no single moral community, apart from the communities of men who are citizens of states living in a system of sovereign states. In short, the base from which natural lawyers seek to criticize the system of sovereign states is non-existent. Second, and related to the first point, in this book I have given an account of what is involved in normative argument. In terms of this account (see Chapter Three

above) the only way in which settled beliefs, such as the one according to which the preservation of the system of states is a good, can be challenged is by showing that it does not fit the background theory which best justifies most of the other settled beliefs within the practice in question. What is not possible is a simultaneous critique of all the settled items of belief within a domain of discourse. Thus if someone wishes to cast doubt on the settled status of item 1 on the list given above, he has to produce a background justification which justifies most of the other items on the list excluding the one he seeks to challenge (in this case the belief that the preservation of the system of states is a good). There is good reason to believe that this would not be possible. One such reason is that a background theory which requires of us that we reject this item requires that we reject several other bits of the settled core which are related to item 1. Of all the items on the list only five could possibly be thought of as totally independent of item 1. In such a case we are being asked to reject too many settled beliefs and are not left with a basis for argument at all.

8 On balance of power theory generally see the collection of texts collected by Moorehead Wright, *The Theory and Practice of the Balance of Power* (London, Dent, 1975).

9 See Philip Windsor, "The Justification of the State" in *The Reason of States*.

10 Quoted in Moorehead Wright, *The Theory and Practice of the Balance of Power*, p. 2.

11 Ibid. p. 39.

12 Ibid. p. 40.

13 Ibid. p. 48.

14 Ibid. p. 72.

15 Hedley Bull, *The Anarchical Society*, p. xii.

16 Ibid.

17 Originally the answer may have been "A Christian one," but for various reasons this theological answer became less acceptable and the authors in seeking some more "neutral" answer introduced the notion of order.

18 Hedley Bull, *The Anarchical Society*, p. 5.

19 Ibid. pp. 17–19.

20 Ibid. p. 20.

21 Ibid. p. 19.

22 Ibid. p. 22.

23 Hedley Bull, "Human Rights and World Politics" in *Moral Claims in World Affairs*.

24 Kenneth Waltz, *Theory of International Politics* (London, Addison-Wesley, 1979).

25 Ibid. pp. 112–13.

26 As far as I know there has been no detailed attempt to justify the system of states on utilitarian grounds.

27 John Rawls has worked out the best known critique of utilitarianism

on these grounds and has sought a theory which fits our considered judgements about fairness and social justice better. Cf. *Theory of Justice* (London, Oxford University Press, 1972).

28 See H. L. A. Hart, "Betweeen Utility and Rights" in *The Idea of Freedom*, ed. Alan Ryan (London, Oxford University Press, 1979).

29 On rule utilitarianism see J. J. C. Smart, "An Outline of Utilitarian Ethics" in J. J. C. Smart and Bernard Williams, *Utilitarianism For and Against* (Cambridge University Press, 1970), p. 9. For a critique of rule utilitarianism see D. H. Hodgeson, *The Consequences of Utilitarianism* (Oxford University Press, 1967).

30 For a very brief but useful portrayal of the utilitarian theory of democracy see J. Roland Pennock, *Democratic Political Theory* (Princeton University Press, 1979), p 126.

31 For a defence of democracy along these lines see Carole Pateman, *Participation and Democratic Theory* (Cambridge University Press, 1970).

32 There may be other possible background theories, but the ones I have considered are the main ones in the field at the moment.

33 Thomas Hobbes, *Leviathan* (London, Dent, 1962); John Locke, *The Second Treatise of Government* (Indianapolis, Bobbs-Merrill, 1952); Jean Jacques Rousseau, *The Social Contract* (London, Dent, 1973); John Rawls, *Theory of Justice*; Robert Nozick, *Anarchy, State and Utopia* (Oxford, Blackwell, 1974).

34 This kind of conclusion is supported by C. B. Joynt and H. Corbett, *Theory and Reality in World Politics* (London, Macmillan, 1978).

35 For the argument presented here against this way of thinking about the relationship between rights holders and the state I am indebted to John Charvet, *A Critique of Freedom and Equality* (Cambridge University Press, 1981).

36 There are significant differences between the ways in which the different theorists picture the initial situation, but these are of no importance to the present argument.

37 John Locke, *The Second Treatise of Government*, Chapter 13.

38 For a detailed account of the problems involved with the notion of tacit consent see John Plamenatz, *Consent, Freedom and Political Obligation* (Oxford University Press, 1968).

39 Walzer's consent theory of obligation is spelled out in his *Obligations: Essays on Disobedience, War and Citizenship* (Cambridge, Mass., Harvard University Press, 1970) and is implicit in his *Just and Unjust Wars* (New York, Basic Books, 1977).

40 *Just and Unjust Wars*, p. 29.

41 Ibid. p. 61.

42 Ibid. p. 72.

43 Ibid. p. 135.

44 Ibid. p. 136.

45 Ibid. p. 61.

46 Ibid. p. 61–2.

47 Ibid. p. 53.

48 Ibid. p. 61.
49 Ibid. p. 107.
50 Ibid. p. 72, emphasis added.
51 Ibid., emphasis added.
52 Ibid. p. 85.
53 Ibid. p. 83.
54 What argument could Walzer advance to show that the individual rights of the Egyptians were not wrongly infringed by the pre-emptive strike of the Israelis? The only one compatible with his general position I suggest is this: the Egyptian citizens and soldiers may be taken to have tacitly consented to an act which their government might have come to intend against Israel and this act in the long run might have infringed Israel's right to political sovereignty. This seems to me a highly implausible argument. The notion that a person may relinquish a right by *tacitly* consenting to an act which *might* (at some future date) be intended and which in turn *might* have the effect of damaging a third party's right is a far-fetched one.
55 *Just and Unjust Wars*, p. 87.
56 Ibid.
57 Ibid. pp. 88, 89.
58 Ibid. p. 90.

Chapter Five

Reconciling rights and sovereignty: the constitutive theory of individuality

1 Introduction

I am attempting to construct a background theory which justifies the list of goods currently accepted as settled in international relations. I considered order based justifications and
utilitarian justifications and found them both wanting. I then
turned to rights based theories which used the notion of contract and found that such rights based theories held promise
with regard to the justification of several of the items on the list
of settled norms. Most obviously it seemed plausible enough to
suppose that a rights based theory would justify the settled
norm referring to democratic institutions within states, the
settled norm which required that states be both internally and
externally concerned with the protection of human rights, and
the settled norm asserting that international law is a good
thing. However, I argued that at first glance it seemed rather
improbable to suppose that the settled norm referring to the
preservation of the system of states and the norm establishing
that state sovereignty is a good could be justified by a rights
based background theory. There seemed to be a basic tension
between those norms concerned with the preservation of the
system of states and sovereignty on the one hand, and those
norms related to individual human rights on the other hand. It

seemed that human rights norms were best seen as setting limits to the ambit of the sovereignty related norms, rather than as justifying those norms. In the course of the last chapter I showed how contract theories of rights which held out the promise of reconciling sovereignty and individual rights systematically fail to deal satisfactorily with the tension between the rights related norms and the sovereignty related norms.

At this point in the argument, we are still faced with the fundamental problem of constructing a background theory which will enable us to justify and reconcile these two sets of seemingly antagonistic norms on the list of settled norms, viz. the norms which assert that state sovereignty and the preservation of the system of states is a good, and those norms premised upon the notion that individual human rights are a basic good.

1.1 *Constitutive theory as an alternative to the contractarian approach*

In this chapter I shall outline a theory which, I contend, does solve the problem of reconciling these two seemingly antagonistic poles on the list of settled norms. I shall call this theory the constitutive theory of individuality. The construction of this theory also involves an attempt to reconcile state sovereignty with individual rights but it involves a different mode of theorizing to that pursued in the contract tradition. Constitutive theory, unlike contract theory, does not seek to show that the sovereign state is a *device* which protects certain preexisting rights. Unlike contract theory it holds that rights are not things possessed by individuals prior to entering into social and political relationships. Rather it contends that a person is constituted as a rights holder of a certain sort within the context of a specific social relationship. Contrary to all rights based theories it argues that rights are not things which a person can be conceived of as having outside of or prior to any and all social and political institutions. A Robinson Crusoe has no rights. Whenever we envisage a person as a rights holder we have in mind a situation in which a person claims a certain kind of recognition from another person or set of people. In a world inhabited by a single being (like Crusoe's island) there would be no point in claiming a right to x, y or z.[1] The typical kind of case in which we invoke a right is in a situation in which our entitlement to act in a certain way is challenged by another (or others). We then invoke our right as giving us sufficient entitlement to act. Eve, for example, may claim that John ought not to have been allowed to publish a certain article. John defends his having written and published the article by referring to his right to free speech. In referring to his right we must suppose John to be speaking to some audience who might acknowledge or deny his entitlement to publish the article. Rights talk always presupposes the existence of a speaker and an audience who between them recognize one another as being able to make certain kinds of claims on one another. Another way of putting this point is to say that rights talk always presupposes a practice of rights: a practice, that is, within which people make claims of right upon one another.[2]

Contract theory envisaged institutions as devices for defending pre-existing rights. On that theory the rights were primary and the institutions were designed to protect them. At first glance it might now appear as if I am making the contrary argument, viz. that institutions are primary and that people only come to have rights once they enter into institutions. This is not my position. I want to argue that neither is prior, but that rights and institutions presuppose and imply each other. As an indication of what I mean consider the following: it is only within the state that people may meaningfully be said to have citizenship rights. To be a person with the rights of a citizen is to be a person who lives within a state-like institution of some or other kind. This might suggest that the state is primary. Yet this is not the case. The state as an institution can only be comprehended within the context of a wider social and political practice. An elucidation of this wider practice would have to refer to citizens, government, police, judges and so on. A state is an institution created and maintained by the people living in a particular territory, i.e. the state depends on there being citizens and citizens exist only within a state.

This difference between constitutive and contract theory has important implications for the way in which the problem of reconciling state sovereignty and individual rights is conceived of in each case. For contract theory the problem is: why would an autonomous rights holder agree to subject himself to a sovereign state? The answer given is the self-interested one that only by entering institution X (for example the state) can a person secure certain of his pre-existing rights. The contract model allows one to argue that the constraining aspects of institution X are actually self-imposed constraints. For constitutive theory the *problem* is quite otherwise. There is no need to show why rights holders perfect in respect of their rights would agree to enter into constraining relationships with other rights holders.[3] For constitutive theory, to be a rights holder at all already presupposes a constraining relationship with other people. To claim a right is to articulate a certain kind of reason justifying an action and constraining the actions of others.[4] A relationship in which rights are recognized is a relationship in which individuals recognize one another as beings who may legitimately constrain one another's actions in certain ways. The problem for constitutive theory is not to show why a rights holder should enter into a constraining relationship (for to be a potential rights holder at all already presupposes such a relationship) but to show how being a rights holder of a certain sort involves the other components of the practice within which the right is situated. The argument will typically not be directed at an outsider who is not a member of the institution in question. It will not be aimed at an outsider in an attempt to convince him that he should enter the institution (this is what contract theory sought to do). Rather it will be aimed at someone who accepts (and acts in accordance with) some components of the practice in question (for example, at someone who accepts and acts in accordance with the norms relating to individual human rights), but who denies another component of the practice (for example, does not accept or act in accordance with the norm in terms of which state sovereignty is a good). The aim of constitutive theory will be to demonstrate to such an interlocutor the connection between his being a rights holder of a certain sort and his being a member of a particular kind of institution. Constitutive theory aims to bring to light the internal connections between being an individual rights holder of a particular kind and being a member of a certain kind of social or political institution, where both the rights and the institution are conceived of as being components of a wider practice.

Where contract theory sought to overcome the objections an outsider might offer against his entering into a certain kind of arrangement (viz. a sovereign state), constitutive theory may perhaps be seen as seeking to overcome a different kind of hurdle. A successful constitutive theory seeks to overcome the *alienation* a person might feel with regard to certain aspects of a practice within which he is living. A person is alienated when he experiences certain aspects of a practice (essential to his full flourishing within that practice) as hostile or detrimental to his well-being. Alienation is overcome where it is made intelligible to the person in question that, for example, there is a necessary connection between his being a rights holder of type X (which he values highly) and his living within an institutional arrangement of type Y (which he may experience as imposing a burden on him).[5] John Charvet portrays the task as the one of "making explicit, or recognizing and developing to its full consciousness, what is implicitly true of an individual's relations to others in any scheme of social cooperation."[6]

The problem then is to show how constitutive theory can justify and reconcile the norm asserting that the sovereign state is a good with the norms relating to individual human rights. As we have seen in the previous paragraph the task is not (as it would be for contract theories) to show why an individual who is outside of a social or political arrangement (i.e. in a state of nature or in inter-planetary transit) ought to become a citizen of a sovereign state amongst other sovereign states. The task is rather to make explicit the moral dimension that is already implicit in the simultaneous acceptance of the state and sovereignty norms (norms 1 and 2 on our list) on the one hand and the rights related norms on the other hand.[7] Constitutive theory does not reason from the "midair" position occupied by the contractualists: an imagined position outside of any existing society. Rather it takes seriously the truth that when we reason about normative issues we do so from within a standpoint defined by specific institutions such as the state and the inter-state system.

2 Constitutive theory of individuality

Let us start by returning to a notion which is common both to contract theory and constitutive theory. This is the notion of the value of the individual. Contract theories usually stress the rights of freedom and equality which they take to be grounded in the notion of the autonomous individual striving for authenticity, i.e. as striving to be the author of his own individual, social and political being.[8] The autonomous individual is presented as having value prior to any community. Constitutive theory starts by asserting that a person only has value *qua* individual in a relationship of mutual valuation with another person or other people, i.e. within a community. Constitutive theory then seeks to make explicit the complex system of mutual recognition within which individuality comes to be a value.

The relationship of mutual valuation is not a contractual type of relationship in which one individual approaches another and says, "I'll value you, if you'll value me." In the contractual perspective the parties do indeed only value one another as individuals who can make contracts. But constitutive theory understands mutual valuation in a different way. Individuality only becomes a value where it is the case that two or more people do, through their reciprocal recognition of one another, give concrete practical expression to valuing one another, rather than merely say that they value one another. Thus the task for normative theory becomes the one of showing how we as individuals are constituted as such through our participation in a particular set of social, economic and political institutions which in turn are grounded in our adherence to certain norms.[9] What we are called upon to do is to stand back from the multiple institutions in which we live in order to show how each contributes to the kind of individuality we value; to show how the kind of individuality which we value in ourselves could not be, were we not members of certain kinds of institutions. This does not mean that institutions should be conceived as means to the realization of certain ends we may happen to have. Rather the point is that we could not be the individuals we are, were we not members of a specific set of social arrangements which are based upon specified sets of norms.

It is apparent from the previous paragraph that the constitutive approach is holist. It insists that we cannot understand individuality without situating it within a whole within which people constitute each other by recognizing one another in specified ways. No independently existing metaphysical whole need be posited. The social practice or institution as a whole is, of course, a human and historical creation, but people are individuals by virtue of being members of certain kinds of social practices.

The foregoing is unacceptably vague. Let us attempt to make the matter a bit clearer by showing an application of the method in practice. Charvet, following Hegel, shows how individuality is constituted within a hierarchy of institutions, viz. the family, civil society and the state.[10] Both Hegel and Charvet take the state (or, as Charvet calls it, "the self-governing political community") as being the constitutive context of paramount importance. It is only in the state that individuality can be fully realized. Both support this contention by examining how our individuality is partially constituted by subordinate wholes, like the family and civil society, and by showing how the shortcomings of the subordinate institutions are overcome by subsequent and higher institutions. This dialectical process then culminates in the state. I do not intend to give a detailed discussion of the whole hierarchy of institutions because my main concern is with the upper end of the hierarchy, i.e. the state and the system of states. However, in order to demonstrate this constitutive mode of reasoning in operation let us briefly examine some aspects of the hierarchy.

The outline of constitutive theory given below draws heavily on Hegel's political philosophy, but it is what may be termed a secular interpretation of his theory. Constitutive theory does not require of us that we understand or accept Hegel's metaphysical system.

2.1 Individuality and the family

Let us examine the historically changing institution of the family. It is within the family that the individual first comes to be valued. Here he is valued as a *member* of the family. An early notion of self-hood is achieved in the recognition accorded him by the other members of the family. Hegel puts the matter thus:

The family, as the immediate substantiality of mind, is specifically characterized by love, which is mind's own feeling of its own unity. Hence in a family, one's frame of mind is to have self-consciousness of one's individuality within this unity as the absolute essence of oneself, with the result that one is in it not as an independent person but as a member.[11]

What binds the members of the family together is love, which Hegel elucidates as follows:

Love means in general terms the consciousness of my unity with another so that I am not in selfish isolation but win my self-consciousness only as the renunciation of my independence and through knowing myself as the unity of myself with another and of the other with me.[12]

We here see that it is within the family that a person gets that special kind of recognition which is to be recognized as a loved self. It is important not to take Hegel as simply making the empirical point that, as a matter of fact, most people do start life as members of families. Rather his point is that in the love between members of a family there is an implicit valuing by each member of the family of the other members; they are ends for him and valuers of his own life. To put the matter another way: in thinking about the family we recognize that the love of the other members for us is partially constitutive of ourselves and that our loving them is also constitutive of ourselves. We could not be the selves which we are and which we value, were it not for the love we receive from, and the love we give to, the other members of the family. We are partially constituted by the common will that exists in the family.

It is important to notice that there is a critical dimension to Hegel's discussion of the family. Throughout history, as anthropologists have shown, there have been diverse kinds of family structures. Not all of these realize or constitute the beginnings of individuality. Hegel argues, for example, that the early Roman family institution in which the father had the right to disinherit his children and even to kill them was an unethical institution.[13] He also says, "A child in slavery is the most unethical of all situations whatsoever."[14] In the ethical family parents recognize their children as nascent autonomous selves who can advance to a more mature form of individuality beyond the family by becoming actors in civil society and citizens of a just state. The Roman family was unethical because it failed to treat children as nascent free people. Although the family is the first on the hierarchy of institutions, it is, nevertheless, a crucial institution at both a micro and a macro level. At the micro level a person who is not recognized within a family as a nascent autonomous individual will not be able to develop into a free individual within the higher institutions. Similarly at the macro level, were the institution of the ethical family to crumble or change it would then no longer be possible for the higher institutions of civil society and the state to persist. These latter institutions are grounded in the family.[15] Thus it is that states must seek to preserve family life. Ethical families partially constitute the individuals who are the citizens of fully formed states.

Viewed in the larger context, however, the family also has inherent defects with respect to the constitution of individuality. Charvet writes:

> But the family, being a small, intimate group, cannot realize the value of the particular personality of its members adequately, for in its intimate bounds there is not the room for the development of the individual's interest that the freedom of civil society provides.[16]

In a general way this may be so, but it does not yet articulate the specific shortcomings of the family. What are these? Two main ones deserve mention. The first is that the family is bound together by love and thus does not provide a fully rational context. About this Hegel says:

> Love, however, is a feeling, i.e. ethical life in the form of something natural. In the state feeling disappears; there we are conscious of unity as law; there the content must be rational and known to us.[17]

Hegel's point here is that a unity based on law, which is consciously recognized as such, forms a more secure bond than a unity based on love. In the family the unit is held together by reciprocal love, but as a feeling this is not something which can be demanded by a member of a family as of right. To summarize this point, the family is deficient in that in it a person's individuality is dependent on something essentially changeable, viz. feeling.

The second shortcoming of the family is that in it the principle of personality is still not fully expressed. Within the family a person is but a member of the family unit. In order to develop, a person has, so to speak, to leave the family in order to seek "the development and realization of his particular needs, interests and purposes."[18] These drawbacks of the family can only be overcome within civil society. In civil society the individual seeks to realize his own ends more fully. But what is civil society?

2.2 Individuality and civil society

Civil society is, amongst other things, an economic system based on private property, within which people work, acquire things, exchange things and generally seek to satisfy their own needs. Amongst the various components of civil society Hegel distinguishes a system of needs, a system for the administration of justice, the police and the corporation. I am not concerned with the details of civil society, but shall look at a few of the ways in which individuality is constituted in civil society in ways which improve upon what is achieved by the family.

On growing up an individual in some sense "leaves" the family. His emergence from the family is characterized by his acquiring contractual rights and rights to property. A minor member of a family is typically not allowed to make major contracts without the consent of his parents and his dealings with regard to property are severely restricted. The acquisition of these rights is generally considered to be one of the reasons why "becoming adult" is a sought after status. But how does our entry into the civil society in which things are made, owned and exchanged constitute us as individuals in ways that would be denied us were we to be condemned to stay as minor members of a family for ever? Or, to ask a slightly different question: "What is the significance of private property for individuality?" There are several levels at which property can be understood. First, a person's appropriating something for himself may be seen as a way in which he fulfils his wants. "I make something my own as a result of my need, impulse and caprice."[19] On this level it would seem that the *raison d'être* of property is the satisfaction of whatever needs a person happens to have. In fact, the satisfaction of wants does not strike us as a particularly important moment in the constitution of individuality (or, as Hegel would put it, in the advancement of freedom). At this level there is not much to distinguish people from animals.

But on a second level property may be seen as a right of personality as such. Hegel says that prior to owning property a person is but a thing amongst things and does not become a personality (we would say "individual") until such time as he is recognized as such by other people who in turn gain their recognition as personalities from his recognition. Property is an important factor in the progress towards mutual recognition of one another as persons. John comes to recognize Joan as an individual, as someone who can own something in her own right and who can cease to own it by selling it, giving it away or whatever. Thus we can see how participating in the transactions of civil society enables a person to become individual in a way that was denied him in the family.

In civil society the individual gains recognition as a free person able to own property and enter into transactions with other people who are free in the same way. The importance of these rights is recognized in a system of law which is impartially administered and enforced. It is important to notice that the rights of personality which are advanced in civil society depend on the property relations being *private* property relations. Hegel writes in this connection:

> The idea of a pious or friendly and even compulsory brotherhood of men holding their goods in common and rejecting the principle of private property may readily present itself to the disposition which mistakes the true nature of the freedom of mind and right and fails to apprehend it in its determinate moments.[20]

Why is this a mistake? In the Addition to this paragraph Hegel gives his reasons:

> In property my will is the will of a person; but a person is a unit and so property becomes the personality of this unitary will. Since property is the means whereby I give my will an embodiment, property must also have the character of being "this" or "mine." This is the important doctrine of the necessity of private property.[21]

In this connection Charvet makes a slightly different point. In order to be fully individual a person needs to be able to distance himself from the collective. Private property is an institution which makes this possible. This aspect of private property is what makes it more satisfactory than family property. On these grounds Charvet rejects collectivist socialism. It would not allow the individual to distance himself from the other members of the community in the way that private property does.[22]

There is a lot more to Hegel's conception of civil society than I have indicated here. The details need not detain us. I have briefly introduced the notion of civil society in order to show two things. First, to demonstrate a constitutive theory in operation. It showed how individuality as a particular kind of self is partially constituted by the institutions within which we live. Second, to show how the shortcomings of a particular institution may be remedied by a further institution which does not replace the earlier defective institution, but operates together with it. Hence there develops a hierarchy of institutions. It is thus clear that in order to understand how individuality is constituted within the context of a given practice we need to examine the whole hierarchy of institutions.

2.3 Individuality and the state

Civil society, although it advances individuality (free personality) in ways that the family did not, is nevertheless itself subject to certain limitations. A simple way of putting the matter is as follows: within the family what the individual gained was a consciousness of himself as a valued member of a whole. Within civil society the individual gained a consciousness of himself as an independent person distinct from the whole. In it he experienced the law and other people's competitive co-operation as necessary for the furtherance of his own aims. Although the whole apparatus of civil society depends on the mutual recognition by the participants of one another as rights holders, the others on whom a person's recognition depends are not experienced as co-determinators of a person's individuality, but rather as threats to it. Similarly the law is not experienced as the ground of a person's individuality, but as a curb on one's aims. To put the matter in a nutshell, in civil society, although the individual is grounded in the law and the recognition of others, he nevertheless experiences them as alien. He feels alienated. It is this tension between the individual and the whole which is resolved in the state. Within the state a person participates in the whole as a member: as a citizen. As a citizen he is accorded a form of mutual recognition by fellow citizens which he lacked within the competitive and atomized civil society. As a citizen a person knows himself to be a constitutive part of the whole and he is conscious that the whole of which he is part is constituted by himself and his fellow citizens. The state is the creation of its citizens and yet it is only in the state that the individual can be fully actualized as a citizen. Hegel writes:

If the state is confused with civil society, and if its specific end is laid down as the security and protection of property and personal freedom, then the interest of the individuals as such becomes the ultimate end of their association, and it follows that membership of the state is something optional. But the state's relation to the individual is quite different from this. Since the state is mind objectified, it is only as one of its members that the individual himself has objectivity, genuine individuality and ethical life.[23]

Here we can see the distinctive break between constitutive theory and contract theory emerging. Hegel criticizes the contract theorists' interpretation of the state on the grounds that it presents membership of the state as something *optional* for individuals. What precisely is Hegel getting at here? The contract position supposes that it is possible to conceive of a fully actualized and free moral person who is not a member of any state, and who may then be pictured as having an option about whether to join the state or not. Hegel's counter is that to become a whole, free and fully ethical self a person has to be a citizen of a good state. It is only in that capacity that individuality can be fully realized. Thus citizenship of a good state is not an option for a free person, but is rather a precondition

for the existence of a free person. This may seem unduly specu-
lative, but in more mundane historical terms Hegel has, *prima
facie*, a good case. Acquiring full citizenship rights has been a
major concern for all those who have been denied them over
the past hundred and fifty years. Even in those cases where
gaining the rights of citizenship has involved taking a fall in
welfare, citizenship has been considered a prize worth having.
It is, indeed, a commonplace of the modern world that citizenship is of fundamental importance. Those who are denied it are
prepared to fight for it. Who, then, would dispute that being
deprived of full citizenship rights would be a major threat to a
person's sense of self? It is this basic connection between individuality and the state which is at the heart of Hegel's
argument.

In the state the individual is conscious that his individuality
is grounded in the whole. But this whole, i.e. the state, is not
something experienced as alien and external to the individual,
for he knows the state and its laws to be the ground of himself
and his fellow citizens. This point comes out nicely in Hegel's
discussion of patriotism. Patriotism is not mere subjective
assurance or feeling, but is "assured conviction with truth as its
basis."[24] It (patriotism) is:

the consciousness that my interest, both substantive and particular, is
contained and preserved in another's [i.e. in the state's] interest and end,
i.e. in the other's relation to me as an individual. In this way, this very
other is immediately not an other in my eyes, and in being conscious of
this fact, I am free.[25]

It is essential to understand that for Hegel the prior institutions
of the family and civil society are not made redundant by the
state. The state incorporates and improves upon them, yet is
also dependent upon them. Here it is relevant to cite *in toto* a
whole section from *The Philosophy of Right*:

As was remarked earlier on, the sanctity of marriage and the institutions
in which civil society is an appearance of ethical life constitute the stability of the whole, i.e. stability is secured when universal affairs are the
affairs of each member in his particular capacity. What is of the utmost
importance is that the law of reason should be shot through and through

by the law of particular freedom, and that my particular end should become identified with the universal end, or otherwise the state is left in the air. The state is actual only when its members have a feeling of their own self-hood and it is stable only when public and private ends are identical. It has often been said that the end of the state is the happiness of the citizens. That is perfectly true. If all is not well with them, if their subjective aims are not satisfied, if they do not find that the state as such is the means to their satisfaction, then the footing of the state itself is insecure.[26]

In sum, the crucial feature of the state is that in it citizens come to self-conscious appreciation of the way in which they constitute the whole and are constituted by it.

Patently such individual freedom is not constituted by just any kind of state. In some kinds of state there is no provision made for private willing, private judgement and private conscience: "under the despots of Asia the individual had no inner life and no justification in himself, in the modern world man insists on respect being paid to his inner life."[27] In the fully developed state the citizens perceive a coincidence between what the state requires of them and what they require in order to be free.[28]

It might seem as if the relevant question to ask at this point is: "In what kind of state can individuality flourish?" The answer would enable us to set about building the right kind of constitution. However, asking this question would show us to have missed a fundamental point about constitutive theory. Posing this question presupposes that constitution building may be used as a means to realize a certain kind of end, viz. a world peopled by free individuals. It also suggests that the would-be constitution builders (in this case us) are, so to speak, standing outside of any constitutional form deciding which constitution to implement. But, of course, we the constitution builders are not outside any and all constitutions. We, ourselves, are constituted by a particular constitutional arrangement, viz. the state. Whatever we propose for the future cannot be the creation of a new constitution, *de novo*, but a modification of the old. Any changes in the constitution will have to be premised on a proper understanding of how we the constitution builders already are constituted by the old arrangements. The relevant question to ask must then rather be: "What is the proper understanding of the institutions by which we are presently constituted as individuals?" The answer to this question will have a critical dimension in that the answer will rule out certain kinds of proposal for a new constitution while it will allow others.

Another important point to make here concerns the role of education in constitutional change. A constitution cannot simply be imposed on a people. It is a set of rules in terms of which they constitute each other. The people have to see the constitution as the proper way of doing things. They have to be educated into accepting it. They have to be convinced that it is necessary to their being who they are.[29]

2.4   Individuality and the society of sovereign states

I have reached the following point in my argument. I have shown rather sketchily how a free individual is partially constituted by being a member of a family, how the shortcomings of this institution are remedied within the arrangements of civil society and how individuality comes to a more complete form within the state. The state, on this view, should not be seen as a device which protects individual rights, but as a comprehensive arrangement between people who by mutually recognizing one another in certain specified ways come to constitute one another as free individuals. The question which needs to be answered now is: "Given that the state is necessary for the flourishing of individuality, in what way is the system of sovereign states and its associated norms a prerequisite for the flourishing of individuality?" The question may be differently formulated as follows: "What is the proper understanding of the link between free individuality and the system of sovereign states?" Yet another formulation would be: "In what way, if any, can our individuality be said to be constituted by the system of sovereign states?"

These questions can best be answered by reflecting on the

respective contributions to, and limitations of, individuality at each level of our hierarchy. In the family a person is aware of himself as a member of a whole, but this limits his development as an individual. This limitation is overcome in civil society within which the individual comes to be recognized as a bearer of rights which he may use or not at his discretion. But once again his freedom is limited in that he experiences other people and the laws to which he is subject as external constraints on his individual liberty. This feeling of constraint on the individual is resolved within the state in that here the individual feels himself to be a member of a whole (as was the case in the family). To be recognized as a citizen of a good state and to recognize others as such is to be self-conscious about the way in which you (the self in question) and others mutually constitute one another within a system of reciprocal recognition.

But the whole within which the individual is reunited with others as a member (i.e. the state) is a whole amongst other wholes, i.e. a state amongst other states. At the level of international affairs the state is an individual *vis-à-vis* other states and its individuality is reciprocally bound up with the individuality of its citizens:

Individuality is awareness of one's existence as a unit in sharp distinction from others. It manifests itself here in the state as a relation to other states, each of which is autonomous *vis a vis* others ...[30]

The point here is that within the autonomous state the individual is constituted as a free citizen, but for his citizenship to be fully actualized his state needs to be recognized by other states as autonomous. Were it not thus recognized his own individuality would not be properly constituted:

A state is as little an actual individual without relations to other states as an individual is actually a person without rapport with other persons ... [it] should receive its full and final legitimation through its recognition by other states although this recognition requires to be safeguarded by the proviso that where a state is recognized by others, it should likewise recognize them, i.e. respect their autonomy; and so it comes about that they cannot be indifferent to each other's domestic affairs.[31]

The necessity of being recognized as autonomous is well demonstrated by the phenomenon of colonialism. People in colonies are not free, because the political entity in which they live is not recognized as autonomous. Few people would agree to their state becoming a colony even if accepting colonial status brought with it substantial economic gain. The reason for this is that in a colony the people are in a subject position and are not free individuals in a way that citizens of an autonomous state are. In short, it is crucial for the individual that his state be autonomous and be recognized and treated by other autonomous states as such. Or to put the matter slightly differently, it is crucial, in order for a person to be an individual, that he be a member of an autonomous state recognized as such by other autonomous states.

In order to be recognized as an autonomous state, the state must meet certain specific requirements. Not just any arrangement may count as an autonomous state. A family, a horde, a clan, a multitude, a tribe, a robber band, a liberation movement, a tyranny, an oligarchy, a totalitarian order ... none of these is an autonomous state. In order to be recognized as an autonomous state, the state must have what Hegel refers to as "objective law and an explicitly established constitution."[32] He continues the paragraph just quoted:

It would be contrary even to commonplace ideas to call patriarchal conditions a "constitution" or a people under patriarchal government a "state" or its independence "sovereignty."

I agree. In order to be recognized as a state, a polity must be one in which the people recognize each other as citizens in terms of the law which they in turn recognize as being both constituted by them and as constitutive of them as citizens. In a patriarchal state the people see themselves as subjects, not as citizens. In an authoritarian state the people see themselves as the oppressed ones, and so on. An autonomous state is one in which the citizens experience the well-being of the state as fundamental to their own well-being, just as a member of a family experiences the well-being of the family as essential to his own well-being. Thus threats to the autonomous state threaten him directly. They do not threaten interests of his which he might then seek to have satisfied in some other way. To threaten the constitution of the state or to withhold recognition of its autonomy is to directly threaten that in terms of which the individual is constituted as an individual.

The argument has now reached the following point. I have been outlining the ways in which, according to Hegel, sovereign states and the system of sovereign states are necessary to the flourishing of individuality. (This discussion forms part of the wider argument in which I have been seeking a way of reconciling the settled norms relating to the preservation of the system of states and to sovereignty on the one hand, with the norms which refer to individual rights on the other.) From what has gone before it ought now to be clear that a failure by sovereign states to recognize one another as such implicitly threatens the individuality of the citizens of the respective states. That this is so can be seen by considering the alternatives to this mutual recognition of one another's sovereignty. In the most extreme case the denial of another state's sovereignty can take the form of seeking to conquer and incorporate the territory of that state. In such a case, apart from the destruction and loss of life brought about by the conquest, the conquest also negates it in another crucial dimension. The conquering state fails to recognize the common will in terms of which the citizens of the target state constitute one another through the constitution of their state. Even in a hypothetical case in which conquest resulted in the conquered state being better off in every respect except self-determination, the individuality of the citizens of the subject state would be severely impaired.[33]

It is important to notice that what is being recognized where states recognize one another's sovereignty is not the rights of the individuals in the states to form an association (where these rights are envisaged as existing apart from and independently of the state in question). What is recognized (or not) is a common will in terms of which the people involved reciprocally constitute one another as, amongst other things, rights holders by recognizing each other in certain specified ways. Where one state seeks to conquer another it does not merely supplant the government but inevitably seeks to place the people in the target state under domination. It seeks to change them from citizens to subjects. The flourishing of individuality requires free citizens, not a subject people.

In the previous paragraph I mentioned one kind of refusal to recognize the sovereignty of a state, viz. a refusal which takes the form of the conquest and subjection of that state and its people. Consider a different kind of refusal to recognize sovereignty. Consider the situation in which the community of sovereign states refuses to recognize a would-be state. Here I have in mind a situation such as that faced by Rhodesia after UDI (and also the situation facing the so called independent states within South Africa, such as the Transkei, Ciskei, Bophuthatswana and Venda). It is important to the argument to see that the refusal by the states of the world to recognize Rhodesia as a sovereign state was not merely a matter of practical significance. Of course, non-recognition did have serious practical implications for Rhodesia. The sanctions policy seriously impeded trade. The refusal to recognize passports hindered the opportunities for travel of the Rhodesian people. Severed links in the sporting and cultural fields impeded normal activity within these spheres. However, over and above these practical consequences of the non-recognition policy followed by the community of states, non-recognition was also of more fundamental significance to the Rhodesian whites who had enjoyed the full benefits of citizenship internally and who had had that status recognized internationally. This group were now denied the *status* which had previously been accorded them. Prior to UDI they had been citizens of a state which had played an honourable role in the recent history of the states in the Western world. Their state had a noble record in the two world wars, and in the Korean War. It had played an important part in the life of the British Commonwealth of

Nations. After UDI the white Rhodesians found themselves to be *outcasts*. Those who supported the UDI suddenly found themselves classed by the international community as criminals in so far as they supported a government which was almost universally condemned as illegal. This loss of status hurt those Rhodesians who supported the rebel government and their hurt was revealed in their repeated assertions that Rhodesia was a member of "the free world." The rhetoric of Ian Smith left no doubt that being recognized as a member of the free world was a major concern for him and his fellow Rhodesians. What was important here was not merely the *results* which recognition would bring (such as increased trading, sporting and cultural links), but the recognition itself. A *de facto* increase in trade and in sporting and cultural contact by clandestine means would not have been a sufficient remedy for the more subtle and basic harm caused by non-recognition, just as *de facto* improvements in the material conditions of the life of a slave do not solve the problem of slavery. What is wrong with slavery cannot be remedied merely by improving the lot of the slaves. It can only be remedied by freeing the slaves, i.e. by according them the status of free men. Similarly, what the white Rhodesians needed was a certain kind of status within the community of states. This was denied them because their "state" failed to qualify for recognition.

The foregoing discussion has implications for the kinds of ways in which the world polity may justifiably be organized. Any attempt to achieve a world state through imperial expansion would, from the point of view of autonomous states, be unjustifiable. Does this rule out the justifiability of a world state altogether? Not necessarily.[34] A world "state" would be justified if it came about through the voluntary action of all sovereign states. The agreed upon polity would have to be one in which the autonomy of the parties to the agreement was respected; it would have to be an arrangement arrived at through a confederal or federal procedure. It must be noticed, though, that the world "state" would have to come about through the confederating (or federating) act of states and not by a dissolution of existing states followed by a contracting in of all the individuals of this world into the new global state. In short, any new order must grow from the autonomous action of *states*. It would be a new order growing out of the old rather than a new order replacing a dissolved old order.

3 The constitutive theory of individuality as a background theory justifying the settled norms of the modern state domain of discourse

In Chapter Four I set out to construct a background theory which justified the list of goods currently accepted as settled in international relations. I examined and found good reason to reject theories stressing order, utilitarian theories and rights based theories. I subsequently outlined a better background theory derived from Hegel which I called "constitutive theory" in which rights are not conceived of as adhering in individuals divorced from any community whatsoever. Instead rights are envisaged as what people come to recognize one another as having within the context of a community with specified social and political institutions. Following Hegel I showed how individuals with the rights which we value are constituted within a system of mutual recognition which includes within it the institutions of the family, civil society, the state and the system of sovereign states. The background theory which we have been looking for is the one which demonstrates how individuality is constituted within the context of these institutional arrangements. This theory then makes it possible to reconcile those settled norms relating to the preservation of a system of sovereign states with those norms connected to the notion of individual rights.

I have not worked out this theory in any great detail. A fuller exposition would have to determine the precise ways in which individuality is constituted within the state and the system of states. A fuller theory would have to indicate the criteria in terms of which states recognize one another as fully sovereign. As I have mentioned, not any polity may justifiably be granted full recognition as an autonomous state within which individuality may flourish. In the exposition we saw how a state in which the individual rights associated with civil society were not recognized would not count as a state within which individuality was actualized and would thus not qualify for full recognition. There is a wealth of detail which needs to be filled in here.

The aim of this chapter has been to find a background theory which would justify the settled norms of the modern state domain of discourse. Constitutive theory succeeds in doing this, but it is a theory with its own characteristic style of theorizing. This mode of theorizing involves bringing to light those dimensions of the moral order within which we, together with others in the order, constitute one another as fully fledged individuals. In the next chapter I shall give an example of how people who accept this background theory might set about reasoning towards a solution of a particular type of hard case in the normative theory of international relations.

NOTES

1 Imposing sets of rights and duties on oneself in such a situation is a sophisticated activity which would involve imagining oneself to be two persons. The two might be envisaged as an actor and a conscience. The actor might claim a right *vis-à-vis* the conscience to do x on Sundays. This way of thinking is derivative from the normal social context in which rights involve mutual recognitions of certain kinds.
2 This point is well argued in R. Flathman, *The Practice of Rights* (Cambridge University Press, 1976), p. 65 and following pages. See also Bruce Ackerman, *Social Justice and the Liberal State* (New Haven, Yale University Press, 1980), p. 5.
3 For contract theory rights holders are "perfect in respect of their rights" in that, as Thomas Paine puts it, "the state grants men nothing ..." (*The Rights of Man* (London, Dent, 1979), p. 44).
4 Bruce Ackerman makes a similar point where he portrays rights talk as constrained dialogue. See *Social Justice and the Liberal State*, *passim*.

5 G. W. F. Hegel, *The Philosophy of Right*, trans. T. M. Knox (Oxford University Press, 1973), para. 187. See also the Preface at pp. 7 and 12.

6 John Charvet, *A Critique of Freedom and Equality* (Cambridge University Press, 1981), p. 164.

7 At this point the objection might be offered that this way of going about things is to presuppose what has to be justified; that is, to presuppose that the system of sovereign states is justified, when what is called for is an attempt to find out whether it is justified. The objection here is that all I am doing is looking for a justification of the *status quo* which justification will not have any critical dimension. This objection is not well founded. The actors within the system of sovereign states may be acting according to a partial or incorrect understanding of the moral dimension implicit in their social arrangements. These actors will, of course, be guided in action by their partial and incomplete understandings. Where a more satisfactory understanding of the moral dimensions implicit in the existing arrangements is produced, this will serve as a criticism of the previous understandings and will also guide their actions in new ways. Thus the charge that constitutive theory merely endorses the *status quo* is unfounded.

8 See E. M. Adams, "The Ground of Rights," *American Philosophical Quarterly*, Vol. 19, No. 2 (April 1982), p. 191.

9 Talking about laws and institutions, Hegel says in para. 147 of the *Philosophy of Right* that they are not something alien to the subject: "On the contrary, his [the subject's] spirit bears witness to them [the laws and institutions] as to its own essence, the essence in which he has a feeling of his self-hood, and in which he lives as in his own element which is not distinguished from himself. The subject is thus directly linked to the ethical order by a relation which is more like an identity than even the relation of faith or trust." A pagan thus *feels* himself part of the pagan order in which he finds himself. But reflection may lead him to have an *insight* about his relation to the order, and thinking may lead the subject to have knowledge of the identity between himself and the ethical order. What is important for my purposes in all of this is that the reader notice that Hegel portrays his (the philosopher's) task as being that of revealing the internal relationships between the subject and the institutions under which he lives. His task is to make intelligible how the subject's feeling of self-hood is bound up with the institutions under which he lives.

10 Hegel uses an architectonic metaphor. See *The Philosophy of Right*, p. 6.

11 Ibid. para. 158.

12 Ibid. Addition to para. 158.

13 Ibid. Addition to para. 180.

14 Ibid. Addition to para. 174.

15 Ibid. Addition to para. 265.

16 John Charvet, *A Critique*, p. 174.

17 G. W. F. Hegel, *The Philosophy of Right*, Addition to para. 158.

18 John Charvet, *A Critique*, p. 177.
19 G. W. F. Hegel, *The Philosophy of Right*, para. 45.
20 Ibid. para. 46.
21 Ibid. Addition to para. 46.
22 John Charvet, *A Critique*, p. 179.
23 G. W. F. Hegel, *The Philosophy of Right*, para. 258.
24 Ibid. para. 268.
25 Ibid.
26 Ibid. Addition to para. 265.
27 Ibid. Addition to para. 261.
28 Ibid. Addition to para. 261 where Hegel refers to this as a conjunction of duty and right.
29 Education here is not to be confused with so called "re-education" as practised, for example, by the Pol Pot regime in Cambodia.
30 G. W. F. Hegel, *The Philosophy of Right*, para. 323.
31 Ibid. para. 331.
32 Ibid. para. 349.
33 In this connection it would be interesting to know whether the citizens of the so called independent homelands in South Africa, such as the Transkei and Ciskei, would regard a reincorporation back into South Africa, which was beneficial to them in every way except with regard to self-determination, as a loss of freedom.
34 Andrew Vincent, "The Hegelian State and International Politics," *The Review of International Studies*, Vol. 9, No. 3 (July 1983), pp. 191–207, reaches similar conclusions on the basis of a close reading of the whole corpus of Hegel's work.

Chapter Six

The justification of unconventional violence in international relations: a hard case for normative theory

The purpose of constructing a background theory was to enable us to generate answers to some of the hard cases mentioned at the beginning of Chapter Three. In this chapter the aim is to demonstrate a practical application of this method. Let us look at the normative problems posed by various unconventional uses of violence in the modern world.

1 Unconventional violence as a normative problem in international relations

In the modern world few conventional wars are fought, yet there is a great deal of violence of one form or another in world politics. We are all acquainted with the typical cases. An embassy in London is raided by Iranian guerillas. The staff is held hostage and demands are made which are of an international nature. West Germany faces a shoot out at the Olympic games with Black September, a group who claim to be fighting for the rights of the Palestine Liberation Organization. Aircraft are hijacked by terrorists who demand the co-operation of several states in realizing their ends. The Irish Republican Army (IRA) is involved in many different kinds of violence, as is the Palestine Liberation Organization. States, too, practise various kinds of unconventional violence, for example sabo-

187

tage against the installations of neighbouring states, active support of liberation movements engaged in violence of one sort or another in neighbouring states, and so on.

These diverse forms of violence pose a problem for normative theory of international relations because there is so much violence and because there are so few settled norms relating to it. This is in sharp contrast to the case of conventional warfare.[1] There is a settled body of norms relating to the legitimate causes of and the proper conduct of conventional war. For example, although it is accepted that war is generally not a good, nevertheless it is settled that going to war in response to aggression is justified in specified cases. There is thus a measure of agreement about when conventional forms of violence are justified. However, with regard to the modern unconventional forms of violence there seem to be very few established norms. Consider, for example, the moral confusion surrounding the violent activities of groups which are often referred to as "terrorist." Most people intuitively judge such activities to be morally evil. However, we cannot simply point to the almost universal condemnation of terrorism and leave the matter there. For we have to take into account that terrorists do not simply disclaim any and all constraints of morality. Indeed, most terrorist actors overtly proclaim a moral position of their own. This deeper concern is revealed in disputes about how such people ought to be described. The people we normally refer to as "terrorists" usually dispute the label. The label has built into it a negative moral evaluation. People called "terrorists" usually call themselves something else: "urban guerillas" or "freedom fighters," for example. Members of the following organizations reject the label "terrorist": The Palestine Liberation Organization, the Irish Republican Army, the Red Army Faction, the Red Brigades, the South West African People's Organization, to mention but a few so called "terrorist" organizations. That disputes arise about the proper classification of members of such groups alerts us to the fact that significant moral importance is attached to the correct description. Why? The answer is plain. The members think that their description of themselves justifies their group and its actions, whereas the alternative description does the converse; it shows the group and its actions to be unjust. If it is important to such groups how they are described (and it generally is so), then we may dismiss a basket of popular myths about the so called "terrorist" groups. Examples of such myths are that such groups are totally indiscriminate killers, that they are arbitrary perpetrators of violence, that they have no standards and are irrational, that they are barbarous, beyond the pale of morality, inhuman and so on. If it is important for such groups to be described in one way rather than another then they have indicated their participation in the business of moral argument. Against the charge "terrorist" the counter claim is made – "freedom fighter." What emerges here is that the "terrorist" groups want to maintain that their actions are justified. The key question thus becomes: "When, if ever, are 'terrorist' type actions justified?" The question is pressing because the kinds of actions in question are dire, viz. killing people, maiming them, instilling terror into them, destroying property, destroying social and political systems. Generally "terrorist" groups would agree that normally such measures are not justified. They argue that theirs is not the normal case, but is a special case and is justified because it is special. No doubt examples can be found of groups who do *not* wish to argue that killing, maiming and so on are usually unjustified. It is difficult to see how such groups would not very soon find themselves in an incoherent position akin to that of the amoralist which was discussed earlier in Chapter Two.[2] But most "terrorist" groups about which people are concerned do not argue in this way. Their argument is that the dire acts which I listed are not normally justified, but are so in their exceptional case.

There are many different forms of unconventional violence which raise difficult normative questions. Such questions arise about: violence against property (for example sabotage committed by individuals or groups opposed to the state against state owned installations, destruction of private property for political purposes, violence by the state against the property of individual citizens for political purposes); violence against persons (for example the maiming or killing of state officials, policemen, military personnel, etc. by individuals or groups opposed to the state, the maiming or killing, by such individuals or groups, of civilians in an indiscriminate manner, the maiming or killing by the state of civilians other than in accordance with the due process of law or in the course of a declared war). All of these forms of unconventional violence get an international dimension when the people committing the violence act across international borders or seek international aid and/or approval.

It is most important at this point to notice that justifications of acts of unconventional violence are not only made by people opposing a state, or the system of states, but may be (and are) made by *states* which do the same kinds of thing against people both inside and outside their territory.

These kinds of unconventional violence raise important normative questions in international relations. Those who commit such acts, be they individuals, groups or states, often act across international borders, they regularly seek international aid and recognition, and the targets of such acts seek political, financial and military aid to combat such violence. Thus most actors in international politics are called upon at one time or another to make difficult normative decisions about unconventional forms of violence. The central question which they have to answer is: "When is the killing, maiming, terrorizing of people, the destruction of their property, and of their social and political systems justified?" This question is too wide and contains within it the question: "When is war justified?" I put it this way to overcome a gut reaction many people have, which is that even to ask whether such acts are justified is silly; to many they seem patently and obviously unjust. But most people recognize that the questions such as "When is war justified?" and "What may justifiably be done during the conduct of a war?" are questions worthy of serious consideration. My contention is that questions about the justification of unconventional forms of violence are in the same class as questions about the justification of war.

2 Terrorism as a hard case for normative theory

In order to demonstrate the ways in which unconventional violence poses difficult problems for normative theory in international relations, let us consider the normative problems which arise concerning the violent activities of terrorists/ freedom fighters. Let us start by contrasting the activities of such people with the activities of mentally deranged persons.

Consider the case of a mentally deranged person who hijacks an aircraft. The hijacker does what he does (for example threatens to blow up everybody aboard unless some irrational demand is met) from some or other compulsion. Such a case would be of interest to a psychiatrist. It would not pose any serious moral issues regarding the possible justifiability of the killing and maiming of people and the destruction of property. In the case of a mad hijacker we do not say that his action was justified or unjustified. It was simply the action of a deranged person. Such cases pose no problem for normative theory. The actor has clearly broken the law and acted contrary to our moral norms, but he cannot be held accountable for these actions. Psychiatrists will probably be able to indicate in a general way why he did what he did. There is also not much dispute about what ought to be done with such a person once he is caught. He should not be punished but ought to receive psychiatric treatment of one kind or another.

Similarly hijackers who are sane but criminal pose no special problems for normative theory. The hijacker who threatens terror in order to get hostages and so to raise money for private gain presents us with an easy case. He breaks the law. If caught, the procedure is clear and the punishment is prescribed.[3] Were a spate of such crimes to occur, the problem of how best to enforce the law might arise.[4] This is a practical problem and not a problem for normative theory.

The major cases in which the normative problems surrounding unconventional violence arise are not at all like this. They are more difficult in that the actor in question argues that although his action would not normally be considered justifiable (indeed his action flouts the conventional legal norms), his action is nevertheless justified. Typically such actors reject the legitimacy of the law (or a legal system as a whole). The important point here is that in order to evaluate this more radical challenge we are called upon to produce a background theory in terms of which the state (and its laws) and/or the system of states (and the international legal system) can be evaluated. It is no use in such cases referring the hijacker to the law and arguing that his action is wrong because he broke the law. The type of hijacker we are considering here admits that he has broken the law, but wishes to argue that there is nothing wrong in breaking the law in his case. Usually he will argue that the law in question is itself unjust. Thus anyone wishing to enter into argument with the hijacker has to proceed to a deeper level of argument about the justice of the particular law (or more likely of the whole system of law) in terms of which his action is judged wrong. In order to make this point somewhat clearer, imagine a woman who hijacked a plane to take hostages in order to secure funds for her political cause and to obtain the release of her comrades who were languishing in jail. Before she was caught she killed one of the hostages. She is brought to trial. At some stage in the procedure she is allowed an interview with a journalist.

Journalist: You admit that you broke the law, terrified the passengers and killed the steward?
Jill: Yes.
Journalist: Yet you claim that such violent action was justified?
Jill: Yes, because life under the junta is awful. The people are starving. They have no real civil rights. They are forced to fight in adventurer type wars which are avoidable. There is no free press, so they do not know what is going on. All opposition to the state is crushed. My comrades and I are trying to change things in the only way that we

can. We need funds and we need support. What I did was done in order to raise funds and publicize our case in the hope of gaining international support.

Journalist: Do you agree that in general it would be wrong to go around breaking the law in this way?

Jill: Yes, but this is a special case.

Readers may continue the dialogue themselves. Whatever follows next has to be some or other normative theory justifying the authority of the state or setting limits to it. It might justify great state power as did Hobbes' theory, or it might set more severe limits to it as did Locke's theory and, more recently, Nozick's and Ackerman's.[5] But it must be a discourse within the modern state centric domain of discourse. This assertion is challenged by Barrie Paskins and Michael Dockrill, who argue that modern man's failure to think coherently about terrorism must be attributable to his being blinded by the theory of the state, blinded by the state centric model of reasoning.[6] Contrary to their position I am arguing that there is, indeed, a prevailing modern state domain of discourse, and this implies that there is more or less universal agreement that it is right that there be in the world a system of states. The terrorist/freedom fighter who ignores this consensus risks being dubbed "mad." The serious terrorist/freedom fighter must distinguish himself from the mad hijacker.[7] His only way of doing so is by justifying his case. This is borne out by experience; for example, serious terrorists/freedom fighters generally seek a high-profile public image in order to put their case across. But, in order to present a justifiable case at all, they must appeal to arguments which will be understood and recognized by the audience to whose attention they have drawn themselves; i.e. they must participate in the state centric domain of discourse. Groups which argue for the demolition of the state and the system of states *in toto* and who may thus be seen as not participating in the state centric domain of discourse at all (such as the Red Army Faction in West Germany, the Angry Brigade in Britain and the Weathermen in the USA) are generally considered to be on the lunatic fringe. Such groups are seen as dangerous in the way that an armed madman is seen as dangerous. But they are not seen as posing any moral challenge or interesting problems for normative theory. They are not interesting because they fail in their justification to enter in any profound way the central political debate which is in the state centric domain of discourse.[8]

Much more interesting and challenging are those groups of terrorists/freedom fighters which do enter this debate, groups who set out to make a plausible case in this central domain of discourse. Such groups cannot merely be dismissed as "lunatic." Here I have in mind such groups as the South West African People's Organization, the African National Congress, the Sandinistas, the Tupamaros, the Irish Republican Army and so on. I suggest that we are acutely uncomfortable in thinking about these cases because on the one hand we want to reject the kind of deeds they are committing as evil, while on the other hand we do recognize that their claim to be a special case does have some force. The regimes which they oppose do seem to be oppressive in special ways, the opportunities for opposition do seem to be limited, the media do seem to be slanted, and so on.

The difficult cases which are posed for normative theory by terrorists/freedom fighters are triply hard. First, they are hard in that we cannot simply deal with the case by subsuming it under an accepted rule (as we did in the case of the criminal hijacker), but are in fact called upon to produce a background justification for the system of rules as a whole. Second, they are hard in that even in terms of the background theory they are likely to be borderline cases. The background theory is not likely to provide a straightforward answer. Finally, they are hard in that once we have admitted that, for example, the PLO's activities may be justifiable, then we are called upon to wage the argument in public. In those cases where a terrorist/ freedom fighter challenges us (where the "we" is the state, or the community of scholars, or the ordinary citizen), we are not simply called upon to sort the issue out in our own minds, so that we may then take the appropriate action. Rather we are required to take up the argument in public. The terrorist/freedom fighter issues a public and fundamental challenge to accepted interpretations concerning the law and institutions of the state and the inter-state system and his *arguments* must be publicly rebutted. Once the issue "freedom fighter or terrorist?" is raised in connection with an individual (or group), executing that individual, or imprisoning him, or having him disappear, or placing him under house arrest, or censoring his written and spoken word will not settle the issue. He has to be shown to have been wrong. His arguments have to be shown to have been faulty.

Pressing normative issues with regard to other forms of unconventional violence in international relations arise in much the same way. In cases (involving state or non-state actors) of sabotage against state or private property for political purposes, in cases of extra legal political executions, in cases of arbitrary terror, in cases of clandestine political, financial or military aid to people involved in the aforementioned kinds of activities the acts would normally be considered to be wrong, but it is claimed by those committing them that in the special circumstances involved their acts are justified. Each of these cases raises core issues within the modern state domain of discourse.

Those committing unconventional acts of violence, as I have mentioned, do not usually confine their activities to the affairs internal to a single state. They often seek material and political aid from other states, and from international organizations. In pursuit of their aims in state A they may commit (or threaten) violent deeds in state B. In acting against state A they may seek bases in state B, and so on. It is thus plain that from the international point of view there is a need to answer questions such as "When are the activities of such groups justified?" and "What ought other states to do when confronted with such actions?"

I have argued that the answer to these questions will have to be within the state centric domain of discourse. More specifically, it will have to be in the form of a background justification for the list of settled norms in world politics. In the previous chapters I have given reasons for rejecting a natural law/community-of-mankind approach to these problems, together with order based theories, utilitarian theories and liberal human rights theories. I indicated why I thought that a constitutive theory of individuality seemed best suited as a background theory. Let us now put it to the test and see if it will enable us to find satisfactory solutions to the hard cases posed by unconventional forms of violence.

3 Constitutive theory applied to unconventional violence

In the discussion of constitutive theory we saw that argument towards the solution of a hard case proceeded by seeking to determine whether the act or institution was a necessary part of the constitution of the community within which certain values are held. Applying this method to the hard cases posed by unconventional violence, the question to ask must be: "Can the practice in question (sabotage, extra legal political executions, terrorism or whatever) ever be partially constitutive of individuality as we value it?" If the answer is positive then "unconventional violence of type x (under circumstances a, b or c) is a good" would have to be added to the list of settled goods mentioned at the beginning of Chapter Four. This list, it will be remembered, included such things as the system of sovereign states is a good, democratic institutions within states are good, international law is a good, and so on.

At first glance it seems unlikely that it will be possible to reconcile any of the forms of unconventional violence with the goods mentioned on the initial list. They seem so diametrically opposed to many of those goods (such as democracy, human rights, law, property, non-combatant immunity, etc.). The practice of terrorism, for example, seems to be in fundamental conflict with most of these norms. But "terrorists" usually see themselves as "freedom fighters." "Liberation movements are a good" seems far more likely to find a place on the list of goods than "terrorism is a good." Thus the general question formulated above may be reformulated as: "Is the practice of unconventional violence in the fight for freedom partially constitutive of individuality as we value it?" Phrased in this way the question does not seem to call so clearly for a negative answer.

3.1 A possible dialogue on justifiable sabotage

In what follows I shall attempt to show how constitutive theory may be applied to the hard cases posed by unconventional violence. In doing so I shall often present the argument in the form of a dialogue. I need to provide a brief justification for this procedure. Arguments presented in this way have, of course, no exceptional logical force. The arguments contained in the dialogue would be as strong were they presented in a more conventional mode. This way of presenting the arguments, though, does have certain advantages. First, it provides a neat way in which argument and counter argument can be presented. Second, it provides a way of dramatizing what might otherwise be a longer and more laborious argument. Third, it is particularly useful for keeping us aware of a central feature of constitutive theory, viz. the insight that we reciprocally constitute one another in certain specified ways. Finally, I must point out that although it is often the case that dialogue forms allow the crisp statement of an argument, this is not always so. Even in dialogue form long arguments are lengthy.

Imagine an ongoing dialogue between a terrorist/freedom fighter, called Seamus, and Critic, who would label Seamus a "terrorist." In order to justify his acts Seamus must show Critic that individuality as Critic values it can be partially constituted by the practice of "freedom fighting" as he, Seamus, portrays it. For the sake of the argument let us assume that Seamus embarks on a series of violent acts, that he does not get caught and that after some of these acts he meets Critic, at which point the dialogues ensue. Both Seamus and Critic may be taken to have read the present essay and to agree with the substance of it. They both agree that the list of settled goods is correct and they agree that these are best understood as indicating a social arrangement in which individuality can be constituted as such. Seamus and Critic will thus not consider the possibility of order based justifications for the practice of terrorism, neither will they reconsider utilitarian justifications nor liberal rights theories, nor will they reopen the debate about natural law theories predicated on the existence of a community of mankind. The first dialogue takes place after Seamus has blown up an electricity pylon.

Critic: This is outrageous. You know that it is wrong to cause wanton damage to essential services thereby disrupting the economy. How can you possibly justify this act?

Seamus: Yes, it is normally wrong (in terms of the settled norms relating to the maintenance of peace and the protection of property rights), but this is a special case.

Critic: Explain yourself.

Seamus: Do you agree that to be a free individual it is important that you be recognized as a citizen of a democratic sovereign state, that it is important that you be recognized as having certain key rights, both civil and economic?

Critic: Of course I do, you know very well that we are agreed upon the list of settled norms which includes norms relating to these matters. But what has this got to do with the pylon you bombed?

Seamus: Imagine that you awoke one morning to find that the state had suddenly withdrawn certain key rights from you; for example, your rights to democratic participation in the central law making authority. You find that you are no longer recognized as a citizen who is entitled to stand for public office and participate in the electoral process. You do not accept the justification for this act proffered by the state as a valid one. Assuming that you are determined to do something about this, what must your ultimate objective be?

Critic: To get people to recognize my rights once again.

Seamus: What people? Are you referring only to the members of the government which passed the laws depriving you of your rights?

Critic: No, not only them. The government's act of passing the laws depriving me of rights must be seen as taking place in a community which recognizes the government's acts as authoritative and binding.

Internationally the act is seen by the community of states as the act of a sovereign state. The state's arbitrary and coercive acts against me depend for their legitimacy on this wider recognition within the society of states. So in seeking to have the wrong done me recognized, I have to address the wider community which recognizes that government as entitled to pass laws. If I cannot convince the government which committed the act, but succeed in convincing the wider community, the government itself will come to lose that recognition which entitled it to act in the first place.

Seamus: Given that you consider yourself to have been wronged, what means would you be justified in using to rectify the situation? Would you, for example, be justified in seeking *power* so that you could force people to recognize your claim to recognition of the requisite sort?

Critic: Of course not. The kind of recognition I presently have (and which I have been deprived of in your example) is freely given and not forced. It is this kind of recognition which I seek to regain. Were I to coerce people into calling me "brother," "fellow citizen" or "comrade" or whatever, their calling me such would not signify that they recognized me as such.

Seamus: What then could you justifiably do to get people to recognize your proper status once again?

Critic: My problem is to get back to the situation of mutual recognition which I was in before. In the prior situation I was recognized as a citizen, voter, property owner, rights holder and so on. I, in turn, recognized my fellow countrymen as having these rights. We constituted one another via this system of reciprocal recognition. It follows that if what I am wanting is a situation of reciprocal recognition, then I cannot get that if I fail to accord to the people I am addressing the requisite recognition. What I want is the recognition of free men and I can only get that if I recognize those whose recognition I seek as free men. This indicates a limit to the means which I can justifiably use to rectify the situation you have hypothetically placed me in.

Seamus: Explain.

Critic: I am constrained in the following way. Whatever I do to regain the recognition I seek, I must not do anything which would deprive the recognition of those from whom I seek it of all value. Let me put the most extreme case. To be a free man is to be recognized as such by other free men, thus it would be self-defeating to enslave those from whom recognition is sought.

Seamus: What are the implications of all this for the situation in which I have placed you?

Critic: The main one is this: in order to regain my rightful status in the community I need to *convince* those who have deprived me of it that they are wrong in denying it to me. In seeking to convince them I must make clear that what I am seeking is a situation of reciprocal recognition and that I am upholding my side of the desired reciprocal arrangement, i.e. I am recognizing them in the proper way. Notice

that this is not only important internally, but is of international significance too. My major source of support against an unjust state is likely
to come from the international community of states. It is crucial that
they see that I use just means to counter injustice.

Seamus: So what may you properly do then?

Critic: Given that my task is not to force people but to convince them,
my efforts must be aimed at *arguing* with the people concerned. Thus
I would seek to address them in as many ways as possible: in personal
conversations, in public debate, at meetings, over the radio, on tele-
vision, in the daily press, through learned journals, via pamphlets
and so on.

Seamus: Suppose that all those avenues are progressively blocked to
you through government action. Your written and spoken words are
censored or banned. You are prevented from addressing people, you
are confined to your house. What may you properly do then?

Critic: If I had tried the previously mentioned methods and had failed to
have my case heard, then I would have to adopt more unorthodox
methods of communication.

Seamus: Such as?

Critic: Getting my case aired internationally. There is an international
consensus that sovereign states, democratic procedures within states,
the rule of law, the furtherance of human rights, etc. are goods. It
would be reasonable to suppose that if my case were a good one it
would find widespread support internationally, both within states
and in international organizations, both officially and unofficially. In
this way I could communicate with those who wrongfully refused to
recognize my case.

Seamus: But suppose that your international hearing was ineffective.
That your case was not taken seriously and that within your state you
were still not allowed to say your say and that others in your position
were put into jail.

Critic: I would have to show the audience that I viewed my situation as
desperate. I could then properly resort to passive resistance and civil
disobedience. In these actions I would break the law (and suffer the
consequences) as an act of communication with my government,
fellow citizens and the international community.

Seamus: Suppose that, once again, this kind of act was treated with the
utmost severity by your government, so that you knew that a single
act of civil disobedience would be your last communication in the
debate. What would you do then?

Critic: I might try and think of a drastic act of communication which
would leave me free to communicate on another day, such as ..

Seamus: Blowing up a pylon?

Critic: Possibly, but I would have to be sure that the act could not be
misinterpreted. It would have to be made clear to my audience that
my act was not merely criminal, that it was not an act of straightforward coercion, that although I was breaking the law by destroying

state property I was not an anarchist, that I had tried all sorts of more
conventional ways of getting my message across, that what I was
trying to convey with my act of violence had widespread support
both internally and internationally, that I had been careful not to
harm any people, that I would not endorse this kind of action in
normal circumstances and so on.

Seamus: I agree with you and my case satisfies all the conditions which
you laid down. I deserve local and international support for what I
have done. Let me explain the history ...

In this dialogue we see how Seamus got Critic to reveal that he
(Critic) was prepared to justify, in certain circumstances, that
very act of Seamus' which Critic had sought to morally
condemn, viz. the blowing up of a pylon. In broad outline
Critic's response may thus serve to show how this act could be
reconciled with the settled body of goods and with the background theory justifying those goods. At no point does he repu-
diate the settled core or background theory. Moreover, these
arguments are aimed at Seamus *and* the reader. The implicit
contention of the dialogue is that between the reader and the
author (me) there exists a community within which we constitute one another in certain ways. We constitute one another in
all the usual ways by recognizing one another as citizens,
voters, rights holders and all those other ways indicated in our
list of settled beliefs. We do not, however, usually recognize
one another as having a right to blow up state property. What
the dialogue sought to bring out (make apparent) is that we *do*
recognize one another as having this right in exceptional circumstances, and that this right can be made to *cohere* with our
usual norms of reciprocal recognition.

Second, the dialogue brought out the centrality of reciprocal
recognition. This works at two levels. For the argument to work
the reader needs to be convinced that in making out a case for
this limited act of sabotage any protagonist of such means is not
failing to recognize the reader in all the normal ways which
constitute him as a free individual (as a citizen in a sovereign
state amongst sovereign states, in a state which is democrati-
cally organized and in which basic rights are respected, etc.). In

short, a person seeking to defend such violent action has to demonstrate his allegiance to the list of settled norms. At a second level a protagonist of such violence must at all times show those against whom his violence is aimed that he recognizes them in the same way. For what he seeks is the just recognition which is wrongly denied him. If he wrongly denies this recognition to those who deny it to him, then neither party has a case and all talk of justification becomes otiose. Slaves who seek to enslave their masters are not engaged in justified action.

Third, the dialogue shows us that whether or not an action is justified depends on a prior history of graduated acts. In this case it clearly would not have been justified for Seamus to resort to sabotage as a first step. In other words, this norm justifying sabotage in specified circumstances is a conditional one. It only applies after the failure of a series of less drastic measures.

Fourth, notice that there is a whole series of ways in which the case for justified sabotage could be weakened. If it could be shown that the saboteur had not been denied access to the media, then no case could be made for advancing to such drastic means of communication as blowing up state property. Similarly, if it could be shown that his arguments, although clearly heard by all those at whom they were aimed, had not elicited much support, then his case would be considerably weakened. For then it is reasonable to assume that what he was arguing for was not consistent with the body of settled goods and its background justification. Thus if the saboteur's message did not find favour within the internal or international community in spite of unimpeded communication, then the odds are that his case is a weak one. If in such a situation he still wanted to maintain that his case was a strong one, he would be entitled to continue arguing for his position, but he would not be warranted in sabotage as a stronger form of communication. The justification for resorting to acts of sabotage is not that other forms of communication did not *succeed* in convincing the target audience, but that the avenues of communication were blocked. Force is not justified as a stronger form of argument, it is justified when it is the *only* form of *argument* available.

3.2 *Application to two examples of sabotage strategies*

Let us apply the conclusions of the previous section to two actual examples of sabotage strategies. In one case the strategy in question emerges as far more justified than does the other. Consider the Red Army Faction in West Germany, which received international notoriety during the seventies. This was a clandestine group of revolutionaries who engaged in the following kinds of acts in support of their programme: robbery, arson, bombing, kidnapping and murder. Their aims were, amongst other things, to "hit the system in the face; mobilize the masses; and maintain international solidarity."[9] To what extent was their action justified in terms of the approach I have outlined? The Red Army Faction (RAF) did attempt to justify their actions, but did so in a somewhat eclectic way. Three main *leitmotifs* to their argument have been identified: first, a strong identification with the armed struggle of the liberation movements in the Third World; second, an argument according to which West Germany is democratic only in form, while in substance it is still fascist, in the way that the Nazi state was; third, the rejection of the consumer society. The *leitmotifs* are not brought into any overall coherence and no clear plan for an alternative social arrangement is offered by the group. The group is against the system, but it is not clear what it stands for.

The RAF's acts cannot be justified in the way that it was possible to justify limited sabotage in the dialogue. It is not possible to construct an argument in terms of constitutive theory which clearly shows that the members of the RAF were being denied a form of recognition which ought rightfully to have been granted them. In terms of the accepted norms they were accorded all the rights which were due to them; their personal, civil and property rights were all well respected. Furthermore, the RAF were not able to make the point that they had been unable to state their case to their national community and the international community. They could not point to a past record of attempts to communicate their case in a peaceful manner and could not refer to a past in which their attempts at such communication had been systematically blocked. The acts of the RAF could not be interpreted as clearly signifying their respect for those institutions in terms of which individuals are constituted as free in the modern world. Nor could their acts be interpreted as acts of communication to an audience whose rights were being respected in the act of communication. Quite understandably, opinion polls during the period in question consistently revealed minimal support for the "terrorists" among ordinary citizens.[10] Nor was there any international consensus that the RAF were fighting for a good cause. We may thus conclude that the RAF policies were unjustified. This conclusion leaves wide open the question whether the West German government's action to combat the terrorists was justified or not. It also says nothing about the very interesting question why the limited activities of the group were of such great public concern in West Germany at the time. An answer might refer to the modern history of Germany or show how the RAF touched upon certain old wounds in the social consciousness.

Let us contrast the activities of the RAF with those of the African National Congress (ANC) and the sequence of events which led the ANC to embark on a programme of sabotage in South Africa. The aims of the ANC as formulated in the 1943 Constitution were:

a. To protect and advance the interest of the African people in all matters affecting them.
b. To attain the freedom of the African people from all discriminatory laws whatsoever.
c. To strive and work for the unity and co-operation of the African people in every possible way.

The constitution of the ANC includes a Bill of Rights with such provisions as the right to vote, freedom of residence, prohibition of police raids on homes, free and compulsory education, equality in social security schemes, collective bargaining rights and equal opportunities rights. The ANC considered that the African people in South Africa were denied their legitimate rights. Initially the organization sought to state its case through conventional channels. For example, at a meeting in December 1951 in Bloemfontein it was decided to write to the government, requesting it to repeal six specific laws which the ANC regarded as discriminatory. In an exchange of letters with the Prime Minister the ANC mentioned a long series of efforts "by every constitutional means" to bring to the notice of the government the legitimate demands of the African people. It served notice on the government that it was contemplating a course of passive resistance against "unjust laws which keep in perpetual subjection and misery vast sections of the population."[11] They made it clear that their action would not be aimed at specific groups, but was a protest against specific laws. The campaign went ahead. African volunteers broke petty laws and then allowed themselves to be arrested, tried and punished, without showing any resistance to these subsequent procedures. The resisters were severely punished by the state, leaders of the organization were detained and banned, the advocating of passive resistance techniques was declared illegal by a new Act of Parliament. Subsequently new legislation and the activities of the police made it ever more difficult for the ANC to operate as a legitimate political group. Finally, it was declared an illegal organization, thus terminating all further options to pursue its aims in open and constitutional ways.[12] At this stage a clandestine branch of the ANC was formed with the express aim of using sabotage as a means of communicating its aims. These aims were still the aims originally propagated. Umkonto we Sizwe ("Spear of the Nation"), as this organization was called, set out to sabotage government installations without endangering human life. It carried out many such acts and they continue to the present day. Clearly in terms of the dialogue the ANC has a much better case for engaging in such sabotage than does the RAF. The ANC's case is strengthened by the fact that at about the same time as it embarked on this campaign it sought and gained widespread international support. At all times it was made quite clear to those who were being addressed that the organization did respect their rights and did not want to deprive any group of their existing rights.[13]

3.3 A possible dialogue on unconventional violence against people

If the kind of justified sabotage discussed in the previous section fails to convince the internal and international audience to whom it is addressed, individuals and groups who claim that they are being denied the recognition which is justly theirs might turn towards more drastic strategies, strategies which involve maiming and killing selected military and official personnel. The IRA is one well known organization which has adopted such a strategy. The question we must face then is: "When are such strategies justified?"

In a second dialogue Critic confronts Seamus after the latter has shot a policeman.

Critic: Seamus, you have now taken matters too far. Last time I agreed with you that in certain special circumstances an act of sabotage might possibly be a justifiable act of communication. But murder is murder and is always unjustified.

Seamus: No, this is just another step in the process which you yourself outlined. For a long time we have restricted our actions to this kind of sabotage and have avoided all violence against persons, especially civilians. But this has been to no avail. Saboteurs who have been caught have been treated with the greatest severity. What is worse, the people of the country have had their rights eroded even further. The government has cracked down on the people's freedom of speech and freedom of movement. Thus the time has come when our cause requires us to go further than sabotage only. We regret the use of violence against individuals. Such violence would normally be wholly unjustifiable, but in our circumstances this is the only possible way open to us.

Critic: Is your task the same one we envisaged in the previous dialogue, i.e. is it to convince those who are denying you the recognition due to

you of their mistake and to convince the international community of
the justness of your cause?

Seamus: Yes, it is.

Critic: If you grant this, then you must agree that your murder of the policeman could only be justified were it possible for you to portray it as
an act which did not in any way indicate a desire on your part to
reject the basic norms in terms of which you and your audience constitute one another.

Seamus: Yes.

Critic: How then by killing a policeman did you convey to your audience that you are still at base committed to the norms of the settled
list? For on the face of the matter killing a policeman signifies a rejection of several of the most fundamental norms. For example, it indicates a rejection of the authority of the sovereign state within which
you live, a rejection of law, and a rejection of the norm according
value to human rights.

Seamus: Yes, but it symbolizes my rejection of *this* state and *these* laws,
not all states and all laws.

Critic: But the message your deed conveyed was that you espoused law-
lessness. Contrast this message with the one conveyed by acts of
passive resistance or civil disobedience. What happens in a typical
case of passive resistance is that a person breaks a law and accepts the
punishment meted out. In doing this he communicates to his audience that although a breach of the law has been committed, he
remains loyal to a more fundamental rule – to which both he (the
passive resister) and his audience (which includes the police) subscribe. Thus someone who burns a passbook to register his rejection
of laws which compel him to carry such documents communicates
his rejection of a specific law. But by accepting the consequences he
also communicates his acceptance of the rest of the legal system.
Compare this type of action to your killing the policeman. There is no
way in which by killing the policeman you could be said to be breaking a law at one level in order to refer to a shared value at a deeper
level. The dead policeman shares no deeper values with you. The rest
of the audience would be justified in interpreting your act from the
policeman's point of view.

Seamus: I did not kill just anyone. I killed a policeman as a symbol of
this corrupt state and I did not kill just any policeman, but singled out
one from the special squad which has been created to suppress the
activities of my group. Furthermore, we had given ample warning to
the state that such attacks might take place. It was not in any way a
random killing.

Critic: Your argument, then, is that your commitment to the basic
common norms is revealed in having given public warning that such
killings would take place (and why they would take place) and in
your choice of target. Is that right?

Seamus: That's correct.

Critic: Do you agree that even in this state within which you live the police uphold some norms listed in our settled list; that some of the laws which they uphold would be essential in any kind of political organization which happened to spring up here in future within which individuality was secured?

Seamus: Yes.

Critic: Thus you cannot be opposed to every law upheld by this government?

Seamus: I suppose so, yes.

Critic: Do you agree that the killing of a policeman in this state does not make it clear that you accept some of the laws and reject others?

Seamus: Yes.

Critic: It is exceptionally easy for your opponents to represent what you have done as unjustified anarchism or mere criminality, is it not? (Contrast this case with the pylon bombing case we discussed earlier. It is very difficult for opponents of your pylon bombing act to represent it as mere criminality or vandalism.)

Seamus: Yes.

Critic: Thus the killing of the policeman appears unjustifiable on two counts. It is a crude gesture capable of too many interpretations and, far more importantly, it undermines one of the basic values which unite you and your audience, viz. respect for one another's right to safety of their persons. Do you agree that if I can indicate a different deed which would have had the same or greater effect as killing a policeman and which would not have been open to misinterpretation in the way that killing a policeman is, then your case for killing the policeman would be undermined?

Seamus: Of course.

Critic: Would a kidnapping of a policeman accompanied by a detailed notice of why it was undertaken have had an equally dramatic significance?

Seamus: Yes.

Critic: Would it not possibly be more effective than the killing because it would hold public attention for a longer period of time?

Seamus: Possibly.

Critic: Would it be possible to interpret such a kidnapping as a straightforwardly criminal act?

Seamus: No.

Critic: Would it show more or less respect for the rights of the victim than killing him?

Seamus: More.

Critic: Thus you cannot argue that killing was the only option left to you in this unjust state in which you live. For there is at least one other option. Nor can you argue that killing is the only effective option left, for there is at least one better one available.

There are some further points which may be made to strengthen Critic's case that Seamus' act was unjustified. The

move justifying sabotage in the earlier dialogue was opened
when the other avenues of communication were effectively
blocked to Seamus. The move from sabotage to killing cannot
be similarly justified. If it is possible for Seamus to undertake
the murder of a policeman, then it is possible for him to undertake further sabotage of the pylon bombing type. It is not possible for a state to effectively block *all* attempts at sabotage.
Furthermore, if sabotage over a period of time did not convince
a large number of people of the case being put by Seamus, then
we have a *prima facie* reason to believe that his case must be a
weak one and that by increasing his activities to include killing
he is not trying an alternative method of convincing his audience, but is trying to coerce them. He no longer seeks recognition for legitimate claims, but seeks to enforce subservience.
The former process requires that he seek to convince his adver-
sary on the basis of certain shared premises; throughout the
argument he needs to make apparent his continued acceptance
of these. The latter process does not necessarily involve argument at all; it also does not seek a relationship of mutual
respect of one another's rights. If Seamus' campaign of sabotage
has not, after a period of time, gained much support then we
would be justified in interpreting any further bombings of his
as the frustrated ravings of an eccentric. Quite different is the
situation in which more and more people come to declare their
support for the policies pursued by Seamus and his movement.
Such an event would clearly increase the strength of Seamus'
claim, especially if it could be shown that the consensus
behind his movement was not forced, but arrived at in some or
other more or less open way. The greater the consensus about
the justice of Seamus' position, the greater the opportunities
would be for effective non-violent methods of opposition such
as strikes, go slows, refusal to co-operate with the implementation of the unjust laws, passive resistance, civil disobedience
and finally very widespread and repeated minor acts of
sabotage.

In the second dialogue we once again see the constraints
placed on normative argument by the condition that in order

for a norm to be justified it has to be shown how due recognition is given to the other rights contained in the settled list of norms. Let us call this the *due respect criterion*. Seamus' act was indistinguishable from that of a criminal in so far as it did not reveal a clear adherence to this criterion. There were other actions available to him which would have satisfied this criterion better.

It might be argued that in the discussion of violence against persons in the previous dialogue no attention was paid to justifications which can be made for *violence*, i.e. no attention was given to those situations in which a group may reject the legitimacy of a whole regime and seek to overthrow it by all means possible, including violence. In such cases those committing the revolutionary violence may be seen (so the argument goes) as seeking not so much to convince the internal state officials who are denying them their rights, but to gain international recognition and aid for their cause. The dialogue ignored, so this argument runs, cases such as that which pertained in Warsaw in 1944 when the Poles of the Armia Krajowa rose up against the Nazis. They expressed their rejection of the Nazi regime *in toto* and used violent means, including the killing of Nazi soldiers and officials. Was their action justified? Did it indicate the Poles' fundamental respect for the core values contained in constitutive theory? What does this example reveal about normative theorizing in revolutionary situations?

The context in which the uprisings occurred was not a stable civil one in which the Poles formed a minority protesting about certain forms of recognition which were denied them. Poland was an occupied state in a highly unstable wartime environment. The occupying Nazis were facing the inevitable advance of the Russian army. The Nazis' treatment of their enemies had always been morally atrocious. It could scarcely be said that there existed a domain of discourse between the Nazis and this Polish underground army at all. The question facing us is: "Given the situation that existed, what forms of violent opposition to the Nazis were justified?" What actions were open to the Poles which would show their commitment to the basic settled norms? Passive resistance and civil disobedience would not work because they require a stable context within which, over time, the effect of these actions may become known and gather support. In a war such acts by a minority would hardly be noticed. Similarly acts of sabotage, kidnapping and other acts which depend for their effectiveness on national and international publicity would not be effective in a time of war when news of great battles totally eclipses any such puny events. In the event it was clear that no act by the Poles would be successful. Anything they did would have failed to convince the Nazis of the justice of the cause. With regard to the international community, we may argue that the Poles did not have to make a case because the justness of the Polish cause was well established. They did not face the task of convincing the international order that their methods of opposition to the Nazis were just. A major portion of the international community was already engaged in a conventional war against the unjust Nazi regime. The international community of states was thus likely to regard whatever form of opposition the Poles adopted as a justified form, provided that it adhered to the just war constraints with regard to the selection of targets and to certain restrictions dictated by international law with regard to the kinds of weapons which may be legitimately used.

The choices which faced the Poles in Warsaw at that time were fundamentally stark: they could either resist the Nazis in whatever ways possible, or they could give up all attempts to maintain themselves as moral beings constituted as such within a practice of reciprocal recognition. This latter option would involve sinking into total apathy and retreating from all discourse and action. They were presented with no subtle moral problems at all. Interesting normative problems only arise where both sides to the dispute claim with some degree of plausibility that theirs is a legitimate position. In this respect modern Poland presents much more interesting normative questions in that there the revolutionaries (those seeking to transform the polity), unlike the underground army in Warsaw, have difficult normative choices to make concerning the means of opposition to use.

The Solidarity movement has achieved a great deal of legitimacy both internally and internationally. It is revolutionary in that it seeks a major transformation of the political system. Were Solidarity to consider whether to embark on a campaign of violence, all the subtleties of constitutive reasoning would come into play. The leaders would have to demonstrate that their planned actions showed full regard for the basic norms of the constitutive model. They would have to show that their action did not erode state sovereignty, law, democracy, human rights and so on. Because Poland is a relatively stable modern industrial state, there is a variety of different non-violent forms of opposition available to Solidarity. Solidarity has chosen these in preference to the more violent methods. The present Polish government for its part similarly tries to choose policies which reveal its commitment to the core values. What is noticeable about Solidarity is the extent to which its political and moral strength has *not* derived from policies advocating unconventional forms of violence. Part of the wide international support which Solidarity enjoys is attributable to the scrupulous care which that organization has shown in its choice of methods of opposition. The adherence by Solidarity to the fundamental tenets of the modern state domain of discourse is beyond doubt. Their case would not be so strong had they used more violent means.

3.4 *A possible dialogue about the use of indiscriminate terror*

Let us consider a more serious kind of terrorism. Here I have in mind those acts in which someone like Seamus commits random deeds of violence such as indiscriminate bombing and shooting attacks on people. A typical case would be the planting of a bomb in a crowded pub. Can a case be made out justifying this type of violence? This brings us to the third dialogue.

Seamus: I planted a bomb in the Pig and Whistle today. Killed several people and got a lot of media time. It gave our publicity wing a platform from which our cause could be aired. Even the quality newspapers have several good discussions about what can be said for and against our cause. The debate is now alive in a way that it was not before. We need some similar bombings in some of the great cities of the world to ensure an international debate. I'm off to London tomorrow.

Critic: Seamus, how can you bring a norm justifying this despicable act into coherence with the norms on our settled list and the background theory justifying those norms? Central to that theory was the link established between being an individual and living within a system of law. The norms relating to the state, to the system of states, to citizenship in a democracy, to human rights and many of the other items on the list all presuppose the centrality of law. Crucial to all law is the purpose of regulating human conduct so that people in their day to day relations with one another will know where they stand. Your act of terrorism goes contrary to that central purpose of law which in turn is a central feature of so many of the settled goods on our agreed upon list. Any member of the audience you are addressing with your terrorist act could be a target for your next attack. By your own confession you do not discriminate between your victims. Thus it is quite impossible for you to claim with regard to any member of your audience that in committing the act you were respecting values which you have in common with them.

Seamus: In all our talks we have been discussing what methods may justifiably be used. Now I want to stress that we have tried the other methods which we have discussed. We tried the ordinary methods of political mobilization using the media and so on. The conventional channels were closed to us. We then tried passive resistance, civil disobedience, sabotage and kidnapping. All to no avail. We are turning to indiscriminate violence as a last resort. We are still committed to the core values we have so often discussed, but this is the only means left by which we can realize those values. By this means we can push up the costs to the government (and its supporters) of maintaining their repressive policies. To use the jargon of political science, what we want to do is nudge along the "asset to liability shift."[14] When the costs of maintaining an asset become too high it becomes a liability and the owner will dispose of it.

Critic: Your argument is that the other methods have failed and you are trying this as a last resort.

Seamus: Yes.

Critic: We need to know precisely in what ways it is the last resort. Are you in a position similar to that of the Poles in Warsaw in 1944 where all other modes of opposition (passive resistance, civil disobedience, sabotage) would not have communicated anything significant over the surrounding din of war? They simply would not have been noticed.

Seamus:　No, the situation we face is not like that, we are not involved in war. The state is relatively stable; it is simply unjust.

Critic:　So the other means that you have tried were noticed, but they did not bring about the desired result.

Seamus:　Yes. We are now trying what we hope will be a more effective method.

Critic:　Throughout our conversations we have agreed that your aim is to convince your audience of the justness of your claims; this is what is to count as being effective.

Seamus:　I have never denied this.

Critic:　For the sake of argument then, imagine that I am a member of the audience you are addressing (I may be a citizen of your state, a member of the ruling group in your state, or a foreign policy maker in the wider international community). I noticed your earlier drastic communications (sabotage, etc.), carefully considered your case and decided that your position was unjustified. In short, you failed to convince me. By escalating your activities to include random terror killings are you likely to strengthen your case in my eyes?

Seamus:　Clearly not, for you are already opposed to our cause.

Critic:　Consider the converse case, viz. the situation in which I was impressed by your earlier attempts. I noticed your passive resistance, civil disobedience and sabotage, considered your case and decided it was a good one. Your efforts have succeeded in convincing me. (By the way, the actions of Solidarity in Poland have impressed me in just this way.) I am determined to support you. Do you need to adopt the methods of random violence against people to strengthen my conviction of the justice of your cause?

Seamus:　No, of course not, for you are already convinced of the worth of our cause.

Critic:　So you admit that such violence will not instil a sense of the justice of your cause in those who were not convinced by your earlier methods, and such violence is not needed to convince those who were impresed by your other methods. How do you justify random violence then?

Seamus:　It is aimed at getting the ruling group to relinquish their unjust policies. We seek to raise the costs to them of maintaining those policies.

Critic:　Your aim, then, is not to convince them of the justice of your case (you have already admitted that violence will not do that if the other methods did not succeed), but to *force* them to change their practices. Violence here is no longer a drastic means of communication to be used in specific circumstances, but has become a means of coercion.

What emerges from the foregoing dialogue, taken together with the earlier discussion of the Polish rising in Warsaw during the

Second World War, is that more drastic violent measures are only justified when the less drastic measures are not available as options which will be heard at all. For example, passive resistance is only a justifiable option when other more orthodox avenues of communication have been closed to the aggrieved group; similarly, sabotage is only justified after the method of passive resistance has been crushed, and so on. Finally, methods of violence against specified classes of people (as in Warsaw) are justified when the situation is such that all the less drastic methods are not feasible avenues of communication at all. Here violence of this kind was the only avenue of expression still open. It is crucial to note that tougher measures of unconventional violence are not warranted in those cases where the "softer" measures were heard by the audience, but simply failed to convince them. The correct metaphor for the conclusions we have reached here is that forms of violence are lines of communication which may only be justifiably used when all the other lines are down. The erroneous metaphor is the one which pictures the forms of violence as a graded set of weapons such that where the small weapon fails to bring down the quarry the hunter may switch to a larger weapon.

There is one final small point to make about the previous dialogue. Where Seamus describes random terror as a method of last resort he is clearly thinking in terms of the weapons analogy just mentioned. His is a means/end argument. He is advocating the use of a force as a means to the desired end. There is a major problem with this approach from the point of view of constitutive theory. The end which Seamus wishes to achieve (viz. the just state in which people recognize one another in certain good ways) cannot be reached in the way he describes. The just state consists in people reciprocally recognizing one another in the ways we have already discussed. This state of affairs can only come about when people do recognize one another in the requisite ways. Where people fail to do so, the only way of remedying the situation is to bring them to see the error of their ways through a process of argument. A person cannot be forced to believe that X is his equal. He may be forced to say it, but not to believe it; hence the importance of argument and education *en route* to the just state. At the end of an indiscriminate terrorist campaign there would not be a people properly educated to be citizens of a free state. The means used would have made the end impossible.

3.5 *Uses of unconventional violence by the state*

In the foregoing set of dialogues we have considered the case of the individual terrorist against the state. Let us now consider whether a case can be made out defending a norm which justifies the state in using similar methods against individuals within the state or against the people of neighbouring states.

Consider a situation in which the agents of state A enter into the territory of state B and commit deeds of sabotage against state installations there. There is in international relations clearly no settled norm authorizing sabotage by one state in the territory of another. This would be counter to the well established norms of non-interference and non-aggression. A state which undertook such actions would have to show that its acts constituted a special case. Before considering whether it is possible to construct a coherent argument in support of such acts let us consider the general justification for the non-interference and non-aggression norms. It is the justification articulated in the previous chapter according to which these norms are justified in so far as they provide a framework within which individuality can flourish. States, by recognizing one another's sovereignty, make it possible for the citizens in those states to recognize one another as citizens in a sovereign state. This is an important component of individuality. Not doing this would involve regarding the neighbouring territory as a conquered territory, a subject state or a colony (to mention but a few of the possibilities). People in a subjected state do not feel themselves

recognized as free individuals *vis-à-vis* those in the dominant
state. In order to justify unconventional violence in a neighbouring state, state A would have to argue that the relationship
of reciprocal recognition between states had already broken
down in specified ways and that it was this breakdown which
warranted A's resorting to sabotage in state B. State A might
make the following allegations against state B:

1. That it (state B) seeks to wrongfully undermine state A's
   legitimacy in the eyes of the community of states.
2. It openly advocates the overthrow of the government in A
   and gives material assistance to those who seek to achieve
   this.
3. It refuses to discuss matters of common concern with the
   government of A.

In the normal course of events it is clear what legitimate
avenues are open to A in seeking redress of these grievances.
The usual approach would be to address the target state
through normal conventional channels. Besides the normal
bilateral channels recourse may be made to the forums of international organizations. In all of these endeavours state A's task
would be to convince the neighbouring state (B) and the international community that B's actions are not justified. It would
seek to show that B's behaviour is not in accordance with the
settled norms and the background theory.

But suppose that the normal channels of communication are
blocked to A. Suppose that state B refused to have diplomatic
relations with state A, that the key international organizations
do not allow A to participate in their day to day proceedings,
that special emissaries sent to put the case for A are not granted
travel documents and access to the key people they wish to
address. What might state A do in these unusual circumstances? Here once again is a situation, with which we are now
familiar, in which a participant in a constitutive practice is
denied the normal channels of communication and has to use
unorthodox methods for putting his case. What might a state
thus placed legitimately do?

There are unorthodox methods which fall short of sabotage which are available to state A; methods which show a full commitment to the settled norms of the constitutive practice. For example, state A could attempt to influence public opinion within the target state by buying space and time in their media to publicize its grievances. It could invite leaders from state B's political, religious, economic, cultural and other spheres to visit state A in order to have the opportunity of putting state A's case to them. Similarly, state A could send citizens from various spheres of activity to foreign states as informal ambassadors seeking to convince the community of states of the justice of A's cause.

Imagine that these avenues of communication are also effectively blocked. Foreign powers might introduce measures to discourage their nationals from visiting state A. For example, sportsmen who go to play in state A might be subject to limitations regarding where else they are allowed to play. Conversely, they might introduce measures to curtail sportsmen from A travelling to play in other states. Similar measures could be applied to other kinds of informal diplomats. For example, organizations in state A which are part of international umbrella bodies could be excluded from those bodies. International contact between academics of state A and academics in other states could be limited in various ways. Multinational companies with interests in state A might be obliged to limit their activities in state A or even to withdraw from that state altogether. In all these diverse ways state A's opportunities for putting its case might be curbed. In cases like this, with so many lines of communication damaged, what might state A justifiably do to make its voice heard? Would state A be justified in resorting to unconventional forms of violence, like sabotage, against the vital installations of neighbouring states?

The answer must be negative. Consider how implausible the example I have sketched is. State A is presented as adhering to the fundamental norms of the modern state domain of discourse. State B is presented as wrongfully failing to accord A proper recognition and as actively promoting the overthrow of state A. Then the community of states as a whole is portrayed as imposing progressively more stringent curbs on state A's right to participate in the discourse of the community of states. At the end of the story state A, a lone just state in a world of injustice, seeks to use extra-ordinary means to communicate with the world of the deaf. The story is supremely implausible because the steps taken against state A by state B and the community of states at large would only be possible if they acted in concert. Such concerted action in a world of many sovereign states would only be possible after the fullest possible discussion of the issues surrounding the claims and the counter claims of state A and B. If, *mirabile dictu*, it were possible to achieve such an international consensus, this, it seems reasonable to assume, would be a *prima facie* indication that A's case was not a strong one.

In this example, as in all the other examples which I have introduced, whether the act of violence is justified or not depends on what is communicated by the act of violence in question. It will be justifiable if it can be interpreted as being in accordance with the settled norms and the background theory. I have argued that it cannot coherently be suggested that the violent act is a desperate attempt at communication following the closure of all other avenues of communication. The consensus required to block the other avenues necessitated extensive debates about the merits of the cases of A and B. How then ought we to interpret such an act? The most plausible interpretation is that it must be seen as an act aimed at intimidating state B in order to get her to act in accordance with A's purposes. If my analysis of this kind of case is correct (i.e. if it is true that this kind of unconventional violence cannot be made to cohere with the settled norms of the state centric practice), then it seems reasonable to expect that A will always seek to deny in the public forum any involvement with such deeds. Complicity in such deeds will be kept secret. B will seek to publicize sabotage attempts by A as widely as possible. Let us now look at a more difficult case.

A more difficult situation to judge is presented in the following case. The troops of state A enter the capital city of state B in
the dead of night and attack several places of residence within
which they know sleep members of a group which pursues a
policy of sabotage against installations in state A. This group
consists of exiles from state A who have formed an organization seeking recognition from the government of state A of
certain rights which it is claimed they (and others still living
within state A) are denied. The aims of the saboteur group have
achieved quite widespread recognition internationally and
amongst the populace of state A as being just aims. After years
of attempting to convince the government of state A of the
justice of their case through conventional means and after the
government of state A had effectively closed down most of the
channels of communication open to the group, it resorted to
passive resistance, civil disobedience and, finally, reluctantly
turned to sabotage.[15] That the group pursued a policy of sabotage was well known. State B, knowing this, continued to allow
the members of the group to live and operate from its territory.
Prior to the night raid state A had repeatedly requested the
government of state B to curtail the activities of the saboteur
group, but this had not been done. On several occasions it had
warned state B that if the activities of the saboteurs were not
curtailed, state A might resort to force to settle the matter.
Again this was of no avail. Finally, before the raid the government of state B was notified by state A that a raid was going to
take place, that no harm was intended towards state B, its
people or its forces. State A asked state B to keep its forces well
away from the proposed scene of action. In the raid the action
was strictly confined to the residences which had previously
been identified as being the places where the saboteurs lived.
Several non-saboteurs who happened to be sleeping in the
same residences were killed in the raid.

Critic in the following dialogue confronts Seamus, who is
now a member of the government of state A.

Critic: How can you justify your government's action of sending troops
      into a neighbouring state in order to slaughter some of its residents in

their sleep? Surely it is in flagrant contravention of the non-interference norm?

Seamus: Those whom we aimed to kill were not ordinary residents of B; they were saboteurs bent on fomenting revolution in A. As the government of A we are obligated to protect law and order, and the security of A's people generally. These people were seeking to undermine it. We had tried several more orthodox means of curbing their activities in order to give due recognition to the sovereignty of B, all to no avail. B refused to curb the activities of these saboteurs; it repeatedly allowed them to stage sabotage raids into our state. In this way they forced us to take more extreme measures which were nevertheless justified in the circumstances.

Critic: Let us consider the position of these saboteurs you refer to. Is their position the same as the one which confronted you some years ago when we had our first dialogue, i.e. do they claim that you as a government are failing to recognize certain important rights of theirs, that they had tried all the orthodox channels of addressing you about this matter, and that you have systematically blocked these, that they tried less orthodox, but still peaceful, channels such as an underground press, and the seeking of international recognition, and that they have at all times taken pains to reassure you that they do not wish to threaten your basic rights? Have they achieved quite significant success in their attempts to gain international recognition and have they gained significant underground support within state A?

Seamus: Yes, they have done all these things, but we still maintain that the case which they are arguing is wrong.

Critic: What is your main aim throughout this process?

Seamus: At its broadest I would say that we aim to establish the legitimacy (both internally and internationally) of our government and of the policies which we pursue. The counter side of this is that we would seek to refute those critics who deny the legitimacy of our government and its policies. Their arguments and actions undermine our international standing and our internal security.

Critic: In short, what you aim at is a situation of reciprocal recognition in terms of which your standing and your acts are recognized as legitimate and where you grant similiar recognition to the standing and acts of other states in the community of states.

Seamus: That's right. To act justly is to act in ways that are recognized as such within the modern state domain of discourse.

Critic: Then you must admit that you cannot achieve your aim by brute force. If you are accused of *not* being a just state worthy of recognition, you can shoot the accuser, but that will not remove the accusation.

Seamus: That's correct. We have been through all this before. What I need to do is convince my critics that their criticism is unfounded. Only if we do so will our actions be recognized as legitimate, and recognized in the desired way.

Critic: But there are two different criticisms to be dealt with in this case,

are there not? First, there is the criticism raised by many in the international community of the way in which you entered a neighbouring
state to deal with the saboteurs with force of arms. Second, there is
the criticism raised by the saboteurs themselves which refers to the
way in which your government denies them their rights. These two
are closely interlinked. Now I can see that you have some defences
which you can offer against the charges of the first kind of criticism.
You can with some justification say that you took great pains to make
it clear to all concerned that your raid was not a challenge to state B
itself. You warned the government of B beforehand that the raid was
going to take place, that it would be limited and that you intended no
harm to state B itself. These arguments may go some way towards
convincing the community of states that your state is committed to
recognizing certain ground rules of the community, for example the
non-interference rule. But it will not silence the second kind of criticism, which refers to the denial of rights to certain groups within
your state. Shooting the critic leaves the criticism either untouched,
or more likely, it reinforces it.

Seamus: Let me ask you a question. What kind of argument from us
would weaken the case of the saboteur?

Critic: Well, consider his claim that he is forced to sabotage because the
normal channels of communication between him and the community
at large are denied him. If you could demonstrate that this charge was
unfounded, his case would be weakened. If you could show that he
and his fellows had full freedom of speech, access to the media, the
right to attend and convene meetings, that he was not threatened with
bannings or house arrest and the like, then his reasons for turning to
bombs would be shown to be spurious and your case for seeking to
counter the sabotage would be considerably strengthened.

Seamus: It so happens that we can erode the saboteurs' position in
much the way that you have outlined. Within our state we have an
exceptionally free press. There is a range of newspapers catering to
most tastes. There is nothing to prevent entrepreneurs setting up new
newspapers. Open discussion is tolerated among the people. There
are universities within which the whole range of political and social
questions may be discussed. The only curbs placed on freedom of
speech are those which prevent people propagating ideas which
would undermine just those rights and liberties which need to be preserved to make freedom of speech possible.

Critic: It is this last contention of yours which is crucial. The saboteurs
argue that they have made it plain throughout their campaign that
they are committed to all the core values on your list. They are not
aiming to bring about a breakdown in the rule of law, they do not aim
to infringe your basic rights, they do not intend jeopardizing your
property rights. In their prior actions they have demonstrated their
bona fides in this regard. For example, in their passive resistance
campaign they demonstrated their respect for persons by avoiding

harm to humans, and to private property. They have avoided arbitrary terror, assassination campaigns and the like. In all this they do not look like people bent on undermining the basic preconditions for a free state. In all this they acknowledged that what they are seeking is a relationship of mutual recognition within the state and they have shown their commitment to recognizing you in the requisite way. Your action against them has not shown a similar commitment. Instead of seeking to induce them to recognize you in the way you require through reasoning, you have attempted to put a stop to their argument, by censorship, bannings, arrests and now finally you have sought to put a stop to their arguments by killing them. Will this not weaken your position in the eyes of those you wish to convince? It seems to me that there is no interpretation of your action which you could have offered the saboteurs killed in the raid which would have shown them that at base you were committed to common core values and a common justification for the core. The most plausible interpretation of your act is that you were trying to frighten the saboteurs into silence; not that you were trying to convince them of the justice of your case. Compare this case with the quite different one in which troops from opposing states who are at war with one another meet in battle. Here in manifold different ways the troops recognize one another as participants in a practice which embodies fundamental values and ground rules which they both endorse. War is a practice within the international community which under certain specified conditions is considered just. There are broad conventions governing how wars might legitimately be fought. Within war there is a strong element of mutual recognition between the antagonists. I mention but one small facet of this: mutual recognition is revealed in according to a killed enemy soldier a decent military burial.[16] Your action in this case has shown that you do not recognize the people involved as rights holders at all. You cannot seriously be seeking recognition from people you portray in such a light, no matter what you protest yourself to be doing. It might be said that you are a true terrorist, in that you seek to frighten people rather than convince them.

4 Conclusion

Several interesting things emerge from the foregoing discussion of various cases of unconventional violence. First, we have seen in each case how important it is, from the constitutive theory point of view, for the person seeking to justify his violent act that he show his audience how his act coheres with the other values in terms of which he and his audience constitute one another as individuals.

Second, in the discussion a particular link between argument and force has emerged. Violent acts which are acts of force *simpliciter* are not justifiable. Only those acts of force which may be interpreted as acts of communication are justified. Violent acts of communication are only justified in those cases in which all other avenues of communication have been blocked. An implication of this is that acts of unconventional violence are only justified where freedom of speech has been curtailed. It follows that a central means of preventing such violence is to keep the channels of communication between people open.

Third, the common adage that violence is justified as a means to a good end blurs more than it reveals. This style of talk suggests that any means to a good end is warranted. However, we have seen in our discussion that violence is justified only when it is used as a *means of communication*. It is not justified as a means of coercion.

Fourth, it has emerged that acts of *random* killing and maiming are never justified because such killings fail to show due respect for the aspect of reciprocity required by justifications in constitutive theory. Even in the case of the Poles in the Warsaw ghetto, the killing which took place was rightfully not indiscriminate, but was aimed at the functionaries of the Nazis. This is not to suggest that all killing of people is always unjustified. In some forms of combat (examples range from formal feuds to wars) there is a form of mutual recognition involved between the parties and it is only in such cases that killing is ever justified. In the relationship between the terrorist killer (or maimer) and his victim there is no such reciprocal constituting of one another as values. Soldiers meeting on the battlefield see one another as representing opposing states in battle. By seeing one another as representatives of their respective states they confer a certain dignity upon one another. The relationship between a terrorist and his random human target involves no such recognition. It is akin to the relationship between a hoodlum and his victim.

NOTES

1 See the sources cited in Geoffrey Best, *Humanity in Warfare* (New York, Columbia University Press, 1980). Also W. V. O'Brien, *Conduct of Just and Limited War* (New York, Praeger, 1981).

2 See Chapter 2, Section 2.1.

3 I am ignoring problems of *legal* jurisdiction which might arise.

4 This practical problem has given rise to several attempts on the part of the community of states to deal with it. One such was the setting up by the United Nations of the "Ad Hoc" Committee on International Terrorism.

5 Thomas Hobbes, *Leviathan* (London, Dent, 1962); John Locke, *The Second Treatise of Government* (Indianapolis, Bobbs-Merrill, 1952); Robert Nozick, *Anarchy, State and Utopia* (Oxford, Blackwell, 1974); Bruce Ackerman, *Social Justice and the Liberal State* (New Haven, Yale University Press, 1980).

6 Barrie Paskins and Michael Dockrill, *The Ethics of War* (London, Duckworth, 1979).

7 Examples of movements which would be concerned to distinguish themselves from mere criminals are:
    the Irish Republican Army in Ireland
    the Gray Wolves in Turkey
    the Red Army Faction in West Germany
    the Red Brigades in Italy
    Omega 7 (anti-Castro Cubans) throughout North America
    the National Liberation Movement (MLN or Tupamaros) in Uruguay.

8 In *The Ethics of War* Paskins and Dockrill are concerned to understand such fringe groups and suggest that we can best do so by viewing ourselves as living in a world in which there is no moral consensus but a mass of people with diverse and divided loyalties. Thus, presumably, we must see the Red Brigades and other such groups as people who feel alienated in a world dominated by huge states and who are expressing themselves in small non-state groupings. No doubt this is, to some extent, true. In the modern world people do have diverse and divided loyalties. But pointing to this fact does not help us in our search for an answer to the question: "What way of arranging the relationships of people in groups is justified and what arrangements between such groups are justified?"

9 Geoffrey Pridham, "Terrorism and the State in West Germany during the 1970's" in *Terrorism: A Challenge to the State*, ed. Juliet Lodge (Oxford, Martin Roberston, 1981), p. 25.

10 Ibid. p. 43.

11 Gwendolen Carter, *The Politics of Inequality* (London, Thames and Hudson, 1958), p. 370.

12 Rodney Davenport, *South Africa: A Modern History* (London, Macmillan, 1977), p. 285 and following pages.

13 The case of the Pretoria bombing in which civilians were arbitrarily killed is likely to be much more difficult to justify.
14 On the "asset to liability shift" see Maurice Tugwell, "Politics and Propaganda of the Provisional IRA" in *British Perspectives on Terrorism*, ed. Paul Wilkinson (London, Allen and Unwin, 1981), p. 17.
15 See the earlier dialogue at p. 198.
16 Such dignified burials were accorded to the dead by both states involved in the Falklands War in 1982.

Conclusion

I have tried to do two things in this book: first, I sought to examine the reasons for the dearth of normative theory in the discipline of international relations and to show that these reasons for eschewing normative theory are not good ones. Second, I attempted to move towards the construction of a substantive normative theory for international relations. In seeking to achieve this latter objective I followed a model of argument first set out by Ronald Dworkin in the context of legal reasoning. This model of argument starts from the settled norms within a given domain of discourse and seeks on the basis of these to construct a background theory which will enable users to find solutions to hard cases. I started with a list of what most actors in international relations accept as settled norms and then sought to construct a background theory which would enable us to achieve a coherence between the different items on the list of settled goods. In the course of this attempt it was found that the following did not suffice as background theories: order based theories, utilitarian theories and rights based contract theories. The best background theory which emerged was the one I dubbed the constitutive theory of individuality.

In the previous chapter I attempted to apply this background theory to some of the normative problems posed by the uses of unconventional violence in world politics. These provide hard

227

cases for international normative theory both because there are no settled norms specifying whether (and under what circumstances) such acts are justified, and because a norm justifying such acts of violence seems to be contrary to so many of the settled norms of international affairs. For example, on the face of it these acts of violence are opposed to the norms relating to democracy, human rights, international law, peace and state sovereignty, to mention but a few. In the course of the dialogues I showed how it is possible to justify a limited class of such violent actions. In each dialogue I showed how it is possible for argument to proceed from the shared premises contained in the list of settled norms and the background theory which demonstrates how individuality is constituted through reciprocal recognition of the list of settled norms, to conclusions about various difficult norms relating to unconventional violence. In each dialogue the interlocutor was faced with this form of question: "Is it not the case that in order for one to be constituted as an individual within a community with other individuals it is essential for others to recognize one as a person who adheres to norms x, y and z (where x, y and z refer to norms on the list of settled norms)?" In seeking to justify the contentious norms relating to unconventional violence the interlocutor had to show that the contentious norm was compatible with the other set of norms, recognition of which was crucial to his individuality. The major substantive conclusion about acts of unconventional violence was that they are only justified when it is possible to interpret them as acts of communication from those who have been unjustly treated to those who have systematically denied the people in question the opportunity of having their case heard. But such extreme acts of communication are only justifiable when they are of such a nature that they demonstrate an ongoing commitment to the corpus of settled norms in terms of which they judge that an injustice has been done them. I have thus outlined a method which enables us to come to grips with a set of normative issues which, at first glance, seemed so difficult to accommodate within our normal modes of moral discourse.

I contend that it would be possible and fruitful to apply this mode of argument to all those other hard cases which were mentioned in Chapter Three. For the present the constraints of space and time prevent me from continuing with this important and interesting task.

Bibliography

Books

Ackerman, B. *Social Justice and the Liberal State*, New Haven, Yale University Press, 1980

Amin, S. *Accumulation on a World Scale*, Hassocks, Harvester Press, 1974

Arendt, H. *On Violence*, Harmondsworth, Penguin Press, 1970

Beitz, C. *Political Theory and International Relations*, Princeton University Press, 1979

Best, G. *Humanity in Warfare*, New York, Columbia University Press, 1980

Bull, H. *The Anarchical Society*, London, Macmillan, 1977

Burton, J. W. *International Relations: A General Theory*, Cambridge University Press, 1965

Carr, E. H. *The Twenty Years Crisis*, London, Macmillan, 1942

Carter, G. *The Politics of Inequality*, London, Thames and Hudson, 1958

Charvet, J. *A Critique of Freedom and Equality*, Cambridge University Press, 1981

Davenport, R. *South Africa: A Modern History*, London, Macmillan, 1977

Deutsch, K. W. *The Nerves of Government*, second edition, New York, Free Press, 1966

   The Analysis of International Relations, second edition, Englewood Cliffs, Prentice-Hall, 1978

Dilthey, W. *Selected Writings*, ed. H. P. Rickman, Cambridge University Press, 1979

Dogan, A. *Philosophy of History*, New York, Macmillan, 1965

Dworkin, R. *Taking Rights Seriously*, London, Duckworth, 1981

Fay, B. *Social Theory and Political Practice*, London, Allen and Unwin, 1975

Feyerabend, P. *Against Method*, London, New Left Books, 1975

Fichte, J. G. *The Popular Works of Fichte*, ed. W. Smith, London, John Chapman, 1849

230

Finnis, J. *Natural Law and Natural Rights*, Oxford University Press, 1980

Flathman, R. *The Practice of Rights*, Cambridge University Press, 1976

Frank, A. G. *Capitalism and Underdevelopment in Latin America*, Harmondsworth, Penguin Books, 1971

Frankel, J. *Contemporary International Theory*, London, Oxford University Press, 1973

Frohock, F. M. *Normative Political Theory*, Englewood Cliffs, Prentice-Hall, 1974

Gardiner, P. *Theories of History*, Glencoe, The Free Press, 1959

Gellner, E. *Words and Things*, London, Gollancz, 1959

   The Legitimation of Belief, Cambridge University Press, 1974

   Spectacles and Predicaments, Cambridge University Press, 1980

Haas, E. B. *Beyond the Nation State*, Stanford University Press, 1964

Habermas, J. *Knowledge and Human Interests*, London, Heinemann, 1971

Hampshire, S. (ed.) *Public and Private Morality*, Cambridge University Press, 1978

Hart, H. L. A. *The Concept of Law*, London, Oxford University Press, 1961

Hegel, G. W. F. *The Philosophy of Right*, trans. T. M. Knox, Oxford University Press, 1973

Held, D. *Introduction to Critical Theory*, London, Hutchinson, 1980

Hobbes, T. *Leviathan*, London, Dent, 1962

Hodgeson, D. H. *The Consequences of Utilitarianism*, Oxford University Press, 1967

Hoffman, S. *Contemporary Theory in International Relations*, Englewood Cliffs, Prentice-Hall, 1960

Holsti, K. J. *International Politics*, Englewood Cliffs, Prentice-Hall, 1967

Hudson, W. D. (ed.) *The Is–Ought Question*, London, St Martin's Press, 1969

   Modern Moral Philosophy, New York, Doubleday, 1970

Hughes, J. *The Philosophy of Social Research*, London, Longman, 1980

Jervis, R. *Perception and Misperception in International Politics*, Princeton University Press, 1976

Johnson, R. W. *How Long Will South Africa Survive?* London, Macmillan, 1977

Joynt, C. B. and Corbett, H. *Theory and Reality in World Politics*, London, Macmillan, 1978

Joynt C. B. and Hare, J. E. *Ethics and International Affairs*, London, Macmillan, 1982

Kaplan, M. *System and Process in International Politics*, New York, John Wiley, 1957

Keohane, R. and Nye, R. O. *Power and Interdependence*, Boston, Little, Brown, 1977

Knorr, K. and Verba, S. *The International System*, Princeton University Press, 1961

Kubálková, V. and Cruickshank, A. A. *Marxism–Leninism and the Theory of International Relations*, London, Routledge and Kegan Paul, 1980

Lenin, V. I. *Imperialism the Highest Stage of Capitalism* in *Selected Works of Lenin*, Moscow, Progress Publishers, 1977

Locke, J. *The Second Treatise of Government*, Indianapolis, Bobbs-Merrill, 1952

Louch, A. R. *Explanation and Human Action*, Oxford, Blackwell, 1966

McCelland, C. A. *Theory and International System*, New York, Macmillan, 1966

Mackie, J. *Ethics: Inventing Right and Wrong*, Harmondsworth, Penguin Books, 1981

Marx, K. *Capital*, London, Dent, 1972

Mitrany, D. *A Functionalist Approach to World Politics*, London, Martin Robertson, 1975

Morgenthau, H. *Politics among Nations*, New York, Knopf, 1973

Nozick, R. *Anarchy, State and Utopia*, Oxford, Blackwell, 1974

O'Brien, W. V. *Conduct of Just and Limited War*, New York, Praeger, 1981

Organski, A. F. K. *World Politics*, New York, Alfred Knopf, 1968

Paine, T. *The Rights of Man*, London, Dent, 1979

Paskins, B. and Dockrill, M. *The Ethics of War*, London, Duckworth, 1979

Pateman, C. *Participation and Democratic Theory*, Cambridge University Press, 1970

Pennock, J. R. *Democratic Political Theory*, Princeton University Press, 1979

Pettman, R. *State and Class*, London, Croom Helm, 1979

Plamenatz, J. *Consent, Freedom and Political Obligation*, Oxford University Press, 1968

Poggi, G. *The Development of the Modern State*, London, Hutchinson, 1978

Popper, K. *The Open Society and its Enemies*, London, Routledge and Kegan Paul, 1945

Pratt, V. *The Philosophy of the Social Sciences*, London, Methuen, 1978

Rawls, J. *Theory of Justice*, London, Oxford University Press, 1972

Reynolds, C. *Theory and Explanation in International Relations*, London, Martin Robertson, 1973

Reynolds, P. A. *An Introduction to International Relations*, London, Longman, 1976

Rorty, R. *Philosophy and the Mirror of Nature*, Oxford, Blackwell, 1980

Rosecrance, R. *International Relations: Peace or War*, New York, McGraw-Hill, 1973

Rosenau, J. N. *The Adaptation of National Societies: A Theory of Political System Behaviour and Transformation*, New York, McCaleb-Seiler, 1970

Rousseau, J. J. *The Social Contract*, London, Dent, 1973

Sewell, J. P. *Functionalism and World Politics*, Princeton University Press, 1961

Singer, J. D. *Human Behaviour and International Politics*, Skokie, Rand McNally, 1965

Stankiewicz, W. J. *In Defence of Sovereignty*, London, Oxford University Press, 1969

Truzzi, M. *Verstehen: Subjective Understanding in Human Sciences*, Reading, Mass., Addison-Wesley, 1974

Tuchman, B. *A Distant Mirror*, London, Macmillan, 1979

Walsh, W. H. *An Introduction to the Philosophy of History*, London, Hutchinson, 1967

Waltz, K. N. *Man, the State and War*, New York, Columbia University Press, 1959

  Theory of International Politics, London, Addison-Wesley, 1979

Walzer, M. *Obligations: Essays on Disobedience, War and Citizenship*, Cambridge, Mass., Harvard University Press, 1970

  Just and Unjust Wars, New York, Basic Books, 1977

Watt, D. C. *A History of the World in the Twentieth Century*, London, Hodder and Stoughton, 1967

Weber, M. *The Theory of Social and Economic Organization*, trans. A. Henderson and T. Parsons, London, W. Hodge, 1947

  From Max Weber, ed. H. H. Gerth and C. Wright Mills, London, Routledge and Kegan Paul, 1970

Wight, M. *Systems of States*, Leicester University Press, 1977

  Power Politics, ed. Hedley Bull and Carsten Holbraad, Harmondsworth, Penguin Books, 1979

Williams, B. *Morality: An Introduction to Ethics*, Cambridge University Press, 1972

Winch, P. *The Idea of a Social Science*, London, Routledge and Kegan Paul, 1958

  Ethics and Action, London, Routledge and Kegan Paul, 1972

Wright, M. *The Theory and Practice of the Balance of Power*, London, Dent, 1975

Articles

Adams, E. M. "The Ground of Rights," *American Philosophical Quarterly*, Vol. 19, No. 2 (April 1982)

Bull, H. "International Theory, the Case for a Classical Approach" in *Contending Approaches to International Politics*, ed. K. Knorr and J. N. Rosenau, Princeton University Press, 1970

  "Human Rights and World Politics" in *Moral Claims in World Affairs*, ed. Ralph Pettman, London, Croom Helm, 1979

  "Human Rights and International Relations," *Daedalus* (Spring 1982)

Donelan, M. "The Political Theorists and International Theory" in *The Reason of States*, ed. Michael Donelan, London, Allen and Unwin, 1978

Gallie, W. B. "Essentially Contested Concepts," *Proceedings of the Aristotelian Society*, Vol. 56 (1965)

Harrison, G. "Relativism and Tolerance" in *Philosophy, Politics and*

Society, fifth series, ed. Peter Laslett and James Fishkin, Oxford, Blackwell, 1979

Hart, H. L. A. "Between Utility and Rights" in *The Idea of Freedom*, ed. Alan Ryan, London, Oxford University Press, 1979

Kaplan, M. "The New Great Debate" in *Contending Approaches to International Relations*, ed. K. Knorr and J. N. Rosenau, Princeton University Press, 1970

Keens-Soper, M. "The Practice of the States System" in *The Reason of States*, ed. Michael Donelan, London, Allen and Unwin, 1978

Kindleberger, C. P. "Scientific International Politics," *World Politics*, Vol. 11, No. 1 (1958)

Kubálková, V. "Moral Precepts in Contemporary Soviet Politics" in *Moral Claims in World Affairs*, ed. Ralph Pettman, London, Croom Helm, 1979

Marx, K. Preface to *A Contribution to the Critique of Political Economy* in *Karl Marx: Selected Writings in Sociology and Social Philosophy*, ed. T. B. Bottomore and M. Rubel, London, D. C. Watts, 1963

Mayall, J. "International Society and International Theory" in *The Reason of States*, ed. Michael Donelan, London, Allen and Unwin, 1978

Navari, C. "The Origins of the Nation–State" in *The Nation State*, ed. Leonard Tivey, Oxford, Martin Robertson, 1981

Oakshott, M. "The Language of the Modern European State," *Political Studies*, Vol. 23 (December 1975)

Passmore, J. "Logical Positivism" in *Encyclopaedia of Philosophy*, ed. Paul Edwards, New York, Macmillan, 1967

Pettman, J. "Race, Conflict and Liberation in Africa" in *Moral Claims in World Affairs*, ed. Ralph Pettman, London, Croom Helm, 1979

Pridham, G. "Terrorism and the State in West Germany during the 1970's" in *Terrorism: A Challenge to the State*, ed. Juliet Lodge, Oxford, Martin Robertson, 1981

Rosenau, J. N., Gartin, G., McClain, E. P., Stinziano, D., Stoddard, R. and Swanson, D. "Of Syllabi, Texts, Students, and Scholarship in International Relations," *World Politics*, Vol. 29, No. 2 (January 1977)

Singer, J. D. "The Level of Analysis Problem in International Relations" in *The International System: Theoretical Issues*, ed. K. Knorr and S. Verba, Princeton University Press, 1961

"The Behavioural Science Approach to International Relations: Payoff and Prospects" in *International Politics and Foreign Policy*, ed. J. N. Rosenau, New York, The Free Press, 1969

Smart, J. J. C. "An Outline of Utilitarian Ethics" in J. J. C. Smart and Bernard Williams, *Utilitarianism For and Against*, Cambridge University Press, 1970

Taylor, C. "Neutrality in Political Science" in *The Philosophy of Social Explanation*, ed. Alan Ryan, London, Oxford University Press, 1969

Thorndike, T. "The Revolutionary Approach" in *Approaches and Theory in International Relations*, ed. P. G. Taylor, London, Longman, 1978

Tugwell, M. "Politics and Propaganda of the Provisional IRA" in *British*

Perspectives on Terrorism, ed. Paul Wilkinson, London, Allen and Unwin, 1981

Vincent, A. "The Hegelian State and International Politics," *The Review of International Studies*, Vol. 9, No. 3 (July 1983)

Windsor, P. "The Justification of the State" in *The Reason of States*, ed. Michael Donelan, London, Allen and Unwin, 1978

Index

237